D1642717

Taming Amy

First Published 2015 by Purple Feather
The Stables, Blair Estate, Dalry, North Ayrshire, Scotland

© Seth Gardner

The moral rights of the author have been asserted.

All rights reserved. No part of this book may be reprinted or reproduced or utilised in any form or by any electronic, mechanical, or other means, now known or hereafter invented, including photocopying and recording, without permission in writing from the publishers or author.

A catalogue record for this book is available from the British Library.

ISBN
Paperback: 978-0-9931728-0-9
E-Pub: 978-0-9931728-1-6

| MORAY COUNCIL LIBRARIES & INFO.SERVICES | |
|---|---|
| 20 39 56 27 | |
| Askews & Holts | |
| F | |
| | |

# Taming Amy

## Seth Gardner

For Andrea, Charlotte and Sophie,
my source of never-ending joy.

# Foreword

Taming Amy is a parable. Like all good parables it starts in the mud - in the quagmire of modern suffering. This is the suffering of the harangued, the stressed, the hounded, the frenzied and the frazzled. The world of exhaustion, depression, anger, anxiety and despair. It is the world of Michael. It is the world of many of us.

And yet in this mire, Michael finds an unlikely friend. This friend leads Michael - and you and me - step by step on a journey of self discovery and growing awareness to the roots of this suffering, both within ourselves and within our shared human condition. Like the author, this friend is an expert gardener. She plants a seed of hope in Michael's life, and carefully cultivates and nourishes this seed until it sprouts and grows - drawing the nutrients it needs from the very mud of suffering that surrounds it - slowly yet surely unfolding into a most exquisite lotus flower of renewed understanding and rekindled joy.

Taming Amy is the retelling of an ancient story, an ancient wisdom. Michael's lessons are your lessons and my lessons. They are perennial lessons. It matters not if you are persuaded more by humanism, science, psychology, religion, spirituality or all or none of these, this parable has insight to offer your life. So put the kettle on, get a slice of cake if you like, and begin your journey. But take the journey slowly. Amy doesn't want to work her magic only in Michael's life; she wants to work it in yours. Listen to her as she speaks to you and shares her insights into our modern world and of the age-old causes of our individual and collective suffering. She brings you a precious gift  A way out

Dr Damian Woods,
DclinPsychol, MA OXON
Clinical Psychologist
Scotland

# Taming Amy

## In The Begining...

I first met Amy stealing sugar cubes from a small coffee shop that doubled as my personal office.

Amy was stealing sugar cubes, not me I hasten to add. In fact she was doing it so expertly, she completely mesmerised me. Skipping and ducking between the tables, she took great delight in lifting a single sugar cube from the small glass dish balanced on each one. Then, undetected by the surrounding adults who were absorbed in caffeine, work and conversation, she munched it noisily. She quickly became aware that I had seen her and sidled back towards my table. My publisher, who was busily speaking into her mobile phone, was blissfully unaware of the commotion going on behind her. Amy meanwhile had snuck behind her back, stolen a sugar cube and then plopped it into her large, skinny, extra hot latte – after sucking it. Noisily!

I laughed, choked and spat out a mouthful of coffee. It splurged across the table, my hefty (recently completed) manuscript and worst of all, my publisher's expensive suit.

That first encounter left me believing that I would soon be unemployed, without a publishing deal and that I had:

a: an incurable brain tumour or

b: an imaginary friend.

Surely things could only get better?

# Chapter One

'What the...! OMG Michael, you clumsy idiot, all over my Armani! I'll have to get it...yow, that's hot!'

My publisher, a formidable and learned lady in her forties, was so startled by my break in coffee shop etiquette that she leapt up uttering a word that made many of the tribe of nearby yummy mummies turn, frown and 'tut' loudly. By jumping up from her seat she'd set off a chain of events that finished with her dropping her brand new and very expensive phone directly into her huge mug of piping hot - and now slightly sweetened - coffee.

'Oh no, my phone! Bloody hell Michael, look what you've done!'

Patricia Blunqvurst was not used to social outbursts. She was used to quiet serious places like libraries, offices and therapy rooms. She did not like coffee shops. She did not like surprises. She did not like my latest manuscript and now, quite clearly, she did not like me.

I tried to calm the situation by explaining.

'I'm so sorry Patricia; I choked on my coffee, erm... the shock of the wrong kind of milk...erm I wanted to warn you.'

'Warn me? Warn me of what?' eyebrowed Patricia, wiping down her phone and suit with all the napkins she could find, further covering my manuscript with splashes in the process.

'That little girl, the one who was stealing sugar cubes. She popped one in your coffee, I was trying to...'

'What little girl?!' demanded Patricia, glaring at me through her severe designer glasses and quickly scanning the room with her laser vision.

'Well that one.' I pointed at the small girl and tried not to smile. Amy was about to steal some cake from one of the mums.

'Which one? I don't see anybody!' snapped Patricia, wiping the half smile off my face in an instant.

'Huh, that one, wearing the flowery dress, beside the lady in....'

I stopped. Patricia Blunqvurst's outburst had drawn the collective attention of the whole coffee shop. It must have been the sheer volume of her voice combined with the pitiful figure that I must have cut. People love public displays of humiliation and I was obviously fast becoming the star of this one.

'There, that little girl, in the corner, beside the ...'

I pointed again. The small girl was standing staring straight at us (well me anyway), a piece of chocolate cake paused at her mouth.

In a voice so icy it would have frozen molten lava, Patricia Blunqvurst completed my rapid descent into coffee shop oblivion.

'Michael, there is no one there. Are you crazy?!'

I felt my face turn bright red. My heartbeat raced like a sports car. My hands got clammy as the occupants of the coffee shop followod my gaze towards the back of the room, eagerly awaiting the resolution of this exciting drama.

Of course she wasn't there. The small, red curly-haired cause of all this embarrassment had completely disappeared. One minute she was there. The next she wasn't. Just like that!

Drama over, villain caught, punishment obvious. Everybody turned away to discuss the next fleeting moment of gossip. In an instant the coffee shop got back to business with its usual hum.

Standing petrified like a fly in amber, mumbling incoherently about visions, ghosts and the effect of too many espressos, my fuddled brain told me that I had just blown my last big chance. After nearly five years of painstaking academic research and many laborious re-writes, my gut told me it had all been for nothing. Patricia Blunqvurst, the esteemed publisher of academic texts and papers, was using the first chapter of my manuscript to drain coffee from the crevices of her handbag. I watched, powerless, as she gathered her belongings and fixed me with her steely gaze.

'Michael the world has changed. People want books that are accessible and readable, books that speak to them. This work is jumbled, incoherent, full of jargon, dense, impenetrable, inauthentic and completely un-publishable. I think you might have become disconnected from the real world. Maybe you've burnt out – ironic seeing as how you've written about the history of madness and its effects on the individual. In my opinion it might be time to consider a new line of work. Librarian maybe? I'm saying this with your best interests in mind Michael. Goodbye and, uh thanks for the coffee!'

With that my last best hope made to leave the café with as much dignity as she could muster. Then she stopped in her tracks and half turned towards me. Maybe it was a last minute reprieve, a lifeline? She was reaching into her handbag, taking out a card – her business card?

'And here's the number of a brain specialist friend of mine. Hallucinations are often the result of brain tumours. Goodbye.'

* * * * * * * *

# Chapter 1

Patricia was right, about the brain tumours often causing hallucinations. Or so I was informed by the bright, young and very enthusiastic neurologist who incarcerated me in a huge CAT Scan machine for what seemed like ages before cheerfully pointing out that 'apart from the usual signs of aging, mild alcohol abuse and an enlarged amygdala,' my brain was free of tumours.

As he gave me my results he noticed my relieved look and smiled for a moment, obviously pleased to have been of help. But then he added,

'Apparently though these kinds of mental health issues, seeing things and all that, don't always show up in brain scans. Could be schizophrenia, exhaustion, genes or maybe the misuse of medication and (cough) substances. Are you on 'medication' Michael?'

As I answered no, my teenage neurologist gave a long slow exhalation. He put his head on one side, observing me for just long enough for me to panic, before suggesting I sought out a psychologist. He gave me a business card with a number on it and was seeing me to the door when he turned, and in an enigmatic voice said,

'There are plenty of 'specialist' self help and support groups these days Michael. It might, erm be prudent to check out a couple. It can be difficult, erm challenging, overcoming these kinds of 'conditions'. All the best Michael.'

Before I could respond, I found myself outside in the brightly-lit hustle and bustle of a busy hospital corridor. I felt myself panicking. The good news of moments earlier had vanished, leaving me in a whirl of confusion and self-doubt. My neurologist had just suggested that I might have mental health issues and had inferred that he thought I had a drug problem. I took a deep breath. I needed a drink  I needed a coffee. I needed a... oh hell, maybe he was right! This week was turning into a disaster. Shoving my hands deep into my pockets, I tried to affect a cheery and carefree attitude and headed along the miles of corridor towards the front door.

I exited the building, turning the corner to head for the car park, and did my best to avoid the ranks of deeply committed smokers. They were all shuffling about in slippers and pyjamas, clutching cigarettes in one hand, saline drips in the other. At times like these I was vulnerable to my own cigarette cravings. I tapped my nicotine patch for comfort and reached into my pocket for my car keys like a child seeking a comfort blanket. Fumbling, I managed to launch the keys high into the air and, to my dismay, heard them land behind some large bins. My embarrassment built as I felt the eyes of a dozen idle smokers boring into my back. I quickly scanned the pavement around me. The keys had vanished. 'Damn and blast today – I should have stayed in bed.' After a moment of negotiating my way gingerly around a massive bin on wheels, I saw my keys and then almost fainted.

The very same small girl that I had seen in the coffee shop - the same urchin that had ruined my chances of publishing my book, the same devil child that had caused me to visit hospital in the first place - was quietly sitting on an upturned red plastic bucket playing with my keys and singing to herself.

My knees buckled and I crumpled to the floor amongst the soggy crisp packets and old newspapers. I rubbed my eyes. I opened and closed them. I pinched myself – that hurt – and tried blinking rapidly. Nothing worked. A few feet away – directly in front of me – the girl sat humming to herself. My mouth was dry. I couldn't speak. My head was a whirlpool of panic. Oh my god, it was true, I was losing it. I must have some kind of rare disorder. I must be suffering from schizophrenia. Maybe I was dying!

> *Don't be stupid Phoney, you're not dying, you great big idiot.*

'Uh...' I gulped like a fish out of water, unable to string a sentence together. The girl who was now staring straight at me had just spoken. Oh my god, I have officially joined the ranks of mentally ill academics! Now I was hearing and seeing things. And, for the

# Chapter 1

second time in two days I was being called an idiot.

'Uh...er...huh. Who, erm...er...what...are you?'

*I'm not a thing. I'm Amy and you are the Phoney. Of
course you can hear me. How are we going to talk if you
can't? Why are you sitting in all that litter?*

I stammered. My mouth was dry. My heart was beating nineteen
to the dozen and I seemed incapable of rational thought.

*I just told you, I'm Amy.*

The small girl yawned with sudden boredom and flung my keys
back at me with surprising force and accuracy. I caught them. It
must have been a pure reflex action. I placed them in my pocket
and tried to speak.

'Am I imagining you or are you real?

*Of course I'm real. That's why you can see and hear me. You do
ask the most stupid questions. I thought you were clever. Why are
you pretending to be a goldfish?*

'I er...if you are real then I must be mad.'

I started to laugh, a torrent of chuckles that rose in me like
a flood and burst the dam. Before I knew it I was laughing
hysterically, wiping tears from my eyes. I started to rock
backwards and forwards on my knees. The laughter took over,
making my whole body shake.

'That's it, I'm mad. I've lost the plot. I'm a complete loony tune!'

*It's not nice to mock people with mental health issues;
you should be kinder than that Phoney! Especially a man
in your condition.*

Amy stood up, walked over to me and slapped me round the face. Oh she was definitely real. And she was strong. She hit me with such force my jaw clicked. I almost bit my tongue off. The sudden shock of pain silenced my laughter, which turned into a gentle snivelling. My body seemed to be quietly convulsing and shaking without asking my permission. Amy was staring straight into my face. Her large blue eyes seemed to bore into my head. I could feel her warm breath. It smelt of old-fashioned roses.

> *Come on Phoney. You're in shock. Let's go home. I want tea and some of that cake you have left. That is, unless you want to be thrown into the bin lorry.*

I spun round on my knees, further ruining my trousers. The huge grey bin was being lifted in the air by the mechanical arms of a massive lorry. As I stood up a slightly surprised refuse worker saw me and raised one eyebrow. I waved my keys at him as if that explained everything and, ineffectually brushing my trousers off with my hands, I quickly turned and headed for the car park. My heart was racing and I kept my head down, desperately trying to remember where I left the damn thing. As I caught sight of my battered old Volvo, I quickly stole a backwards glance towards the bins. Just as I'd expected, there was no one there. No small girl in a red mac and wellies with curly red hair and a gappy smile. Not even the bucket remained. I took a deep breath and dived gratefully into the spacious interior of my old car. My nerves were on edge. I started the engine and took a swig of cold coffee from the dregs of my large, skinny, extra hot, double shot latte or, as I called it, my early morning rocket fuel.

As I raced out onto the main road and headed back to my Glasgow flat, my mind began to jitterbug around like a grasshopper on hot sand. My heart was having palpitations and my nervous system was more activated than a navy seal on manoeuvres. But here was the weird thing. I realised, as I sank deeper into my driving seat, that for the first time in ages I felt truly alive! It was as if I'd just been shocked back into life. My senses were on high alert and I felt as if my whole idea of reality had somehow been picked up and turned inside out like a cheap umbrella in a tornado. I tried to focus on the road and saw that I was exceeding the speed limit by almost double. I slammed on the brakes and drove the rest of the journey at the heady speed of a pensioner driving a lawnmower.

My flat was small and almost empty apart from hundreds of books, papers, journals and papers. Okay, it was stuffed full of enough paper in various guises to circumnavigate the globe several times. It wasn't a comfy place. Well it wasn't designed for living. I had bought the flat as a quiet place to study and write. In the beginning it had worked well. I would kiss my indulgent wife goodbye and then travel the half a mile to our 'investment' to write my masterpiece. As time passed I forgot to go home on more than one occasion. So I set up a small camp bed. Then I got a few basic utensils. I even bought a microwave – banned in my home where my highly intelligent and eco-friendly wife had forbidden them. A few bottles of whisky joined me. Then some more books moved in – hundreds in fact. And then, remarkably, most of my belongings had moved in with me as I was firmly evicted from my home.

My long-suffering wife had had enough of my moods, my moaning, my shouting and temper tantrums. She had called time on my growing frustration and anger at not being able to finish my masterpiece. Quite simply, one morning, just after breakfast she calmly asked me to leave 'until I had learnt to give her the same attention as I gave my books.'

Of course the tiny flat was now too full to study and write in. The fact I had to be there full-time now meant that I resented it. That's why I moved my office to the local coffee house. I had never mastered the art of creating coffee worth drinking – or even any kind of food beyond baked beans. I spent a great deal of my time moving back and forth from the coffee shop carrying food and beverages. So it seemed prudent to work from there instead. I would arrive early and occupy the table at the back - near the loos with the power supply - and rely on the cheerful and professional staff for company. As they were often bored and caffeine fuelled like me, there was no shortage of conversation.

The coffee shop had actually galvanised me into action. Driven by coffee and the desire to try and restore my relationship with my wife – who did occasionally join me when she needed me to sign cheques – I had managed to finish my epic book. As I approached the street where I lived, I wondered if, after my last public humiliation, I would ever be able to face going back to the coffee shop again. All the staff had known how important my meeting with Patricia Blunqvurst had been. They had all made sure that I got my usual table. Coffee had flowed freely and the best cakes had been reserved. I shuddered as I recalled the pitying looks they'd all given me as I had chased after my now ex-publisher.

The morning that Amy had materialised was the morning my world was destined to change. I had fantasised about my lecture tour, my speaking engagements and of course the welcoming arms of my proud wife. Now, as I pulled the car into my expensive parking space, I realised that my dreams were as dead and cold as the dregs of my coffee. As I walked up the steps to open the door, I felt as if there was nowhere I belonged. My newfound thrill for life vanished into a fog of self-loathing and depression. Maybe it was time to get some serious medication. As I turned the key to open the front door I remembered that a guy in the coffee shop had once boasted that he could get any kind of 'performance-enhancing' drugs available. I understood he'd meant illegal and therefore 'mood enhancing' rather than performance enhancing, but even that sounded OK right now.

I pushed my front door open and gasped. My mouth hung open. My head swam and I felt panic rise up though me like wildfire. I had been robbed!

My flat was empty. Not a book, magazine, journal or newspaper in sight. No bookcases, no boxes, no anything. From the door I could see right through to the front window. My two rooms and small hall were stripped bare. As I approached the living room I glanced into my small kitchen. It was empty too. More than that, there was something peculiar about it. As I stepped into my living room/ writing space and looked around, a niggling

Chapter 1

doubt replaced the rush of terror. Apart from a single chair, my
writing desk/kitchen table, a lamp and my laptop, nothing else
remained. I began to breathe heavily. My mind was playing tricks.
Something was wrong. This was far worse than being robbed.
What was it?

I sat heavily on my chair as the room swayed into focus. I glanced
at my laptop. I looked at the desk and then it hit me. There were
no coffee stains. No ring marks. In fact, as I leapt up and strode
around the flat, I could see that everything was gleaming and
clean! Not a mark on the wall, not a stain on the carpet. No sign
that I had lived here at all. No sign that I had even existed, apart
from my desk, chair, lamp and laptop. Then it hit me, what my
olfactory system had been screaming at me from the moment I
walked in. There was no smell. No odour of damp washing, crusty
dishes, books, dust, dirt and stale TV dinners. Hang on, that
wasn't quite true. There was a slight smell. A slight aroma. No
way. It was the subtle yet distinctive scent of wild roses!

I spun around. There, perched on the edge of my table, her little
legs swinging happily, her small toes wiggling in the air without
shoes, was Amy.

> You were ages. I ate the cake. Sorry. It wasn't very nice. It
> was old and stale, just like one of your socks. Yuk!

I don't know if it was the shock, the relief or just my shitty day but
I exploded.

'Right that's it, young lady! What the hell do you think you're
doing? What have you done to my apartment? What the ****
are you? I've had it. Enough! Now you just tell me what on earth
is going on here or else I'm going to… '

Amy was laughing and didn't coom to be the slightest bit worried
or scared of me. She flicked her small head so that her profusion
of bright red curls seemed to dance in the air around her.

*Hey Phoney, you are SO funny when you are angry. All
your veins stand out. Your eyes are all bulgy.*

'This is not a LAUGHING MATTER!!!' I shouted at the top of
my voice. 'What is going on? And my name is Michael – not –
Phoney!!!!!'

Amy just laughed some more and started to unwrap a lollipop
which she'd produced from the pocket of her flowery dress.

*I didn't do anything to your apartment. You did. I am
helping you get better. My name is Amy. You asked me to
help you write your book so why don't you sit down and
start?*

Her calmly spoken answers silenced me. My mind circled again,
trying to work out what she had just told me.

'I did this? I cleared out my own flat? I threw away all my
belongings, all my books? My valuable books! Me?'

*Yes Phoney, you did it. Oh and me. It was fun. You said
you should have done it ages ago. I told you that's what
I thought too. Now come on, sit down. You have a lot of
questions to ask me.*

'Stop calling me Phoney.'

*No shan't. 'Cause you are.*

Amy began to suck her lollipop and then fixed her unsettling
clear-eyed gaze on me.

*Sit down Phoney. Now!*

I felt my body obey her tiny command. Amy had remarkably
intense blue eyes and seemed ancient and child-like at the same
time. She had the authority of a much older person. I sat down

inches away from this small devil child.

*Oh my darling Phoney. Here, remember.*

Amy reached out her arm and touched my temple with her small index finger. Its gentle contact was warm and sticky and covered in essence of lolly.

What followed was the most disconcerting experience I'd had so far, and by now I'd had more than my fair share. It was as if a film fast-forwarded inside my head. I was like a child in the cinema watching a movie screen far away in front of me. It was a movie that I starred in. Yet it wasn't a movie because I could smell and feel everything. I saw myself return home from the coffee shop fiasco. Then I saw me - and AMY - move around my flat like whirling dervishes. Books, papers, magazines, litter, rubbish, cups. Plates, saucers, bottles – in fact everything was bundled into black refuse sacks and then hurtled down the stairs into a next door neighbour's mini-skip. Then, as an even greater shock to my frazzled system, I saw myself scrub and wipe every surface until it gleamed. And then toss the cleaning materials into a black refuse sack, which joined the rest in the skip. I was dimly aware that it had got dark and then I saw myself curl up on the floor and go to sleep.

The vision came to a stop. I remembered. It was as if I was recalling a dream of a dream that had once been told to me by a friend while recovering from a hangover.

'Was that real?' I croaked to Amy who was now balanced on the open window ledge.

*Of course Phoney. We had fun. You don't have much fun do you?*

'Ha!'

Before she could continue I leapt up and tore out of the flat. I literally went down the stairs two at a time. I shoved open the front door, almost taking out my neighbour's cat in the process, and raced down the short path to the street. Diving round the corner I skidded to a halt beside my neighbour's mini-skip, expecting to see all my belongings at the bottom of it.

'Oh no it's all gone!'

I cried out. The mini skip was completely empty. Not a crumb lay inside. Not one piece of paper, not one journal, not one book remained. I stood on tiptoe, desperately scanning the vast interior of the mobile steel cavern. I gulped. I blinked. Then I held onto the sides of the skip as my head did a strange cartwheel, closely followed by my stomach. At that moment I heard a loud cough. I had only just managed to regain a modicum of composure when my neighbour peered round the edge of the rusted steel container.

'Hello Michael, have you lost something?' he said throwing armfuls of broken plasterboard and bits of paint-splattered wood into the skip. As the rubbish clanged off the inside he paused, wiped the dust from his eyes and scanned me closely.

'Are you alright?' he asked with genuine concern as he took in my look of anguish.

'I erm, yes, fine thanks, couldn't be better; I was just surprised that it was erm...empty already?'

'Ah yes don't worry there's plenty of room if you need to dump anything. Don't know what happened. Somebody fly-tipped in it last night. Must have emptied the entire contents of their flat into it. We had to get it emptied first thing so we could carry on decorating. It was bizarre, plenty of quite nice stuff. Jean made me sort it and give loads to the charity shop. Erm, are you alright, you look quite white?'

'Oh, er I see.' I mumbled. 'No no, I'm quite fine, erm, maybe I'll pop in a couple of old bits and bobs later if you don't mind Jim?'

'Not at all Michael. Well, must get on, see you. Maybe grab a pint later?'

'Sure thing, love to.'

I croaked and turned back towards my flat. Oh my god, all gone! All my stuff. All my notes!!

I entered the flat cautiously. She was still there. Sitting on the windowsill. Singing to herself.

> You don't need notes. You don't need books. You just
> need to ask the right questions Phoney.

I sat down heavily on my chair and stifled a sob.

'Don't call me phoney, my name is Michael.'

> No it's Phoney. 'Cause that's what you are. Going round
> the world, speaking to all those people, telling them
> all that stuff about how to be happy healthy and sane.
> All those words. All lies. You are the most stressed out,
> lonely, miserable, grumpy person in the whole street.
> So glad you deleted it all. Now we can start from the
> beginning.

'Huh, deleted it...all!?'

In moments I had fired up my laptop. With growing panic I searched the desktop, the hard drives, every digital nook and cranny. Nothing. My laptop had been wiped. This time I sobbed for real.

'Why? Amy why would you do this to me? Who are you? What are you? Are you the devil?'

*I didn't do it, you did. I'm Amy, I keep on telling you that. I am a small girl aged around five or six. Thought you didn't believe in gods and devils anyway Phoney.*

'I er, don't, didn't, oh hell, I don't know anything anymore...!'

*You know tons and tons of stuff actually. That's been your problem Phoney. You believe that by knowing tons of things you will find peace. Knowledge is your god, confusion and delusion your hell. That's why I'm here to help you.*

'What the... of course knowledge is important! That's my whole life I've thrown away.'

*You haven't thrown your life away. You are still here. Still sobbing. Still breathing. Still being a Phoney and still not asking the right questions.*

'Oh great, a philosophical and metaphysical debate with a six-year-old.  Brilliant, just what I need!'

*What you need Phoney is to stop and then let go. You've done the material stuff. That was easy peasy. Now it's the hard stuff.*

Suddenly the small girl was beside me. She was stroking my hair and her voice was kind and gentle. I couldn't help it. I felt myself calm down as Amy spoke.

*We are going to start again. You got lost. If you don't get found again then I can't go home. I am going to teach you how to stop and let go. You need to stop all your fancy knowings and practise simply being. You are just a simple being, simply being human. That's it, nothing more. You just forgot - that's all. You are actually a nice man Phoney, you just forgot how to be nice to yourself.*

# Chapter 1

'I've got to stop?'

*Yes, it's easier than you think. That is, you do a lot of thinking trying to work it all out. All that thinking has made you ill. Stopping is simple. It's the first step towards healing.*

'Healing?'

*Do you think that you are well Phoney?*

'Yes. No. I guess not. I'm hallucinating you aren't I?'

Amy put her small curly-haired head on one side and looked at me, waiting, patiently waiting for me to speak some sense to her.

'I mean to say, well...erm... I have no idea how I feel. Maybe lost, like you said.'

*Good. Now let's start a new book. Let's live your story. One that I can read. One that anyone can read. One that is not phoney and full of lies and made up stuff. There are a lot of Michaels who are lost in the world and a lot of Amys who want to go home out here. You just need to keep it simple.*

'Are you an angel?'

*Keep it simple Phoney. I told you I'm a five- or six-year-old girl and now it's time for sleeps.*

Then as she vanished from my sight, she added:

*Angels are huge and I am little. Silly Phoney.*

So here I am, hands shaking, at my laptop, trying to work out how on earth I'm going to write this madness down.

# Chapter Two

*The first thing, Phoney, is learning to Stop. It's not as easy as it sounds. Yet it is easy. It's like trying to stop eating a delicious cake that you know is bad for you halfway through. You have been munching a huge cake Phoney for far too long and now you have to STOP.*

Amy was sitting in her usual place on the windowsill. She was cross-legged and wearing a strange orange dress that resembled a monk's robe. As she was speaking she was munching on a huge slice of chocolate cake that she had sent me to the coffee shop to buy. In front of me were a peppermint tea and a small fruit salad. My tummy rumbled and I felt a stirring of anger.

*The second thing is to stop you being scared of me my dearest Phoney. This is a very special thing we have and for it to work you mustn't be scared.*

'Scared? I'm not scared of a little girl who eats cake and is obviously hypocritical...'

*Yes you are Phoney. You are very scared of me. You are scared of what I represent to your poor work-wearied mind.*

'Pardon?'

I was not used to Amy using long words and as she spoke she turned to me. She stared straight at me and I felt a shiver of alarm ripple through my body. I took a calming sip of my herbal tea, wishing that it were coffee. I felt drowsy, tired and grumpy and now my pulse had started to race.

> *You are not dying Phoney. My being here does not
> mean that you are ill. My being here means that you are
> going to have to accept something in order to let go of
> something. My being here means that you are getting
> better...well starting to anyhow.*

I nibbled my fruit salad. It actually tasted really good. There was
something in Amy's tone of voice that began to settle me down
again. Amy's voice was either commanding or reassuring. She
was small but she seemed tough and gentle at the same time.

> *You are like a skittish horse. You are scared of everything.
> You do not need to be scared of me. I am your spiritual
> guide.*

I spluttered on my pineapple chunk.

'Spiritual what? Spiritual!? I'm a scientist, I'm an academic,
and spirituality is for the weak of mind and the deluded. I am a
materialist, an empiricist, a man of science. Spiritual guides were
invented by self-seeking nutters to feed off the goodwill of others.
Religion has done nothing but murder, maim and extend the
suffering of the world since it was created. It was conceived as a
means to control the masses. Religion is a...'

> *Quiet Phoney!*

Amy's voice silenced me. Under her gaze I felt slightly ridiculous. I
swallowed my pineapple chunk.

> *Well if you don't want your very own spiritual guide than
> I'll be off. If you want to believe that you are really ill and
> might be dying then you can. It's just that I won't be able
> to help you. You'll make yourself worse, not better. Sorry
> Phoney. Goodbye.*

Then Amy vanished. Disappeared. Leaving a lump of chocolate cake lying on the floor where it had been dropped. The room was suddenly silent. It felt different. It felt empty, really empty.

Well that was that then. I was cured. The hallucinations had stopped. I could start my life all over again. I scrabbled around for my logical brain. I took a deep breath, held it and then exhaled as I reached for my intellect. I might have held my breath for a moment too long, as I felt a bit dizzy. I shook my head and moved towards the window, bending down to pick up the dropped piece of cake. As I lifted it slowly up to my face I froze. There was no denying it. One perfectly formed bite mark indented the small expanse of chocolate deliciousness. I felt my hand shake. I lifted the piece to my mouth in slow motion. I opened my mouth wide and peered at my reflection in the window. There was no way that my mouth could have created that small bite.

My mind cartwheeled again. I held my breath and gulped. Come on brain; let's get a grip. We can do this. Obviously there must be some rational explanation. In my confusion I must have taken a piece of cake from the coffee shop along with my new diet fad purchases. I must have taken it from someone else's plate by mistake. It must be the remains of a slice left by a small child. My subconscious must have used it to support my delusion that I had a small five- or six-year-old friend. That was it. That explains the flat, everything. I must be suffering from schizophrenia. I am hallucinating a world to justify my mental breakdown in order to rebuild myself. I was a classic case.

I turned to reach for one of my many medical and psychological books and then stopped. Of course, I had thrown them all out. I had thrown out all my precious belongings. All my work! All my papers, my research, my notes! Oh my god. I really was losing it. I must be flipping out. Maybe the tumour was hidden in the scan. Maybe I should get a second opinion.

Just for a second my imagination flickered on inside the gloom of my mind like a candle in a black-out. What if the results of the test were right and I was okay? What if spirits and metaphysical stuff really did exist? What if Amy was my spiritual guide? As absurd as it was, maybe I should just entertain the idea for a moment. I mean, wouldn't that be the scientific thing to do?

I sat down heavily on my chair and took a deep breath. I peered carefully at the small bite mark in the cake and allowed my aversion and resistance to the idea that Amy wasn't real to dissipate just for a moment. And as I did I felt a strange sensation come over me. It began at my feet and slowly progressed all the way up to my head. The bird song outside seemed to stop. All my movements became slow. My breathing softened. My heart rate seemed to slow. It was as if time itself was decelerating. I turned my head ever so slowly towards the window. Outside the trees seemed to be motionless. Not a single leaf stirred. A cat on the wall beneath the tree sat immobile. I looked around the empty flat and marvelled at how the dust motes seemed to hang, static in a shaft of sunlight.

By the window, on the floor, were loads of crumbs. In fact, the space beneath the window was covered in crumbs; crumbs that had been made by many small bites and much careless chewing of chocolate cake. Just above them a spider was suspended from a gossamer thin thread of silk. I slowly picked up the piece of cake again. I lifted it as if I was cradling the most delicate substance known to man. I became aware of every crumb of the cake. I could see the individual grains of flour and chocolate. I could see the minute glistening granules of sugar exposing themselves to the sunlight. I could see the delicate carvings made by small teeth that formed the most perfect bite mark I had ever seen. I let out a long slow breath, which seemed to come from my boots. Then, like the small trickle of melting chocolate oozing down my thumb, a realisation dawned on me. As my logical mind gave up and capitulated to the present moment, my whole perception of life shifted. With it came a sensation of warmth and wellbeing, an awareness of deep calm. It was an idea that worked its way slowly up towards my consciousness from the very centre of my being. Maybe Amy was real!

*Hey well done Phoney. You've stopped being scared of*

*me.*

I jumped, startled at the sound. The room whirled back into life. City noises and bird song roared in from outside. The piece of cake fell from my hand and splattered into pieces on my desk. My pulse raced. And I spun round to see my little orange-robed friend sitting once more on the windowsill.

'You, you're back, oh hell!'

> *Well that's nice. Glad to see you too. Now Phoney, don't think. Don't move. Stay seated. Oh, and keep on breathing.*

I realised as she gave me her orders that I was holding my breath.

> *Breathe deeply. That's it, in and out. Nice and slowly. Good. You must keep on accepting that I am real. Otherwise you are going to be afraid. Your fear will stop you enjoying my wonderful company. Your fear will keep on trying to persuade you that you are ill. Your fear will persuade you that you are dying. I am your spiritual guide. You are really a very lucky man. You are what we guides say, blessed. Now, say it out loud Phoney.*

'Huh?'

> *Say out loud that I am your spiritual guide.*

So I did. There, in the middle of my cleaned out flat. At my desk upon which I had verbally slain every idea of non-rationalist thought or non-scientific reason ever written down; there at my shrine for intellectual illumination, I threw in my scientific and academic towel. I let go of my whole sense of self. I dropped my idea of the aspiring professor, lecturer, writer and broadcaster and dared to believe that a small and slightly chocolate-covered hallucination of a girl was indeed my spiritual guide.

# Chapter 2

'I believe that you, Amy, are my spiritual guide.'

*There you go Phoney. Now then. How do you feel?*

'I feel kind of calm, relieved on all levels, disbelieving and believing at the same time. I feel as if a weight has just gone. Oh my god, I'm healed. Wow!'

*Oh poor little Phoney. That's great but you are just starting out. This is just the beginning. I just had to get you to stop being afraid of me. Hey, I'm glad it worked. I wasn't sure.*

'You weren't sure? I thought you spiritual guides knew everything?'

*Oh we kind of do. It's just that I've never done this before.*

'You've never done this before. Never done what?'

*Well I'm probably the first Amy ever in the whole history of everything.*

'The first?'

*Yes the first Amy. Brilliant isn't it? That means our story will be the first as well.*

'Never done what?'

*Oh, never guided someone before. I thought the cake might work. Just couldn't be sure.*

'You thought it might work?'

*Yup the whole cake thing. You see, Phoney, you've spent all your life being afraid of me. Well, allowing me to be*

31

*the cause of your fear. So you see you were hanging on to
your fear for dear life. I had to trick you. And it worked. I
think I'm good. I think this will all work out fine. As long as
you do what I say.*

My head was starting to whirl again. Amy was jumping up and
down and twirling round and round in a state of obvious delight.
Part of me was chuckling and part of me was confused and even
a bit angry. I tried to slow the spinning child down.

'You said that you are the first?'

*Yup sure am! Well I guess you humans have had all those
chubby cherubs helping you learn not to be afraid of love.
Maybe fairies I guess. Hmmm quite a lot of little folk, but I
am definitely the first real Amy-spiritual-guide.*

'Fairies, cherubs? Oh come on, you don't expect me to believe in
fairies!'

*Well Phoney. You believe in little old me. Can't say you
don't. Can't take back what's said.*

My head was aching slightly now and I was beginning to feel
tired. The day had turned into night and my view from the window
had vanished. I could clearly see our reflection in the glass. Amy
heard my tired thoughts.

*Time for bed, Phoney. You've been through a lot today.
First thing tomorrow we'll go for a walk. We'll find
somewhere nice to practise stopping. You have been
running for ages and ages. You need to learn how to stop.*

'I can't go out with you.'

*Why not?*

'Well even if you've convinced me that I'm not mad, erm...

32

suffering from mental health issues, everyone else will think I am.'

*Am what?*

'Mad...suffering from mental health issues.'

Amy was stifling a laugh with her small chocolate-covered hand.

'Seeing me babbling away to myself is the quickest way to getting locked up...I mean interred in a medical institution.'

*There is nothing to be ashamed of. Everybody in the whole world has mental health. Many people need help at times. I'm helping you. I can lock you up if you want.*

'No Amy I don't want that. It's just...'

*Oh I see Phoney. You are still scared of how people see you, aren't you? Hey, just speak to me in your head. I can hear everything that huge brain of yours says anyway. I am just trying to shut out all the noise.*

'Oh, erm, I see. Well if that works.'

*Of course it works Phoney, I'm your spiritual guide. I'm the first ever...*

'I know, I know, the first Amy ever.'

I chuckled, I might be thinking my part of our conversation quietly inside my head but I could hear Amy as loud as any excited child.

*The quieter your head becomes, the clearer you will hear. Now go to bed Phoney. You need your beauty sleep, a lot in fact.*

Amy laughed at her insinuation and pointed back through the flat to where a single blanket and a cushion would have to do for a bed. I threw out my bed?!! I sighed and stood up, unsure if I even had a toothbrush left. I felt very tired but slightly excited at the same time. Stuff like this just didn't happen to me. Not even after a large bottle of good malt whisky.

> Go to sleep Phoney. It will be nice outside tomorrow. I want to go to the park and have an ice cream.

Amy followed me through into the small bedroom. As I lay down she wrapped the thick blanket around me, popping the pillow under my head, and peered into my face.

> Stop frowning Phoney. Never frown before sleep otherwise your wrinkles you might keep.

She chuckled at her terrible rhyme. I was sure that I could never sleep on this uncomfortable floor. My frown was one of discomfort. I was just about to explain that to Amy when she reached her small hand out. As her red curls tickled my forehead she simply said:

> Sleep now.

That was the last thing I remembered until morning.

# Chapter Three

*Once upon a time there was a man sitting down on the side of the road...*

'Once upon a time?!'

*Look Phoney I'm telling the story. It's all part of my guiding you so be quiet.*

'Amy, just before you begin. If you are my spirit guide, how come you are a little girl of five?'

*Or six.*

'Exactly, five or six.'

*Oh we'll get onto that later Phoney but the simple truth is your ego is as large as your brain and you wouldn't listen to a grown up. You'd think that you knew better. In fact you think you know better than everyone you meet. You have to be right about everything.*

'That's not true! I am an academic. We strive to be egoless in our search for knowledge '

*See what I mean?*

'Huh?'

*See what I mean? You have trouble hearing truth. All that knowledge and no wisdom. Anyhow I'm telling a story so shut up!*

Chapter 3

I smiled and tried to sit cross-legged on the sweet-scented and recently mown grass of Kelvingrove Park. I had chosen our spot carefully, far away from the crowds of bleary-eyed students picking their way home from all-night parties. We were well away from the small groups of early morning mums trying to pass the time with their toddlers before the coffee shops opened.

But even though we were up high on the hill I was concerned that I might look rather foolish. I had my academic reputation to think of. It was a reputation that might need some salvaging now that my masterpiece had been rejected. What was I going to tell the head of department and the Dean? I needed to publish regularly to keep my post. I had been working on this for years. What was I doing here? Were these the last vestiges of my sanity? I had to try to control my rising sense of panic and get grounded. Where was I? Oh yes, I was sitting on a sunny elevated bank in my favourite park in the city. I let my breath slow down as Amy had been trying to teach me all morning.

Amy had woken me early, just like any young child would. I had slept surprisingly well for a night on the floor under only a single blanket. My body felt as stiff as a board though. I had awoken with a very small face peering into mine. Amy's warm rose-tinged breath had tickled my cheek like a gentle summer breeze. I felt pleased that she was still there and her presence brought a smile to my face where normally my early morning frown would have been.

My tiny slave master hadn't allowed me any coffee again. There was no food in the flat, which meant that my tummy was rumbling. Yet here, on the hillside, looking out across the trees and the duck pond with my diminutive guide sitting beside me, I felt a strange kind of peace. I hadn't done this since student days.

*Phoney! Your mind's drifting off all over the place. Take it off your belly. Now sit still and stop wiggling around. Keep your back nice and straight like how I taught you and listen to my story.*

'Sorry Amy.'

I straightened my stiff back, crossed my legs and focussed on Amy's voice whilst reminding myself not to reply to her out loud in case I was noticed.

*Once upon a time.... erm...so anyway, there was this old man sitting by the side of the road. He looks up and he sees a man on a horse racing down the lane towards him. He can see that he is hanging on for dear life. He can see the look of panic on the man's face. The old man shouts to the man on the horse as he draws near. 'Hey there. Where are you going in such a hurry?' As the man on the horse rushes past he calls back. 'No idea, ask the horse.'*

I laughed out loud. Amy was actually a great storyteller. She put her whole heart and soul into it and made all the right faces to convey emotion.

'Great story Amy.'

*Don't patronise me Phoney. I know I'm a great storyteller. You've been buying into my stories for longer than you think. Now, what's the meaning of the story?*

'Huh, well you don't have to be like that. I ...'

I stopped, aware that I was shouting, or speaking loudly with passion (as I had told my poor wife on many an occasion). Some students had started to watch me carefully. If students notice your existence from within their bubbles of learning and self-exploration, it means you had better check yourself. Either you are being weirder than them, or doing something so weird that they would like to join in with you. Thankfully they were not my students so I returned my attention to the small guru who was leaning towards me, frowning.

*See what I mean Phoney? Off you go again. The horse*

*of your self-conscious mind is racing off down the road
of distraction and confusion and you are hanging on for
dear life.*

'Huh?'

Amy was using long words again and it was a shock. I wasn't
even used to her presence in my life yet, let alone as a highly
precocious small child who had eaten a dictionary for breakfast.

*Your poor old mind is chattering away and chasing after
ideas and thoughts and stuff that you just don't need to
be giving any attention to.*

'I was only trying not to look mad and you keep using long
words...I thought that you were only five.'

*Or six - Phoney, I thought we had agreed to stop saying
things like crazy and mad and see it's all just mental
health. It's time to get your mental faculties healthy. Now
focus. Concentrate. Listen.*

I shut up. Amy was being forceful and when she was being
forceful it was as if a very small, powerful and wise old woman
spoke out from behind her large blue child's eyes. I felt
momentarily alarmed.

*Phoney, stop being scared. Breathe. Relax. You have
to learn how to stop. You are like a small mouse that is
scared of its own shadow. You are always running away
from things. Or you are chasing after things.*

'But Amy, I am an academic. My mind is like a detective. I am
always searching and thinking. Thinking is what I do. Sometimes
it takes days to formulate an idea, to extrapolate...'

*Phoney!*

'Huh?'

*Please shut up and stop using long words. They don't impress me. Listen.*

Amy leant in close. Her little face was calm and her blue eyes sparked and held me transfixed. I could smell her rosy breath and see the freckles on her nose.

*Phoney. You need to learn how to stop. You have a very bad habit. Your very bad habit is the horse that you are sitting on. It is racing all over the place and you have no idea where it's taking you. You might think that it is being so very helpful but, Phoney, most of the time it's just running away from things or chasing after stuff. None of which you need. None of which will help you.*

'Help me what?'

I squirmed. This was sounding true but...

*No buts Phoney. If we are going to get you better, you have to learn to Stop. It's the first step of healing yourself.*

'The what ...of ...what?'

*Baby steps Phoney! Now sit with your back straight and breathe nice and slowly.*

I tried but my back was sore. My backside was aching from sitting for so long. Grass was beginning to tickle my ankles and I was sure that a spider had crawled up my trouser leg. I began to scratch and itch.

*Oh heavens to Betsy Phoney! You have a total grasshopper mind. It's springing off all over the place. Right this isn't working. Come on, stand up - we are going to the pond.*

I stood up and tried to massage my legs and backside and check if there was anything up my trouser legs all at the same time. There wasn't and I failed. I slipped on the grassy slope and fell over, sprawling face-down in front of the shocked students.

As I picked myself up I became aware of the purest laughter I had ever heard. It seemed to rise like a bubbling brook to surround my senses. The laughter was infectious. It was childlike, pure, carefree and wonderful. I realised that Amy was overcome with mirth at my pratfall. The sight of a small girl doubled up and crying with laughter set me off. For the first time in ages I felt myself laugh. It seemed to start low down near my boots, work its way up my body and then burst out of my surprised mouth. This sent Amy into more squeals of laughter.

> *Your laugh Phoney...it sounds like...a startled donkey...ha ha he he...*

This accurate description made me laugh all the more. I remembered an awkward dinner party when my first wife had snapped at me to stop embarrassing her with my laughing. I had stopped, mortified. Oh my god, maybe that was the last time I had really laughed. And then I was off again, vaguely aware that even the students had started chuckling too. Oh well it will be all through university in no time: the mad professor losing it in the park. I stopped laughing.

We were almost at the duck pond and Amy span round on me.

> *Oh Phoney you are funny. See. You've run off into self-doubt and worry again. They might think what a wonderfully happy man you are and all choose to do your stuffy old history course.*

'It's not stuffy!' I snapped at her, and then felt immediately bad as she turned her huge blue eyes on me in shock.

> *Touched a nerve Phoney? The History of Madness in*

*the Age of Post Modernism and Its Effect on Collective
Action!!!' I mean really?! How's that not stuffy?*

Before I could argue or defend my great work she had grabbed
my hand and turned me to face the pond. I stood up against a
low black iron railing. In front of me was the ornate duck pond. In
the middle was an island covered in green bushes and trees. One
tree, directly opposite me, had become the perch for countless
birds over the years. Their acidic excrement had stripped the
tree of leaves and bark and now it stood like a big, bleached
white skeleton amidst the colour and vibrancy of the park. It was
covered in pigeons and circled by happy ducks milling around on
the water.

Amy squeezed my hand hard and looked up at me, squinting into
the sunlight with her huge blue eyes.

*Now Phoney, let's get real for a moment. I want you to
breathe slowly. Look at that tree. Relax your vision. That's
right...just focus nice and gently on the tree. Relax your
body. Now, become still.*

As she said the words I felt myself become still. It was not the
stillness that you might get if you heard a noise downstairs and
were straining your ears to work out whether it was an intruder.
It was more like the stillness of a deep sleep, but with my eyes
wide open. My heart was beating gently, not pounding with fear.
I felt relaxed. I was simply and quietly aware of the skeleton tree
opposite me, covered in birds. Even the gentle breeze seemed
to cease. The other trees became motionless. Everything went
quiet. The whole world seemed to slow down. My shoulders
dropped and I felt a moment of deep relaxation. I just let go of
everything other than my concentration on the tree opposite.

*Now.*

Amy whispered the word and gently squeezed my hand.

# Chapter 3

At that moment all the birds on the tree took flight. They lifted from the branches as one. Yet they moved as if in slow motion. They took off effortlessly, gracefully and silently.

Once airborne they slowed further until they all flew towards me, across the pond, in an unhurried, precise and leisurely fashion. It was as if time was crawling. The huge flock of pigeons, gently flapping their wings, climbed upwards in a deliberate and synchronised motion. I could see the individual feathers of their wings as they became airborne. I could even sense their small muscles straining. Their wings seemed to make a soft, leisurely thrumming sound. They moved so slowly. I was entranced. I watched each bird swim through the air until, as one, the flock soared over my head and up into the blue sky. What was happening?

The instant I sought to question my experience, the world around me burst back into a cacophony of light, sound and movement again. I felt the breeze. I heard the sound of laughter and talking, of ducks swimming and I could hear the squadron of pigeons as they circled overhead.

*How do you feel?*

Amy was looking up at me, smiling.

'I, er, don't know. I feel really peaceful. I feel quiet, relaxed...I erm...what happened?'

> *Don't question, just see. Try to stay in the moment for a few minutes longer. You became still Phoney. You haven't been still in years. I needed to show you so that you would have something to aim for. I needed to give you a gift You needed to remember the joy of stillness. We are just at the beginning Phoney. You are going to need some hope and faith. Now you can have faith that it works.*

I felt different. As I looked around the park I noticed everything.

The colours, the sounds, the smells, the warm summer breeze and one single soft white feather floating gently down in front of me. As I scanned the park I could see that people's faces seemed to be like expressive books. I could see the flickering of emotions move across their faces like ripples on a calm pond. In fact I felt just like the calm pond that the ducks were paddling on. Amy was right, once you let go of all of the whirring thoughts in your mind the world turns Technicolor. I realised that I was actually seeing the truth of the world around me. I wasn't ignoring it. I was noticing everything but I was doing it effortlessly. A great sense of peace seemed to envelop me.

I held Amy's hand and turned to look back up the hill. The trees were resplendent in their summer dresses and I could make out the spaces between their branches. I could see the leaves, I felt their presence. The world was no longer flat. The whole park had become three-dimensional. I was aware of the spaces between everything. I sensed that I was part of this entire wonderful and vibrant universe. Just noticing things brought me pleasure. I remained standing at the edge of the pond, my hand still in Amy's, as if letting go of it would mean letting go of this amazing vision. As people passed us by I felt myself smiling and found that my smile was returned. I couldn't believe how beautiful everybody looked. Every time a question or doubt popped into my mind I brushed it away. I was not going to let anything stop this experience for me, not even me.

> *My dearest Phoney, as your poor old mind gets all cluttered up with ideas and fears and stuff, it keeps on making up lots of new versions of who you are.*

I let Amy's words wash over me.

As Amy spoke I glanced up at a lazy V of geese, high overhead, making their way towards the highland lochs. The world was as peaceful as the slow beating of their wings. A seagull swooped past and another single white feather mesmerised me as it slowly drifted up and over the pond, caught up in the gentle eddies of the warm breeze. Amy squeezed my hand gently and brought my mind back into a relaxed focus.

> *Don't go into a trance Phoney, stay with the moment. You see my dear Phoney, when you are truly still, when you are present, the real, eternal you emerges. You are free of all the fluttering chatter of a hundred little personalities flapping around inside your mind. Because being who you really are is just so wonderful, you will learn to choose to just be yourself. You won't be scared to be yourself any more.*

Amy was right. At this moment in time I couldn't even entertain any idea of myself other than the one I was experiencing right now. I was so calm, so peaceful and so clear and present. A small smile flickered across my face as I realised that I actually quite liked myself, I was actually fond of the person I was right now. He was the kind of chilled, relaxed, joyful person that I would like as a friend. I squeezed Amy's hand in return and took the fragrant air deeply into my lungs.

'Wow Amy, this is amazing! You are good, what are we going to do next?'

As I spoke I felt my reverie slip just a little. My mind was building up an avalanche of questions. Amy let go of my hand and gave the cutest chuckle I had ever heard. It was the chuckle of a small child who was most definitely in charge of the game.

> *OK Phoney that's enough for today. Besides you need to keep practising. Practising how to stop all on your own, without me being here, before we can move on. This is just a first step my dearest Phoney. Well done and thanks for trusting me.*

'Huh?'

I looked down. The upturned face of my remarkable new-found imaginary friend was glowing with pride. Somehow she seemed smaller and even slightly see-through at the edges.

*You did well Phoney. You let go.*

'I did let go didn't I? Now I see what you mean. I was hanging on to all that stuff. I wasn't really here was I? I wasn't really seeing everything as it was.'

*Good Phoney. You let go of all the chatter, the moans and the doubts. You let go of the horse. You got off. You stopped riding off into the vastness of nowhere, thinking that it was somewhere.*

'So that's what people mean when they say stop the world I want to get off then?'

*It's not the world Phoney. It's your world. This is the real world, right here, now. It just simply is. Now you are just simply a human being, being simply here. Not on your horsey of bad habits.*

'How long will this last Amy? Can I do this whenever I want to?'

*Right now Phoney you are not doing anything! You are being everything; that's the difference.*

I turned my head upwards again and marvelled at the clouds as they gently scudded across the treetops. Even the clouds seemed different, full of light and shade and texture. The natural world seemed so real and so vibrant. The sandstone facades of the beautiful Georgian buildings were lit up in the morning sunshine and shone like gold. The air seemed to buzz with insects and the sound of bird song. I was sure that I had never realised just how many birds sang inside the great parks of Glasgow. Maybe all I had heard before was the drone of traffic. Now their song seemed like an orchestrated symphony of happiness.

As we walked, somewhere deep inside me, like old echoes, I

became aware of a clatter of questions and doubts and thoughts rising up. Every time this happened Amy gave my hand a small squeeze so that, with her help, I let go of them as soon as they started to arrive.

Saying nothing we walked ever so slowly all around the pond. I felt as if I was gliding. I was aware of my every step. I was aware of my gentle breathing. I was aware of everything and my awareness was effortless. Eventually we came to a gentle stop right back where we had started. The pigeons bedecked the bare tree branches again like old socks on a washing line and the laughter of children in the play area tinkled musically in the air.

Amy looked up at me and let go of my hand. She seemed to shimmer like the sunlight on the pond's surface. She was almost transparent. She had a big smile on her face and had somehow managed to make an ice cream appear in her other hand. She was happily licking it and humming gently to herself. Amy looked up at me and I smiled at her sticky, sugary smile. She looked very pleased with herself.

> *Well done Phoney. I'm very pleased with you. It must be because I'm a good guide. Now then Phoney, keep on practising Letting Go. Don't pause. Not for a moment. Not even when you sleep. See you tomoz but don't forget to buy a new bed. I mean, who wants to sleep on the floor?*

Amy grinned at me, swallowed the last of her ice cream and then vanished, leaving me to enjoy the park for the first time in many years.

# Chapter Four

It took me all day to find a bed. I eventually chose a small, single sofa bed that I could load into the back of my cavernous Volvo and just about carry up the stairs on my own.

I tried not to rush. I tried to slow down. I tried, honest I did.

But truthfully, as soon as I was in town. As soon as I had to speak with shop assistants. As soon as I had to drive through the Glasgow rush hour traffic. As soon as I stubbed my toe and jarred my elbow carrying the couch. As soon as I saw the pile of bills on my super-clean hallway where once there had been a doormat. As soon as I put the couch together, wrong, three times!!! As soon as I realised I still had no food and no milk to make tea, and no kettle. As soon as I had to rush to the café before it closed. As soon as I drank heavily from a huge skinny latte, extra hot to go, and burned my mouth. As soon as I started to think about work, my wife, my daughters, my book and the lack of clothes in my wardrobe...

As soon as all those hectic experiences began, I quickly felt all my peace, calm and gentleness disperse and drip away from me. By the time I eventually sat down on the couch my head was once more full of the usual roar of whirring thoughts and distracted whims. My head felt busier than the approach flight path of Heathrow airport.

I swear I actually felt more anxious than I had before.

I know that we all stress about money. Paying the bills, paying maintenance, just affording to live in this crazy consumer-based reality always makes me anxious. Hazel, my clear minded and clever wife, had always done our accounts. She'd used carefully created spreadsheets and had shown me how to fill in the columns; how to plan and run my affairs. She'd helped me calculate my tax and National Insurance payments and shown me how to save. Since she had politely requested me to sling my hook and move out, my finances had transformed into a huge pile of receipts and bills that I'd been cramming into groaning box files.

Opening my morning mail I had found myself staring at the latest round of utility bills and a reminder from my accountant. I realised that my accounts were soon due for completion. It was then that I felt the cold grip of terror around my heart. I no longer even had my box files! I had no receipts. I had no way to calculate my returns. Oh my god, was I ever going to get stung for tax! That would mean I'd be late with my payments on my insurance, rent, loans, credit cards. Even worse, my maintenance payments would be delayed. As if on cue my mobile phone buzzed and I saw that I had a message from my first wife. It was demanding an early payment of monies due to 'unforeseen circumstances' with my kids.

I tried to shake my brain awake. How many lectures did I have? How many speaking engagements were coming up? How much was I going to earn? When would I get paid? Could I still salvage my manuscript somehow? Oh hell, could I honestly remember even a quarter of what I had written?

Grown men don't cry very often. I'm not ashamed to say that a very small tear found its way into the corner of my eye. Damn Amy. Somehow she had made me feel vulnerable. How was I going to resolve all this mess? I needed a coffee. Maybe a change of scene would help.

As I stood up from my sofa bed I sensed a familiar presence behind me.

*Oh poor Phoney. You aren't very good at stopping are*

*you?*

I spun round. Amy was jumping up and down on the new couch. She was hopping from one foot to another, testing out the springs. Her curly red hair bounced up and down with her and her red dress billowed out like a miniature parachute. At least she didn't have her wellies on. I noticed that I didn't react to her sudden appearance with surprise or fright. I guess I had grown used to her appearances already. I realised that deep inside I'd been kind of hoping that she would show up.

> *You know that you are going to have to sort all this out for yourself Phoney? Only you can be responsible for your own happiness. Only you.*

Amy had pinned her laser vision on me as she bounced up and down, making the sofa bed groan and creak. I frowned and tried to wiggle out from under her intense gaze.

> *You have to stop Phoney. Unless you learn how to become still, you are going to carry on racing around until you are all frazzed out and no good to anyone.*

'Everyone gets 'frazzed out' at times Amy!'

Amy smiled at me and stopped bouncing. She popped her head onto one side and, flicking her cute curls away from her face, sucked her thumb for a moment. She frowned at me as if in deep thought whilst playing with her long curly hair. Then she rubbed her nose on her sleeve and tried again

> *You are hanging on to your charging horse for dear life Phoney. And you keep on trying to build the road for the horse to rush down. It is like trying to lay down the tracks for a runaway train. The thing is, you don't know where it's going. That's why you are suffering. I'm surprised your arms don't fall off with all the hanging on that you have to do. You just need to get off the horse, step off the train,*

*and get off your pretend world for a moment and chill out.
It's really easy my dear Phoney.*

Amy looked impressed with herself. Her mixed metaphors
irritated me and I felt patronised. Financial worries were real and
challenging. Besides she had thrown out all my accounts - well
she had made me do it - of that I felt certain. I felt anger rising
in me as years of frustration and tension burst up through the
spring of my consciousness. I felt myself getting ready to shout.

'You have no idea how hard it is. You have no idea Amy. Day in
day out. Just trying to survive. Just trying to get by. Constantly
reinventing yourself. Working all the hours God gives you. 24/7!
On and on. I'm exhausted Amy. I've had enough. No-one on this
planet can stop. If you STOP all that happens is you have to run
even faster the next day. I am constantly running, just trying to
make ends meet. If I'm not physically working then I'm planning
what to do next or I'm evaluating what I just did to make it better.
On and on, it doesn't ever stop until you're dead!  I'm exhausted,
I'm knackered, I've had enough. Don't you see?'

Amy was still standing on the couch. Her big eyes were looking up
at me and her eyes were full of tears. I felt awful. I realised I was
shouting again. Even though Amy was standing on the couch I
was towering over the small girl like a raging giant.

'I'm so sorry Amy, I didn't mean to make you cry. I'm just stressed
out that's all...'

*No Phoney it's OK. I was upset for how much you are
suffering. But this is fabby dabby doo. It's wonderful. It's
actually rather brilliant.*

'Huh?'

Amy was smiling again and clapping to herself. All tears had gone
and she was even doing a strange kind of dance, hopping from
one foot to the other. My brand new couch creaked alarmingly. I

had a sudden flash of the few screws and odd bits that had been rather worryingly left over when I'd put it together. I tried to calm her down in case she caused it to collapse. I sighed. Amy had distracted me from my rage again.

'What's brilliant?

My anger quickly passed as Amy's eccentric movements and bizarre bouncing movements made me smile. Her sheer enjoyment of life, the universe and everything was infectious. It was like having a small whirlwind of playfulness exploding into your life without the actual parenting duties. Amy was doing a slow dance from foot to foot whilst pretending to be some sort of bird. She squawked, jumped in the air and looked at me sideways as if she was a largish red chicken.

> It's brilliant Phoney. All that stuff. Everything you just shouted at me. That's it. That's the beginning. You did it. You found your suffering. You woke up. You called it out. You spoke of your fears and wanting them to stop. You said them out loud. You now know that you want all of your nasty old fears to stop so that you don't get angry and shout at small and very lovely little girls who are only trying to help you.

'I froze. That was not what I expected to hear. Anyway, of course I'm suffering. The whole bloody world is suffering Amy. Life is suffering.'

> Exactly Phoney. It is. At last you have realised that. You have noticed truly, deeply. You are waking up. All of your life is suffering. You suffer all of your life.

'I'm what, I've what... you what..?'

> You are waking up to the fact that you are suffering. Remember the man on the horse? He didn't know where he was going. He didn't know where the horse was going.

56

*He didn't even know that he was suffering by hanging on to the horse for dear life.*

'Well of course I know that I suffer. Life is hard.'

*Yes Phoney it is and that's why it's brilliant. You get to practise so that it's not.*

'What? Practise what?'

*Your first challenge is to practise stopping. Stopping to stop your suffering.*

Amy gave me her triumphant look again. I felt confused and tired. I am a university lecturer. I don't deal in extreme emotions and, to be honest, they wear me out quickly.

'I'm exhausted, worn out Amy. To be honest I don't know if I can go on. I have no more energy left for your games.'

*I'm not playing games my dearest Phoney. Maybe we could later though. Now listen. You have just noticed that your life is all about suffering haven't you?*

Amy sat on the edge of the sofa bed and pulled a lollipop from her pocket. She looked so content and peaceful that I experienced a sharp contrast within myself. She was peaceful and happy; I was in turmoil and suffering the effect of that. Oh hell maybe she was right again.

'Erm...I guess so Amy, when you put it like that. Oh don't wipe your sticky fingers on the sofa bed! I...'

I let the words hang in the air. Amy was looking up at me with a serious frown on her face and was sitting very still, lollipop suspended half way to her mouth. I could see that she wanted me to get this point. She was waiting for me to understand. It was like being at school again. Under her severe gaze I sighed and wracked my brains.

'So, what you are saying Amy is that all the bad stuff that happens to me is just my suffering. You mean that all my life has become one great big state of suffering?'

I paused, looking for an answer, but Amy just slowly sucked her lollipop and waited for me to continue. I took a deep breath and tried again.

'So all of my life really is some sort of suffering. But life should not be the true definition of suffering? Life just is what it is and I choose to respond to it by suffering?'

A small smile was creeping across Amy's face yet she was trying hard not to show it. I felt encouraged and ploughed on.

'So then, all of this suffering is in fact caused by my own perceptions and ideas and beliefs. It is my thoughts that are causing me to suffer?'

Amy gave me a huge grin and then launched into one of her stories.

> *Well done Phoney you have arrived at the beginning. You have been able to wake up. You have arrived at the very start.*

Amy put her half-sucked lolly back into her pocket, wiped her face with her sleeve and continued.

> *So Phoney, this is where your story has to start. This is where everybody's story starts. Once upon a time...there was a man called Phoney who woke up to see that all of his life was built on suffering. All the earthquakes he was experiencing in his life came from his own faults. The fault lines ran deep inside him. They ran deep in his ideas about his world and who he was. They were so*

*deep within him that they caused powerful tremors and quakes which collapsed everything he built. He suffered as his home collapsed, his work collapsed, his friendships collapsed, his job collapsed and even his marriage crumpled into a pile of rubble.*

Amy somewhat over-emphasised the earthquake by making a loud crashing sound and falling to the floor where she lay as if crushed by falling debris. I decided Amy was a terrible ham actor but her theatrics had hit home.

'So it's my fault, all of this suffering then?'

I sat down and felt a deep sadness wash over me like a tsunami of grief. Amy was right: I was a complete failure. I had mucked up everything in my life. Every time I had tried to build something good it had literally collapsed. All my best and bravest efforts to create a great life had crumpled and fallen into disrepair. Now I was sitting here with literally nothing. I was in a bare, empty flat. The sum total of my life was zilch. This had to be the nadir of my little inconsequential life. This had to be...

Amy had stopped her heroic gurgling sounds and death twitches and sprung up to confront me with her small intense face.

*I won't have you being so nasty to yourself. Us spiritual guides can't have our wards heading off down those bumpy roads. Those horrible, negative beliefs are just a recipe for more suffering.*

'But Amy, I am agreeing with you. It's my entire fault. I'm a complete loser. I mean look at my life - it sucks!'

*No Phoney you are not getting it. Those beliefs are the fault lines that cause the earthquakes deep inside you. Those kinds of beliefs were there all along. Those painful beliefs are the root of all your suffering my poor dear Phoney. The truth is you are a fabulous, wonderful human being just like everybody else. You have just believed your own bad press. Deep inside you my dearest Phoney you have accepted that all there is is suffering. You have not noticed that you have gone on to create a world that agrees with you. You believe you suffer and then go on creating a world in which you really do suffer.*

Amy came closer to me, her little face a picture of concern. I could smell her rose tinted breath and she swept her bright red curls away from her face to get a better look at me.

*Look my dear wonderful Phoney. This is a great breakthrough. This time we have managed to collapse all the nasty old suffering bits and not the good bits. This is a spirit guide's job. I have to wake you up. There is an intruder Phoney.*

I span around, alarmed.

*No Phoney, not out there, in here.*

Amy prodded my chest, just above my heart.

*A nasty old thief has broken in and stolen all your joy. Not just a thief in the night but a thief in the day as well.*

Amy couldn't help herself; she was beginning to prowl around my small bedroom as if she was an international jewel thief. She was taking huge silent steps and was holding an imaginary magnifying glass out in front of her. I realised that Amy was trying to get me to play, in fact I had a sneaking suspicion that Amy thought that all learning should fundamentally originate from play. However, I was an adult feeling rather vulnerable and slightly confused so I folded my arms in mock disapproval. Amy's daft role-playing did bring a small smile to my face though. She crept up on me as I sat watching her and brought her large imaginary magnifying glass up close to my face. She blew a curl out of her eyes and continued.

# Chapter 4

*So, my dear Phoney, you've just noticed that you suffer all day long by making up make-believe worries and troubles all the time. You have just woken up to the fact that your life is one big bundle of hurt as you try to hang on to your nasty old habit energy of fear. That's all suffering is, down deep and dark inside you making smelly old fun with fear. That's where it all comes from. It all comes from your deepest fears my dear Phoney. In fact, you live in a world of fear. You are riding the horsey of fear.*

Amy leapt away from me, making me jump as she let out a very realistic neighing sound. Then off she went playing horses and cantering around the room at breakneck speed. I wondered if the noise of her galloping feet was real and how I would explain it to my neighbours. I tried to slow her down.

'Fear, Amy? I'm not fearful am I? I mean not really?'

*Yup you sure are, all the nasty terror of all those worries gobbling you up and stealing all your energy. They suck you dry of all your life force, all your joy, all of your play energy.*

Amy stabled her imaginary horse beside the sofa bed and stood in front of me with her hands on her small hips. It was true, all these emotions had left me feeling exhausted and in need of a large coffee.

'Well yes I guess you're right Amy. I know I always seem to be exhausted these days. You're right, this whole mess, it's my fault and...'

*There is no fault Phoney. This is not a blame culture. Blame is wrong. Judgment is wrong. You must never blame or judge anybody and that goes for yourself too. Judgment is just another nasty old fear habit. Look my dearest Phoney this is just the first step to finding your true happiness again. Once you wake up and grasp that your whole life is one of suffering, then, at that moment,*

*you can choose to change it. You take back your power.*
*Only you can choose to change it. That's all there is. It's*
*that simple.*

Something in the way Amy was speaking got through to me. Her voice was so kind and loving and gentle and firm at the same time. Suddenly I realised just who the grown up was in this conversation and it wasn't me. Amy whispered to me.

*You can step out of your nasty old prison Phoney. The*
*door was always open. You just need to realise that your*
*prison exists. Once you can see that your prison exists*
*you can see that the door has always been open. Until*
*you wake up to this fact you can't choose to put one giant,*
*size eleven, foot in front of another and simply walk out of*
*it.*

Amy was actually stroking my cheek as she said this. I realised that my face was wet. Tears of self-pity had been quietly moisturising my entire face like the melt water of a distant mountain range. Lakes of saltiness had formed on the lower slopes of my chin. I wiped the crags of my cheeks dry with my sleeve and gave what I thought was a very manly sniff.

'Oh Amy, I just feel so tired sometimes; it's all just a bit too much, my small cake-eating friend. So what must I do?'

*So now you are awake my dearest Phoney, you can*
*practise living differently so that your life isn't all about*
*suffering. To heal properly you will need all your energy*
*back. You can stop hiding deep inside yourself, all*
*huddled up in the corner of your mind.*

I sat up straight and took a couple of long, slow, deep breaths and tried to regulate my breathing again. My miniature guide had nipped off to the kitchen again where I heard the fridge door open.

*Phoney we are all out of cake, biscuits and general good quality munch! You must have eaten them all, you great big piggy.*

Before I could react with an indignant remark Amy was beside me, looking up into my face.

*Go on Phoney, you need a quick breath of fresh air and a short mindful walk will do you the world of good. I'll wait for you here and then we can get down to business when you come back.*

Before I could protest I found myself at the front door with my coat on, ready to head to the local cake shop. I glanced back to see the small head and shoulders of a curly-haired girl waving at me from my half open door. Amy's big grin lit up my senses for a moment and as I descended the steps I realised that I was humming a tune to myself. I was halfway to the shops before I knew it. There was something comforting about having your own spiritual guide, even if she seemed to eat her body weight in cakes. I felt a smile glowing deep down inside. Maybe all this stopping, becoming present, letting go and ceasing suffering was going to be fun after all.

# Chapter Five

After I'd returned laden with cakes, Amy had made short work of devouring a rather large cream bun and was turning her attention to a doughnut whilst happily smiling to herself and wiping her sticky hands on her dress. I noticed that even though she kept doing this, her dress never really seemed to get dirty. Not like my kitchen. Nearly every surface was covered in small sticky handprints.

Just as I finished a more modest bun and my herbal tea, Amy fixed her big blue eyes on me and frowned.

> *It makes me so sad when you get all depressed about stuff Phoney.*

I finished my cake and felt a small trill of alarm deep down in my rather full stomach. I was grateful for Amy's concern but I had never considered myself a depressive. Amy wiped her sticky face and continued.

> *I watch you sleepwalking all the time Phoney. I know why you keep on staying asleep and all sad and depressed. It's because you are still fearful about most things but you don't even know just how depressed and all deflated you get sometimes. You are a bit like a big old weather balloon that has come down to earth and got caught on a branch.*

I wasn't sure where she was going with this but I didn't much like her animated similes. I wasn't as fat as a weather balloon! In fact since Amy had burst into my life I hadn't been eating much at all.

Just watching her stuff her face was enough to make me feel full. Amy rattled on, getting up to speed with her observation.

> You are all wrapped up inside in a big old grey damp blanket of despair sometimes Phoney. Your depression steals all your energy and uses it to make nasty old images and ideas of suffering which you then watch inside your head all day long. It's no wonder you feel like you can't get out of bed sometimes.

My good mood was vanishing as I reflected on what Amy was saying. As she was speaking it was as if she brought me directly face to face with an old familiar, impenetrable wall of grey despondency and gloom. So that was what she was talking about.

> Sorry Phoney, but I've got to get you to wake up today. You need to wake up and see the big old floppy energy-gobbling depression monster that you have been feeding for most of your life.

I began to feel uncomfortable under her gaze. She was doing that guru mind control thing again. Her piercing blue eyes were so bright that I couldn't flinch away from her gaze. As she stared at me, the huge wall of fog came clearly into my line of vision, hanging damp and still in front of me. As I saw it I sensed that my good humour, happiness and energy was leaving me. I could see myself huddling down for warmth. Amy's voice was very gentle now and I knew that she was sharing my vision.

> Your suffering keeps on growing inside you Phoney because you keep on feeding it. You put all of your attention onto it. You allow it to exist and you do this because you are not aware that you are doing it. You are not awake and you are living in a dream world. You use it as a great big excuse to not face your fears.

As Amy spoke and I sniffed with controlled sobs I realised that the heaviness of my sudden depression really was a place where I was hiding. As I looked at Amy's deeply concerned face I realised that this covering of greyness had been with me for a long time. It had become my friend, a place I hid in; it was the place where I chose to stay and conceal my real, fearful self from the world. I noticed that with my depression came a profound tiredness, a very real and deep exhaustion. Amy smiled at me, wiping away one of my tears with her sleeve, and then raised her finger to touch my forehead. As she did I was immediately transported to a world I recognised. I was a small boy, all alone, sitting in the corner of my bedroom unhappily playing with some wooden bricks. Amy tapped my forehead again and peered into my face.

*Fear is suffering Phoney. Suffering often reveals itself as despair because it wants to hide from you. It wants to grow like a big old lion or weeds. The big grey cloud of depression starts when we are so little Phoney. It becomes our comfort blanket before anyone notices. We don't know what it is so we try to hide it. We pretend it's not there. We play make-believe and pretend that it's not there even though it's walking alongside us all the time. We pretend that it's not in all our games. We lie to ourselves that it's not our constant companion.*

It was as if Amy was peering deep into my very soul. She was like a single ray of light illuminating a far-off forgotten part of myself. She was all serious but kind and gentle at the same time.

*Depression becomes your best friend when what you really need is a fabby little guide of light and happiness just like me, my dearest Phoney. But as we grow older our silly old brains grow old too and our grey blanket of flumpyness gets all hard-wired into who we are. Our depression becomes who we are. By the time we are big children it's too late. We think our greyness, our misery, our flumpyness of fear is part of us. We believe our brains have changed for good. Then silly old doctors give us drugs and we wobble off like down the road of life like a child who can never stop having stabilisers on his bike. The secret truth is that it's never too late to change our*

*silly old brains. Brains are just like children's putty, like*
*clay, they can be moulded to be different. It just takes*
*time. It just gets a little bit harder the older we get my*
*dear little Phoney. We can un-learn our suffering.*

Amy was reading my thoughts again and even though she was
being so gentle and compassionate she couldn't help herself
from having a laugh at my expense. She had started to mimic me.
She had slumped her shoulders, and pouted her bottom lip. She
was doing a complete Eeyore and mimicking my sighs. I caught
her eye and couldn't help but laugh at myself. As I did, my cloud
of greyness shifted ever so slightly and let in a small ray of hope.
Immediately a huge grin spread out across Amy's face and she
drew back a bit and began to twirl her hair with her fingers.

*So my dearest Phoney, today's challenge is to stare the*
*big old grey flumpy blanket of depression in the face*
*and tell it that you see it and that you no longer need it*
*because you are not hiding anymore. It's time to say NO!*

I took a deep breath and felt some of my energy return; a ray of
light and warmth beginning somewhere deep inside me.

'You're right Amy, to do this, to beat this thing, I will need all of my
energy back.'

Amy chuckled and then took a deep breath and began a small
dance. She began to hop from one foot to another whilst holding
the ends of her hair out in front of her at the same time. She kept
laughing as she spoke.

*Yes Phoney, we need all of our energy to have fun. Real*
*fun: living for real, and having fun. Playing takes up a lot*
*of energy but it also makes a lot of energy. Living isn't*
*meant to drain you Phoney. Living is meant to refill you*
*all the time. The sheer joy of living is supposed to sustain*
*you and charge your spiritual batteries up whilst you*
*play. That's why little children and small spiritual guides*
*have loads and loads of energy. Now Phoney, answer this*

*question. How do you try to replenish your energy?*

'Huh?'

*When you are feeling exhausted and beaten down into a pulpy thing by your great comfort-blanket of depression, like now - how do you try to get your energy back?*

I frowned; I screwed up my eyes like Amy who was staring intently at me again.

'I er, sleep?'

*Oh Phoney you try to sleep. I watch you try to sleep. Even when you sleep your old habit mind is chasing after stuff and running away from stuff. That's not sleeping.*

'Yeah I guess you're right Amy. It's true, I can't remember the last time I had a great night's sleep. If I've been drinking I guess it all just blacks out but then I wake up feeling terrible.'

*It's because you don't stop Phoney. You don't get off your horse of fear and suffering. You are never actually still. You are never in one place at one time. One of the many reasons that you are a Phoney is because you don't really exist.*

At this moment Amy finished a biscuit that she had plucked out of the air and swallowed it with an air of victory.

'Huh, hang on Amy, that's a bit much. I may suffer, I may be tired but of course I exist.'

*Do you? Do you really Phoney? To exist you have to be present. You have to be here, really here in space and time. You have to be like the mountain, solid, real, in one place, not moving, still. Phoney, you are never really fully present. Your mind races you off all over the place. Bits of you are off into some fantasy world while other bits of you are in a miserable memory of your past. You feel guilty about the past and you worry about the future. You spend most of your play energy, your life force, practising not really being here.*

My mind was beginning to feel like treacle. It was trying to run away from what Amy was saying but she was doing her 'spiritual guru thing' where she stared straight at me with her big blues eyes like some wise old woman. I couldn't wriggle free although I felt some rising resentment.

'Of course I'm here Amy.'

*No you are not Phoney. Most of the time you exist in tomorrow or yesterday.*

'That's impossible!'

*Exactly Phoney! IT IS an impossible place to be in. Impossible, because there is no future. There is no past. There is only now. There is only the present moment. It's called a play-day. Not a play-tomorrow or play-past. All children know that.*

Something deep inside me was beginning to understand.

'Is that what happened yesterday, by the pond? Did we become still and present? It felt like I was present. Was I?'

*Yes Phoney. Wasn't it wonderful? Isn't it fun? All that amazing human potential actually, truly, being. You were an actual 'human being'. Not a 'human pretending to be'. You were simply being in the present moment. Not spread out thinner than cheap margarine on a piece of toast.*

'I'm like thin margarine?!'

*Yup, most of your energy is spread out way back into your past and the rest of it is flung into the future. You give all your energy away to past guilt and future worries. And you need to wake up Phoney! It's all a dream, it's an echo, made-up. It's not real and it's stealing your life-force.*
*It's like you are a big cake with all of the nice chocolatey chunks and the cream middle gone. You are the dried up bit that has been left out all night.*

Amy was pulling a face of complete disgust and I wasn't sure that I appreciated yet more of her vivid images of myself. I tried to save the moment.

'So is that what you meant by stopping? Learning to let go of the past and future...erm...and stopping and becoming present?'

*Yes.*

Amy looked victorious and I could tell that she was pleased with herself.

'So what was all the suffering lecture about then?'

*The first step of power means that you have to wake up to the fact that YOU ARE SUFFERING. Otherwise how can you practise stopping it? Past and future can be a prison that your poor old mind cannot escape from Phoney.*

Amy had pulled a funny face and was enunciating every syllable so that I understood. She was speaking to me as if I was the small child.

'I am suffering because I am not stopping suffering? Huh!'

*Oh dearest Phoney, you are suffering from a huge pile of smelly old habits but yes, you are suffering because you don't know how to simply be yourself.*

Chapter 5

'Be myself?'

*Yes my dear Phoney. Being you is simply being in the moment. Being present. Being a 'human being'. Not a 'human doing'.*

Amy looked pleased with herself and then frowned when she realised that my poor old slow brain was still struggling with the whole concept of time and suffering.

'Yesterday, when I went shopping for the sofa bed, it was so hard to....Amy you have to be thinking about where you are going and where you have come from or else you get lost and...'

*No Phoney. First you need to wake up to the fact that you are suffering. You are stressed off your nut. You are exhausted. You are constantly living in a dream world and you need to wake up from it. Your fantasy dream worlds are stealing all your life force.*

'But Amy it's so hard to keep up this breathing stuff and not rushing and be...present.'

*Oh dearest Phoney, I know it is, that's why I'm here, to help you practise. Now that you are waking up, all you need to do is keep on being awake. I'm going to help you.*

'Usually I use coffee to stay awake.'

*You use coffee to stay in the future or past and very rarely in the present Phoney. It's because you are scared.*

'I'm not scared!'

*Yes you are, you all are. You live in a world of fear when it should be a world of fun and happiness.*

'Life isn't all fun Amy; it's not just about having fun!'

73

*Why not Phoney? Why isn't your life fun? Don't you want your life to be fun?*

'Yes of course I do Amy.'

*Yippeee. Fabby. Amazeballs! Now you have seen the next step.*

'Huh?'

*You have chosen to see that you - yes you my dear Phoney - can choose to make your suffering stop.*

Amy was really taking me on a roller coaster ride of learning. I felt like I was now just hanging on hoping that I wouldn't lose all my marbles as we careered around each new curve of wisdom.

'So the first step is to see that all of my life is made up of suffering and the second step is to see that I am causing it and the third step is that I can make it stop.'

Amy was doing her strange slow motion victory dance, which entailed her hopping from one foot to another whilst waving her hands in the air and clapping.

*Yippee, wow, well done my clever Phoney, but no running ahead. Right now let's just focus on the fact that you have understood that your suffering can stop and that you can practise to make it stop. That will do today. It's a very powerful first couple of steps Phoney and I'm actually quite proud of us you know.*

Amy was doing a small celebratory dance around the kitchen whilst eating a chocolate biscuit.

'How do I do that? I don't have any free time to practise your strange ideas.'

*You don't have any free time because you are not free to stop worrying. You are not free to stop stressing. You are not free to stop jumping around like the proverbial grasshopper. Free time simply means being free in time. Time is freedom. The only place to find freedom is in the present moment. That's one of the reasons that you suffer so much Phoney. That's why you're not happy.*

I realised that I was feeling the light of a gradual dawning fill my mind. My whole being felt as if it had just been thrown up into the air and then put back together again but with every one of my molecules slightly adjusted. I felt exhausted and invigorated by our session. Listening to Amy was a bit like being immersed in a free-jazz concert.

'I guess there are many reasons why I'm not as happy as I could be, it's just that...'

*Don't choose to worry Phoney, I know. We don't need to do all the steps all at once. Just practise the breathing I taught you and practise Stopping. Next we can practise Calming.*

'Calming?'

*That's going to be the next magic moment for us my dearest Phoney. OK that's enough time, you are beginning to melt a bit. Good though. Your brain is becoming all soft and malleable again. Excellent. Now call the number on your phone and get practising. See you later Phoney, and well done.*

Amy gave a small victory twirl and then slowly vanished in front of my eyes, leaving behind only the softest fragrance of classic roses. The room became still once more. I was alone again. It was amazing how such a small person could somehow fill up a space.

I sat still for a few moments with Amy's words ringing in my head.

She really knew how to bombard the senses and somehow trick you into seeing around corners in your mind. She had reduced me to tears, flung me into a pit of depression and doubt and then revealed, like a miniature magician, that it was all an illusion and that I was really a wonderful human being. My intellectual and rational mind seemed to have taken a small vacation and just for the moment I felt okay with that. I rubbed my still- moist eyes and sniffed loudly to try and make sense of what had just occurred.

It had all been a bit of a blur of information and ideas. This whole 'being still' and 'being present' thing seemed to be important to Amy. I was glad that she had introduced me to the full effect of this practice earlier in the park. I wasn't sure that I would have believed her if she hadn't.

I straightened my back and focussed on my breathing. I tried to be still. I tried to be present. Almost immediately a stream of past and future ideas filled up my head. I experienced a flood of anxiety about bills, my failure to get published, worry over work and money issues, thoughts of disappointment and uselessness, all of which stressed me out in an instant. I took a deep breath. This time I put all my attention on breathing slowly and gently like Amy had taught me. My mind began to quieten down. Amy was right. Many of my thoughts were about things that had happened. Many of my fears were about what might happen. I wondered just how much time I spent with this endless wall of noise in my head. I guess that's what Amy meant; all these anxieties were making me suffer. All of these past and future concerns were concerned with the smallest of things. I was suffering because I invested all my energy into worrying about stuff that had happened or that might happen. She's right; I guess I am fearful.

I breathed gently and counted the thoughts that rushed through my head – I was amazed at how many there were. This time I didn't get caught up in them. I just watched them rise up inside me like rats up a drainpipe. My list was extensive.

I thought: what food have I got in for later, can I pay my bills tomorrow, will I get paid enough this month, can I pay my ex-wife's maintenance, will my children resent me if I can't, does Hazel miss me, will she have me back, what am I going to tell the Dean about my rejection, can I ever go back to the coffee shop, did I offend my publisher so much that she won't speak to me again? I ruminated on how tired I felt. On and on and on. So many anxieties all in the space of a couple of minutes. Wow, Amy was so right.

I stood up and shook myself, literally, trying to shake off my fears and worries. I tried to stay calm and centred and focus on one thing at a time. Now then, what had Amy said about my phone?

I cautiously approached my mobile, which was lying on the table. In my messages I saw a new telephone number. How did she do that? How had Amy managed to get a telephone number onto my phone? I didn't feel even the smallest bit alarmed by that fact though. Amy wasn't alarming, surprising maybe, but not alarming. I had a sneaking suspicion that keeping it simple was the only way I would survive whatever was happening to me. Breathing slowly and gently, I pressed the call button and waited for the phone to ring.

'Hello, Glasgow Meditation Centre, how can I help you?' A gentle and calming voice was speaking in my ear.

'Um, er, well a friend gave me this number and suggested that I give you a call.'

I wasn't sure what to say; meditation still seemed like some weird religious kind of practice. Still the man on the end of the phone sounded sane, in fact quite calm and relaxed.

'Sure, we get many recommendations and we can get quite full some days. Are you a beginner?'

I paused for a second; I didn't feel like sharing the past couple of days with anyone so I just mumbled that I was and that I would like some lessons.

'Maybe you would like to consider our beginners class? Come along and give it a try, shall I book you up for a trial session? There's actually one at four o'clock today. You're lucky; it's day one of a six week course.'

I heard myself say a slow yes and then give my name and details. After the call had ended I glanced at the time and realised I actually had to rush for my first class. I threw a few soft clothes into my only remaining bag and attempted the hilarious feat of rushing whilst not rushing. Moving quickly but not being stressed or panicked. I kind of got it but just as I thought I had mastered it I realised that I had left my wallet behind in the flat, then panicked about how I was going to pay for the session and bumped into a lamppost.

So a bit later, slightly sweaty and with a nice bruise on my knee, I found myself sitting in the tranquil, clean, white space, of a non-denominational meditation centre. I was one of about a dozen beginners being taught by a nice young lady on how to sit with our backs straight whilst breathing slowly and gently.

OK it was nice. Maybe it was the atmosphere, maybe it was the soothing voice of the instructor, and maybe it was the meditation practice. Almost immediately I felt much calmer. Within a few minutes my mind seemed to jump around less. I did yawn out loud, and I was aware of my stomach burbling away merrily and that my knees creaked, but I persevered. We all seemed to be suffering the same kind of beginner anxieties and challenges to our bodies. One woman fell asleep and one man lost the battle with his insides and, as Amy would have described it, delivered a huge bottom burp that momentarily drowned out the gentle music.

After the initial introductory short meditation practise session, the rather gorgeous and waif like instructor explained to us that feeling tired was perfectly normal. I put my hand up and complained about the pain I was experiencing in my legs, I could barely unfold them from my earlier kneeling position.  Our slightly mystical meditation elf smiled knowingly at me and then suggested that I use one of their orthopaedic chairs to save my knees. This may have been because when I stood up my knees had gone off like a rifle. I didn't feel patronised, or old, just grateful. I tried the chair and, to my carefully concealed delight, almost instantaneously found my body's equilibrium. I decided that from now on I would meditate sitting on a chair. None of this lotus position stuff for me! Another gentleman and a lady appreciatively joined me for the longer session.

The next half an hour seemed to pass in minutes. With gentle instruction I soon found myself visualising the pond in the park again. I saw it as it had been with Amy - smooth, calm and still. We were guided to imagine the pond as a mirror for our minds. We were encouraged to become still so that not even a ripple broke the surface. As I gently concentrated my breathing and my mind I found that I also became still. Not as still as when I was with Amy but I was freed from the incessant buzzing of my thoughts. The hour seemed to be over in moments. A final bell softly chimed and then everybody stood up and moved peacefully towards the door where our shoes waited patiently for us in neat little rows. Everyone exchanged shy glances and I realised that we had all enjoyed the experience. A low buzz of gentle conversation filled the hallway as we all exchanged our reasons for being at the meditation session. Nearly all of us had sleep issues and some of the younger ones were feeling stressed out at work. One guy said that his wife had made him attend the session to chill him out. We quickly realised that we all shared some kind of concern about our anxiety and energy levels. Some admitted that their doctors had referred them to the meditation centre. I noticed that one young girl had some rather frightening marks on her wrists. Just as I tried to avert my eyes she noticed me. She saved my embarrassment by smiling and saying that she was hoping that meditation and the practise of mindfulness would help her to come off her medication. I was amazed by her unworried openness.

Picking up my battered brogues, I smiled sheepishly at two friendly and relaxed looking fellow meditators who were obviously a couple. As we stepped out into the evening I was relieved that nobody else seemed to want to talk. I was rather selfishly enjoying my newfound sense of relaxation. I left feeling rather pleased with myself and very sleepy.

Leaving the tranquil space I headed for home. I wondered why I hadn't achieved the same world-altering experience that I had enjoyed with Amy. I guess that's what she'd meant by giving me something to aim for. I was aware that I was walking slowly, moving gently between shoppers, students and the traffic. I felt a gradual realisation that maybe Amy was right. If my whirring mind was a source of suffering for me then maybe my meditation session had shown me that my suffering could cease, if only for an hour.  Maybe she had shown me a way to stop suffering. Could it be this easy?

I stood at one of Glasgow's seemingly endless processions of traffic lights and watched them turn from green to amber then red. It was now rush hour. I watched a whole cycle take place. Hundreds of people were darting along like a pulsing flood of a river. Every few minutes they swapped positions with bikes, cars, lorries and buses. Then the sequence repeated itself. I turned and looked back at the flood of people as I practised some of the day's breathing techniques.

In my stillness I witnessed the phenomena of the city as a large pulsing body with the packed streets and pavements as a huge arterial network of living energy. It was as if a big slow heart was pumping people and traffic ever forward in a synchronised pulse of life. Round and round the city we went, carrying life, thoughts and energy. The stiller I stood, the less people seemed to notice me. They flooded around me, some almost on top of me. Yet they all seemed repelled from me like the positive charge of two magnets coming together. Nobody bumped me however close they came. People then cars. Cars then people. On and on. Old and young, happy and sad, they all swept around and past me not noticing the middle-aged, grey haired man standing quietly beside the traffic light. No one seemed to be aware of their actions as they rushed home. It was as if humanity was moving with one unified sense of purpose but unaware that they all shared the same goals. It was as if they were sleepwalking, sleep-driving, sleep-rushing. People's faces expressed emotions of stoic determination. Every face had the grim look of someone trying to get somewhere fast.

It was only small children and the occasional older person that looked around and noticed the surrounding and overhanging trees of the park. One smiling black gentleman paused for a moment to take a lungful of the sweet fragrance of the lime trees before diving back into the river of life.

I realised that I would usually have been one of the many pointy-elbowed, grim-faced, grumpy, sweaty and stressed people racing for home. I could see myself, clutching my rucksack full of books and notes, talking into my mobile phone, eating a tasteless sandwich, sipping a coffee, all whilst trying to get home as quickly as possible. I guess Amy was right. I would have been too absorbed with doing to actually experience my reality. What was it she had said? Too busy as a 'human doing' to be a 'human being' – simply being, being simple. I wondered how often I had passed this way without noticing the trees and inhaling the sweet late summer fragrance of the lime flowers that cut through the fumes and dust.

Gradually I became aware that my feet were beginning to ache and my tummy was rumbling. On the next red light I joined the flow of human activity and let the tide of life carry me down the street towards my flat.

I was still dimly aware that, on some level my usually whirring and panicked mind was responding to something I had not yet fully grasped. I realised I was still unsure about the causes of this suffering. However, tonight was a breath of fresh air. Tonight was not the moment to break the spell. After a light supper I knew that I had to sleep.

Maybe it was because I was genuinely exhausted by the past few days, maybe it was due to the meditation practise, maybe it was due to the fact that my mind had stopped shouting at me.

All I know is that night I slept for the first time in years, deep and dreamless.

Taming Amy

# Chapter Six

I don't usually go to the zoo. I'm not sure that I like them. I'm not sure that I trust them. I think that zoos might actually make me feel guilty. I feel guilty enough most of the time anyway.

I always feel kind of sorry for the poor animals staring back at me. I have an old fear of being sent to prison, a recurring dream from childhood. One from which I awake, covered in sweat and very stressed. Not too sure that I'm much good with enclosed spaces actually. Anyhow, here I am, at Edinburgh zoo. It's a miserable grey Scottish morning, I haven't had any breakfast and I'm feeling grumpy. Meanwhile a small child, clad in a bright red plastic raincoat and wellies is blowing kisses to a weary old lion sitting under a cover scowling at us. She is laughing and smiling. I am sure that I have the beginnings of a migraine. It wasn't this hard with my real children when they were small.

'So come on Amy, spill the proverbial beans. I'm cold, getting wet and I'm hungry. Why are we here?'

*Oh Phoney just chillax and enjoy for a moment. We can see the giant Pandas later.*

'I don't care about....'

*Yes you do!*

Not letting me finish, Amy span round so that her little face was looking straight up at me. I could see the freckles on her small snub nose peeking out from beneath the brim of her red plastic hat. She wagged her finger at me.

# Chapter 6

*You have loved Pandas ever since you were little when you had a toy Panda that was bigger than you. But Phoney, right now I want you to meet this lion.*

'Why Amy?' I sighed wearily. Then, seeing that other bedraggled tourists were beginning to look in my direction, I tried to think the words I was speaking rather than speak them out loud. I was still finding this difficult and Amy said the effort of my concentration made me look as if I had swallowed a wasp.

*Because Phoney, after Stopping you have to Calm Down.*

I moved towards the bars of the enclosure. The fine rain was causing droplets to run down inside my collar and make me shiver. Amy had pronounced the words calm down like she often did, as if it was a proper noun.

'I am calm. I'm just wet, hungry and ...'

*It's only water and you eat too much anyway Phoney. Now, look at the lion.*

I followed the direction of her small finger and made eye contact with a large, damp male lion. He was still quite impressive even if he looked miserable. I looked at his face. He had enormous golden eyes. He gave a huge yawn and licked his lips. He made me feel despondent just looking at him.

Then, without warning, Amy gave the shrillest and scariest sound I have ever heard. Both the lion and myself were startled, but we both had very different reactions. I merely took a sudden intake of breath and clenched my fingers. The lion however leapt up, pounced forwards towards the double fence that separated me from his enclosure, and roared in my face. It was deafening, fierce, terrifying and much too close for comfort. I could smell his warm meaty breath. I screamed. I dived for the floor. I shook like a leaf.

In the next instance the lion stopped dead, glanced down at me cowering and trembling on my hands and knees in a large puddle and then, with a look of complete disdain, headed off into his hut and out of the rain.

My heart was pounding. My breath came out in rasping gasps, and my body was shaking. All around me children were laughing and pointing at me cowering on the floor. Even when I shakily stood up, whole families were still laughing at me. I felt ashamed, embarrassed and very angry. I was so pumped up with fear that I stormed out of the big cat enclosure and headed for the small café without looking back. Still trembling, I ordered a large coffee and a huge slice of banana cake and seriously thought about taking up smoking again. I was furious with Amy yet, as I turned from the till to find a seat, I saw that she was sitting quietly and demurely at the only free table in the café. I had no choice but to sit down beside my miniature daemon.

'That,' I said, moving my cake away from her, 'was the meanest and cruellest thing you have ever done.'

I could see that Amy was struggling to keep her composure.

'Don't you dare!' I bellowed to the surprised café but it was no good.

Amy's infectious laughter spilled out of her. She was bent double, holding her sides, and her laughter seemed to transform the whole place. Within moments the general chat and hubbub of the café increased and soon everyone was merrily laughing away to themselves for no apparent reason. And, to my annoyance, her laughter soon set me off. I quickly held my mobile phone out in front of me as if I had just received a humorous text. Once Amy's laughter hit you there was nothing you could do.

*Oh Phoney you were so funny. I thought you had poo'd your pants! You actually dived into that puddle. You screamed like a little girl.*

## Chapter 6

She broke down with another fit of the giggles.

*Mr Lion gave you a right old scare, ha ha, he he...*

I took a long and noisy slurp of my coffee and ate some cake as my heart rate began to subside back to normal. After a few mouthfuls I capitulated to Amy's pouting lips and mournful expression and pushed a small slice of my massive piece of cake over to her side of the table where she quickly worked on making it disappear.

'Look Amy, you still haven't told me why you brought me here, and why you were so mean just then. That poor old lion and me could have died with fright.'

*That's right Phoney.*

Suddenly Amy was serious again and she looked straight at me whilst stealing another huge chunk of my cake.

*You can die of fright. It's not just physical death. Your dreams can die, your ideas can die, your hopes can die, your relationships can die and all because you see lions roaring at you wherever you go.*

I paused, annoyed.

'You are the one who nearly made me die of fright Amy. You are the only scary entity that I seem to be seeing everywhere and, to be honest, this morning, I really wish I wasn't.'

*No I'm not Phoney. You see lions everywhere. You see lions hiding in your bills, in your relationships, in your work, in your life all the time. And they are always roaring at you, making you almost die of fright. There are so many lions in your world that you live in a constant state of fear.*

'I don't understand Amy I...you make it sound as if I live in a jungle.'

Amy licked the remains of the gooey cake from her fingers and took her hat off. She leant conspiratorially across the table to me. Her breath smelt of roses and bananas.

> *You were right to be scared of that lion my dear Phoney. If you were in Africa out in the open on the huge plains and he got a whiff of you standing there, you would be right to be scared. Your fear would make you run very fast. Your fear would make your heart pound like a drum pumping blood to your legs. Your fear would clear your head so that you knew exactly which way to run. Your fear would make you pee your pants and even poo. You would be able to run very fast. And, if he caught you, your fear would calm you and make you feel no pain. If you were just injured your fear would make your blood clot to heal your wounds. Your fear would be very important to help you survive the day. Your fear would be your friend.*

'Fight or flight. I know Amy, our autonomic defence mechanism. It's from the ancient part of our brains. What I don't understand is why you had to inflict that fear on me just then.'

> *Was the lion going to eat you Phoney?*

'Erm no, but he was close and...'

> *Were you actually in danger Phoney?*

'Well no I guess not but...'

> *That's the point Phoney. There are no lions running around in Glasgow where you live. If you walk down Byres Road you are not going to get eaten. When the bills pop through your letterbox they are not going to attack you. When you mess up something - a lecture perhaps - the students, your friends, your colleagues are not going to*

# Chapter 6

*kill you.*

I know that Amy. That's obvious.

*So why did you get an ulcer last year then?*

'Huh?'

*Why did you get an ulcer?*

'It was due to micro-organisms living in my gut which...'

*No Phoney, it was because you were living in a complete fear-based reality. Everywhere you looked you saw lions so you were stressed out of your box all day and every day, just like a poor old antelope being chased by lions and coyotes from dawn to dusk.*

'I don't get it Amy.'

I tried not to speak out loud but kept forgetting as I started to feel agitated by Amy's lecture. Sighing, I realised that I really had become one of those poor souls who sits in the corner chatting away to themselves. Amy snapped her fingers in front of my eyes.

*Lion Phoney. Self-doubt. Hah!*

I grimaced. I kept forgetting that Amy could hear my every thought. She peered into my eyes.

*Look Phoney. The moment the antelope gets chased she is very scared. Her fear protects her. She races to her freedom. Then she stops. Calms down and then relaxes so that she can get on with the business of the day, which is eating and digesting grasses and leaves. After you have a genuine fright you just forget to stop and calm down. I think you may have forgotten how to calm down a very long time ago actually. Being calm really isn't your thing anymore. It's sad, and very tiring for you. Still, you have me so we can practise together.*

I went to take another bite of cake but Amy had scoffed the lot. How can she speak and eat at the same time? My coffee was cooling but still delicious so I consoled myself with a satisfying gulp. Part of me knew that Amy was right but part of me was still resisting her childlike metaphors.

*Most human doings and beings live to be very old. Most have well fed lives. Most have doctors to cure their illnesses. So why do they see lions everywhere? Why do they run around in a state of fear, of stress and anxiety?*

Amy looked directly at me, wiping her face and looking triumphant. She could see that the penny was dropping.

'Because they see everyday things as lions that could hurt them?'

*Hurt them, no! Kill them yes. That's how bad most humans have got it. Loads of stress every day becomes a habit. That makes you weak. You can't recharge. Your immune system gets weak. You get colds and ulcers and cancer and then you really do die. Truth is you are dead well before that.*

'So that's why you brought me here then? To teach me about fear and chronic stress?'

*No I made you bring me here so that you could see the pandas and learn about Calming Down.*

Well if you wanted me to be calm why did you scare me half to death?

*No point learning from fancy ideas like you always think you can Phoney. It's time to get real. It's time to wake up. It's time to start living. Nobody can live if they feel terrified all the time. You are so addicted to fear that you even drink huge cups of coffee every hour to make your poor old body more scared. You think that caffeine and cigarettes make you feel alert and alive. Really you are falling asleep and then deeper and deeper into your nightmare. The more severe your nightmare, the more you believe it. You can't stop. You can't calm your poor old body down. You can't relax and you can't heal and recharge. The poor old antelope is better at living than you are. Yet I bet you think that you are cleverer than her.*

'I do relax sometimes Amy.'

*When?*

'Erm...when I am with my friends...'

*OK, sometimes you do, but you always get drunk don't you? You all use drink to fall asleep together. You are all running from your fears. As soon as you have dulled your senses with alcohol you think your fears are not there. You feel strong and confident. But really, you are falling deeper into the nightmare. Besides Phoney, you are not a good drunk. Your fears always rise up to meet you and you get manic and start shouting at everyone.*

Amy was right. Drink and drugs had played a huge part in my past and, when drunk I always ended up falling out with everyone. My ex-wife said I ruined every family occasion. I hardly touched a drop since I had been with Hazel, well not in her presence anyway. I felt as if Amy was a miniature lion attacking me.

'That's quite heavy Amy. You are saying that this whole world is neurotic and living in fear and even when we think that we are calming down, then we are not? In fact we are just making it worse.'

*Yup you just party and abuse yourselves so that you are*

*completely exhausted. You mess yourselves up so much your body literally throws the off-switch and you collapse and have a mini-death.*

I felt alarmed at the idea of a mini-death; in fact any idea of death alarmed me. Some rather dubious memories of very drunken nights flashed across my mind. I could see myself dancing, shouting, debating and laughing hysterically until I collapsed into a drunken sleep.

'Is that why I always feel relaxed the morning after a party? Even though I have a hangover I feel nice and calm and relaxed and, well, deeply chilled?'

*Phoney's re-boot. Phoney's first aid kit. Poor old Phoney, falling asleep so that he can wake up. Your half-dead mind is trying to flush poisons out of the body. No wonder the poor old mind goes quiet. It's blatted and flattened by all the abuse Phoney.*

'So do we all do this then, I mean, abuse ourselves to scare off your proverbial lions?'

*Many do Phoney, yes. Don't worry about other people yet Phoney. It's just you that I'm here to help. You are the one who is still mostly asleep.*

Amy gave a big yawn and wound her curls around her finger at the same time. Her yawn was infectious, it caught me, and then I noticed that I set off a chain reaction of yawns around the room.

'So you are saying that I am still asleep to all this then? You think that I still exist in this nightmare of unconscious reality and negative perception that you just described? You are saying that my perception of life is wrong? That what I think is normality and a great life is in fact a nightmare that I can't wake up from?'

Amy drummed her little fingers on the table as she acted out an antelope being chased by a lion.

> *Look Phoney, the antelope knows what is. She knows*
> *when to be scared. She doesn't create a whole world*
> *around her that is based on her fear of lions does she?*

'Erm no, but she's not conscious like me is she? I mean she's
not sentient like humans so she can't conceptualise anything
differently from her experience of her immediate reality...
therefore she doesn't have the ability to imagine fears that aren't
there. As soon as the lion is gone she's forgotten it and so she
returns to eating and digesting grass.'

> *Don't believe that horse poo Phoney. Many animals in*
> *harsh captivity can die of stress. In fact it can happen*
> *very quickly. You are right about one thing though.*
> *Animals don't go on to create a whole world built on fear*
> *and suffering. They always look to return to a safe, calm*
> *place as quickly as they can. And that dear Phoney is*
> *what I am here to teach you.*

'Ah, now I get it, to calm down?'

> *To Stop, be Still, so that you can Calm yourself down. Yes*
> *Phoney. Only then will you begin to cease to create your*
> *all-encompassing nightmares. Only then will you begin to*
> *wake up. You have to learn how to tame your lions by first*
> *seeing that there really aren't any and that you have been*
> *making them up all along.*

I looked at my empty coffee cup. So many questions swirled
around my mind; I tried some of the meditation breathing which
helped a bit. I felt depressed. It was as if a thin veil had been
lifted from my eyes. In the dregs of my coffee I saw a whirl of
images, of scenes in which I was the central character. There
were literally hundreds of occasions when I had been less than
relaxed. Visions of times when I was acting out of panic, stress
or anxiety flashed in front of me. I could see plenty of occasions
when my panic and stress had turned a good day into a bad one.

Time after time I was shouting or sulking, or cross, or aggressive or judgemental or ...

*Come back to me Phoney.*

Amy was leaning into me and her clear blue eyes calmed my mind.

*You were about to dive into another nightmare of guilt and regret Phoney. You created your own jungle of lions and tigers. Can you see how you go from being nice and calm and then, Bingo, you spot a lion and off you run screaming and shouting?*

I sighed. Amy was right. As she spoke I could see myself sitting enjoying my early morning coffee, all nice and relaxed until a pile of bills dropped through the letterbox. I could sense how my immediate reaction was one of stress, worry and anxiety which would then last me most of the day. In fact just about any thought about money would trigger me off recently. She was right; I had created lions of fear to chase me out of my personal savannah of solace. As I flicked through my memory index of my typical day I realised that in fact almost everything triggered my own personal flight or fight response. Even mundane telephone calls could become roaring lions the longer I left them. My writing deadlines were more like a pack of wolves hounding me all day and all night long, never ever really stopping to let me relax and recover my breath. The thought of public speaking engagements would chase me like a pack of killer whales until I was reduced to a shivering bag of nerves at the side of the stage. I cast my mind further back and realised that even the walk to school had been an expedition through the hostile wastes of the African savannah for me. Would I get picked on, would the bullies see me, would I get a good mark for my homework and avoid a beating, would Jenny Jones even notice me at choir practise? I guess I had started creating my jungle early on. Phew – Amy was right, it wasn't a jungle 'out there', it was a jungle 'in here', in my own head. I was a complete idiot, I had let my own fears and psychogenic phobias ruin my life and the lives of others. Amy snapped me out of my trance again.

*You must keep practising staying in the present with me Phoney. There is no blame. There only is what is. All you need to do is wake up and see what is real, what is truth and just how amazingly wonderful this world is. Now then! Shall we finish all this learning later on? Let's go and Calm Down and relax with a panda. Pandas are great at teaching us the art of Calming Down.*

So that's how, a few minutes later, I came to be standing, like a small and excited child, in front of the Giant Panda's enclosure. I'm sure that Amy had something to do with it. The sun came out. The pandas came out, and for my allotted few minutes, I got to see these wonderful animals up close. They were lying on their back chewing every ounce of nourishment that bamboo has to offer in the calmest most relaxed fashion I swear it is possible to be in. The more I just simply stood and noticed them, the more I could sense my own personal menagerie of ferocious beasties vanishing until I became wonderfully calm and still. For a few minutes the Pandas and myself existed in the perfect relaxed harmony of my mind. At one point Amy looked up and then, to my surprise, stuffed her small, hot, sticky, pink hand into mine for an instant.

*See Phoney, it's all quite wonderful when you wake up from the nightmares isn't it?*

Just for that moment, standing in the quiet sunshine, I had to agree.

# Chapter Seven

I hadn't had the best week. I had started to feel vulnerable and unsure of myself. My meditation classes were actually quite wonderful yet I soon realised that I had a long way to go. Some days I would achieve my calm, other days my mind just raced around torturing me. For every positive breakthrough I experienced an old habit-energy of fear which would pounce on me like a lion. The quieter I became, the more I missed the hustle and bustle of life and worried that I might be missing something or may be becoming a dullard.

Plus, every time I sat to meditate at home I realised that I was really missing my wife, Hazel. As soon as I became peaceful and happy again I wanted to share that experience with the woman I loved. Then, as I reflected on Hazel, even more lions of guilt chased my poor old mind around its self-made jungle. I reflected on how stressed I had always been around her when in fact I had thought I was being exciting and interesting. Hah!

I kept on returning to breathing mindfully and being still though. Bit by bit I would experience longer periods of calm and positive stillness. People at work were noticing that I was not my old frazzled self. Bizarrely everyone kept asking me if I was alright. It was as though I had fallen ill or something. One morning I found myself peacefully opening the door for an old battle-axe of a lecturer. This unusual action made her stop in her tracks. I swear she thought that I did it to patronise her or mock her age or something. I could almost sense her own lions roaring at her and stealing the moment from both of us. Summoning up as much scorn as she could muster for me, she suggested I was losing my touch. She implied that recently the other academics had started to worry that I'd 'turned simple' because they found my smiling at everyone disconcerting. Then she added that maybe I should take a writing sabbatical. Little did she know that every time I tried to write, the blank page defeated me quicker than a black belt ninja.

I was now plagued with an even greater growl of self-doubt and anxiety. I was no longer sure how to run my day. Usually I just threw energy at it, shouted and ordered the world around me to do what I wanted. Now that I didn't feel that this was the appropriate attitude and action to take, I felt like I had lost my ability to steer my own ship. I felt rudderless and set adrift on a stormy sea. I felt swamped with self-pity. Even though these sharks of anxiety were obvious to me, I ignored them and allowed myself to wallow.

My corporate clients didn't seem to notice. I knew my training material was good but somehow the days left me feeling hollow and empty. I was no longer sure that teaching people how to lie professionally to dupe shareholders, colleagues and the public was such a great job. I went home with a migraine more often than not or with a howling thirst for wine.

I'd still had no calls from my publisher apart from a terse text message that suggested that I might be better off writing academic papers. What this meant was that my material was too dense for anyone other than myself to understand. My self-belief in my creative ability took a nosedive and plunged me into an abyss of misery. I sensed vultures of despair circling overhead.

Even I was quite amazed at how quickly I could plummet from grace and my nice feelings of deep relaxation. The moment I gave up all hope of ever being able to write again, I dropped into a deep hole of despair. I sought the company of fellow moaners. I'm not proud to say it but I spent three very drunken nights with friends and colleagues until the unforgivable happened – I got barred from our favourite drinking den for excessive shouting, swearing and cheating at the pub quiz. To add to my list of dubious achievements, I was now a social pariah.

To top it all my ex-wife kept on pestering me for more and more money until her text messages became so toxic that my cherished mobile phone took a hissy fit and went into a full meltdown. So now I was un-contactable and unable to access my database of clients. I felt marooned on an island of despair.

I was a mess.

It was early on a Saturday morning that I was rudely awoken by the very real discomfort of someone forcing my bleary and whisky-soaked eyes open. Small but determined fingers forced my eyelids apart and the scent of sweet roses huffed over my face.

> *Oh dear Phoney. What a smelly-breathed mess you're in. What on earth have you been doing to yourself?*

I groaned and tried to turn over but it was no use. Amy was amazingly strong for a small girl of five or six and she held my head fast and my eyes wide open so that tears of sun-scorched pain ran down my cheeks. She barked an order at me.

> *Right Phoney, get up, get showered, get dressed. We are going out. Now!*

So, that's how, half an hour later, I found myself standing at the entrance of a large garden centre, blinking in the morning sun.

> *'What on earth are we doing here Amy? I am not going to buy you any flowers!'*

Amy answered by prodding my ribs with her sharp little fingers and directing me through the garden centre, past the inevitable café, past the trees, shrubs, pots and piles of compost until I was standing in front of a large nursery greenhouse.

'Amy we are not meant to be here. This is private, I mean this is not for the punters, this if for the staff only and ...'

# Chapter 7

*Shh Phoney. Open the door - we're going in.*

With a sigh, I did as my small guide demanded and carefully slid open the door and stepped into the warm, damp interior of a huge greenhouse. In front of us, stretching out as far as the eye could see, were rows upon rows of seedbeds and juvenile plants. Some were potted, ready to sell but most were just sprouting. On one side was a large patch of ground that had been allowed to lie fallow. Already a host of weeds were rising up to threaten the ordered beauty of the vast glass warehouse. Amy prodded my ribs and propelled me to stand beside the bed of weeds. To its right were rows of carefully marked plants, their small green shoots just poking up above the judiciously raked and sifted soil. The weeds seemed incongruous, as if their chaos challenged the perfect order of the rest of the greenhouse.

'How come this bit is full of weeds Amy?'

> *It's full of butterfly and insect plants that protect the others Dumbo.*

'Huh, now listen that's not fair. I don't know anything about gardens so...'

> *It's OK Phoney, just be quiet and practise your breathing. For the purpose of today these plants are weeds.*

'I just thought you said that...'

> *Weeds, Phoney, are what you are full of!*

I spluttered, coughed and then laughed, thinking that Amy had made one of her jokes but she was staring at me with the look that I had come to know meant 'pay attention'. Her steely blue eyes ordered me into silence.

> *Breathe Phoney. Breathe deeply and slowly. Let go of all your tension as you breathe out. Breathe in fresh new*

*energy from the universe. Now be quiet and listen.*

I did as I was told. I stood still and tried to let my breath rise and fall slowly and naturally. As I did, my hangover seemed to momentarily subside. I felt calm for the first time in days. How did she do it? Before I could ask, Amy began.

*Your mind is a garden. Your thoughts are the seeds in it. You can grow flowers or weeds.*

'Huh, oh I know this one. That's a biblical reference, seeds falling on stony ground and all that...'

Amy turned round and pinched me so hard on my leg that I squeaked like a mouse who's just discovered that the lump of cheese is in fact the cat's nose.

*Shush your drunken mind Phoney and listen. Deep within you is your huge store of all your limitless possibilities. It is your store mind. It is vast. Within it are seeds of suffering and seeds of happiness.*

I found that I could easily imagine an underground room full of piles of seeds. I remembered when, as a child, I had visited an arable farm. We had all run into a huge shed and were amazed to find that we'd been allowed to climb mountains of bright golden grains of corn, wheat and barley. Once we had reached the top we'd spent hours plunging our hands deep into the seeds. We were surprised and delighted that dozens of small mice had joined us. It was no wonder that the farmyard cats were so fat. Amy prodded me again and told me to open my eyes.

*Now look at what you just called the weeds. What do you see? Go on. Take a proper look. Tell me what you see.*

I looked. I squinted. I got down on my haunches to get a closer look at the strip of wilderness. I got cramp. I stood up again. I could only see weeds.

# Chapter 7

'I see loads of weeds Amy. Weeds everywhere. So what?'

*Describe the weeds Phoney.*

'Erm... well they are green.'

*Yes, go on.*

'They have leaves and stems and things.'

*Go on.*

'Erm...some have small flowers and some have larger flowers and...'

*Exactly Phoney. Some ARE flowers.*

'Oh yes, now you come to mention it.'

I bent down again and viewed the patch from the same height as my diminutive spirit guide. As I looked closer I could see that between the 'weeds' were a few random flowers. They must have self-seeded from the  other flowers in the greenhouse.

'So go on then Amy, what's the significance of the weed/flower arrangement?'

*Your mind is full of weeds, full of the sources of suffering, yet even in your overgrown and cluttered mind Phoney, you still have a few flowers of happiness.*

'Oh well, that's not really fair Amy but...'

*Turn round Phoney.*

I turned around. In front of me on a low shelf were two identical trays full of carefully sifted soil, both sporting identical green shoots.

'Erm, very nice Amy, so what's the significance of these?'

*One is a tray of weeds. One is a tray of flowers. Which is which?*

I looked closely. I bent forwards. I brought my nose up close to smell them. I put my reading glasses on and peered at the shape and outline of the leaves and stems. I couldn't see any difference. They all looked the same to me. I felt annoyed and ignorant at the same time. It reminded me of a time in school when I couldn't understand basic trigonometry.

'They all look the same to me Amy.'

*So what is the only way we can tell them apart then?*

'Erm, let them grow?'

*Exactly, that's all you can do. So how do you separate all the weeds that clog up your poor old mind from the flowers of happiness then?*

Amy turned me round to face the weed or 'wild flower' bed. My mind hurt. My thinking was slow and kept darting off to argue with me about things I thought I should be doing and positing how ridiculous this whole exercise was and how I really was losing my mind. After letting out a long slow sigh I stood still for a moment and practised my breathing. After a couple of deep and gentle breaths I felt a sense of calm return and was rewarded with the dawning of a slow realisation. This was simple.

'I have to weed my mind. I have to pluck out the offending plants so that only the flowers remain. That's what you are saying aren't you? I have to pay careful attention to all the 'weeds' - my negative thoughts and emotions - and then carefully weed them out. Then I will be left with that state of calm and happiness you keep banging on about. After that the thoughts of happiness can flower in me once more.'

I experienced a kind of momentary elation.

*Go on then.*

'Huh?'

*Go on Phoney. Get weeding. Don't worry, no one will come in, or mind you weeding even if they do. Just say it's your chosen form of therapy. I mean, you will be doing them a favour.*

Knowing that resistance with Amy was futile, a few moments later I found myself carefully plucking out thistles, nettles, briars and all manner of weeds from the large patch of ground in front of me. I slaved away for what seemed like ages but when Amy made me stop to survey my success, I was disappointed.

My pile of weeds was large but I had left the ground looking moth eaten. There were patches of bare soil beside the flowers. I could see that many of the weeds I had plucked were in fact flowers and some of the plants I had left in were weeds.

'I'm not much good at this am I Amy?'

*No one is Phoney. It's almost impossible. As quickly as you pluck them out more will grow and truly, my dearest Phoney, how can you tell a weed from a flower when it is so small?*

I felt tired and thirsty and really annoyed. This was going nowhere fast. My feeling of elation had been replaced once more by a feeling of heaviness mixed with tinges of self-loathing.

*Phoney, snap out of that rubbish thinking habit. Now!*

I jumped. Amy had jolted me out of my pity-party. She looked hard at me, gave a loud tutting sound and then made me turn back to the two identical seed trays on the shelf.

*Think, Phoney, think.*

I stared vacantly at the two seed trays. My mind was blank. I thought. I thought some more. It hurt my brain. Even trigonometry hadn't been this challenging. Then I had another eureka moment.

'I know! Just plant flower seeds. Just plant flowers. It's easy. Just plant flowers in the first place.'

I looked expectantly at Amy - surely this time she must give me some credit. Instead she smiled a warm and loving smile at me and almost whispered.

*Your mind doesn't work like that Phoney. The universe has filled your store mind with all seeds of possibility before you were born. All your seeds are already planted deep within you. You have to choose.*

'Well that's just not fair then is it?'

My head was really aching now and beginning to thump out a beat that an early punk band would have been proud of.

'I've had enough of your games, Amy. I can't win. You keep moving the goal posts,' I sulked.

*Oh Phoney, this isn't a game. This is real life. Now think. How do you make flowers grow Phoney? How do we tend flowers to make them grow? What do we do every day, carefully and with our greatest attention?*

I paused and tried my breathing exercise again. In this lesson I felt like the clown who kicked his hat away every time he bent down to pick it up. I glanced around and saw a pale green watering can beside a rain bucket. Aha, of course!

'We water them Amy. We water them so that they will grow.'

*Yippee, well done Phoney, well done!*

Amy leapt up and down with delight. Her smile lifted my flagging spirits again. Now I could head back home and get some well-earned sleep.

*You are not quite there yet Phoney.*

My heart sank.

Amy had grabbed the corner of my jacket and stopped me from moving towards the door. I felt annoyed. The warmth in the greenhouse was making sweat trickle down my back. I really wasn't in the mood for her games. But she held me fast and turned me back towards the weeds.

*If you water the seeds in the trays Phoney BOTH weeds and flowers will grow, so you are back to square one.*

'But if I don't then they will die. They won't grow. Nothing will grow. I'd be like a zombie. I'd be dead and devoid of life. My mind would be like a desert.'

*Oh Phoney, the universe is much cleverer and more amazing than that. Because it cares about you it gives you the choice. Always you have a choice. Now then what is the choice?*

'I only water the flowers?'

*And how are you going to tell which are which? How are you going to make sure that the water only reaches the flowers of happiness and not the weeds of suffering?*

'I can't,' I said sullenly like a spoilt child.

> *Exactly Phoney. You can't. Well you can't yet. The first thing you have to do is choose what you water your seeds with.*

'Huh?'

Weeds of fear and suffering cannot be nourished by the water of love, compassion or calmness.

'Love? Compassion? What are you saying Amy?'

Amy went over and picked up the green watering can. It was almost as big as her. I momentarily marvelled at her strength. Then she began sprinkling my feet with water.

> *In the beginning you have to start by learning how to nourish the seeds of happiness, of joy, of awakening. Otherwise you will be overrun with weeds in no time at all. You can't separate out the seeds of weeds from the seeds of flowers Phoney. As fast as you pluck, new ones will grow. And, as you just found out you can't tell the difference and so will pluck out flowers when you meant to pluck out weeds.*

'So I've got to water my seeds with love? I've got to make sure that my only thoughts are loving ones?'

> *Exactly Phoney. Woods of suffering cannot respond to love. They get no nourishment. They do not grow.*

'So this was a long-winded way to tell me to love myself? I have no idea what that means.'

> *All the weeds of suffering that have wound around you this last week, ruining your life, have been watered by your fear. You have chosen to be fearful Phoney. You ran*

*away from your fear. Your lions defeated you. Your horse of bad energy habit ran off with you. You allowed yourself to fall asleep again.*

'I was awake all week and for most of the nights actually!'

*You didn't sleep Phoney because your ego was chasing you all night. Worrying you like a sheep dog, herding you until you shut yourself tightly off from reality in a pen of your own drunken making. And, as you slept, with your eyes wide open, you continued to water all your seeds of suffering until they grew up to choke all the flowers of happiness. They are like so many thorny briars that pull you to the ground and steal your nourishment. They take all of your vital life-force. Weeds of suffering are nourished by fear. They cannot be nourished by love. They simply cannot grow.*

Amy had picked up a weed and a flower in one hand whilst she continued to sprinkle my feet with warmish water from the can. She was looking up at me intently. Suddenly I was overcome by just how deeply my little helper really cared for me.

'Oh so it's all about fear again!'

*Yes Phoney. It's always fear. Your poor old mind has been riding off on its fear habit again. It's been doing it so much that all the weeds have sprung up inside you and choked the tender shoots of your awakening.*

I cast my mind back to the week that I'd just had. Amy was, of course, right. I remembered how light it had seemed at the beginning and then how, as the week went on it got darker and darker: just as if the weeds had grown up and blocked out the light. Maybe Amy's gardening metaphor was working after all.

'Is that why the meditation wasn't working?'

*Hmm, your practise always helps you Phoney. It was just that you were practising fear and suffering about 100 times more than you were practising love, peace and compassion.*

'So if I simply breathe, stop, calm and practise loving myself, only flowers will grow?'

My voice was mocking. I felt slightly ridiculous. This seemed too simplistic, too flaky.

*Don't mock me Phoney. It's not big and it's not grown up. When you mock me you mock yourself. You mock me because your ego is scared that you have found a simple way to defeat it. Without fear your ego will cease to exist. A lot of your reality will simply dissolve and vanish.*

'Oh so that's what's been happening. That's why I haven't felt like myself. That's what all this stress has been about. My life has been vanishing in front of my eyes ever since you showed up. People at work are beginning to think that I've lost the plot. They think that I've gone soft or something. It's your fault. This meditation stuff is making me weak. I'm less of a man. I'm a...'

*Oh Phoney. Once you stop being fearful you will see that what you are losing are your weeds. All the habits that have been running you and sabotaging your life have been vanishing. You will realise the deep strength within you. Don't worry dearest Phoney. It will take some time. We are still at the beginning.*

'Oh my god, what do you mean still at the beginning?'

*You have had a lifetime of living in fear Phoney. Your poor old brain has to get all nice and malleable again. It's going to take a while to re-wire your whole head.*

I was beginning to feel alarmed. Every time I thought I'd got it,

Chapter 7

Amy seemed to move the goal posts. Besides, I was lousy at wiring and things like that. The last time I'd wired a plug I'd blown up Hazel's new food processor. Amy must have heard because she started to laugh yet somehow still maintained her stern schoolmistress demeanour. Not bad for a five- or six-year-old spirit guide.

> It's just practise Phoney. I'm showing you how to make it easy peasy. I mean, allowing yourself to be loving and compassionate with yourself is a wonderful way to get healthy. I mean, it's the only way to do it in my opinion. Water your mind with the gentle rain of loving-kindness.

My feet were quite damp now and I was standing in a small puddle. I looked down and gasped. All around my boots were springing up beautiful flowers. They were growing right in front of my eyes. Soon they had opened their heads, unfurled their brightly coloured petals and had risen to the height of my knees. I was transfixed.

> Hold onto your clear and wonderful insights Phoney. Hold on to all the good stuff. Let the good stuff guide you. Not the scary fearful stuff. Think what you have learned. You can now see that your life has been all about suffering.

I was amazed by the flowers that Amy had made spring up. There was no denying them. They were really there and all around my feet. I picked one and sniffed the small bloom. The whole greenhouse was being filled with a heavenly rose tinted aroma, not unlike honeysuckle.

> You can now see that your suffering has causes. Am I right Phoney? Your suffering is caused by all your lions and tigers and your fearful old habit energy.

Holding a delicate bloom between my fingers, I gave in to her logic. I crumbled. She was right. I couldn't deny it. She had highlighted my suffering and had shown me that I was the one who caused it. Amy smiled at me, noticing that my fists had

113

uncurled, that my shoulders had dropped and that my face had softened. She continued gently, her eyes full of compassion.

*Listen carefully Phoney. You can now see that your suffering has causes. It begins deep within you. So now you can actually begin to choose to ease and eventually stop your suffering. Your suffering exists for reasons that no longer need to be your reality. You are learning that with gentle practise and loving kindness and compassion for yourself you can become free of suffering.*

As Amy was speaking she held my hand and stared up into my eyes.

*I love you Phoney. I am here to show you how you can save yourself. You are safe and you are loved. All you have to do is to choose to believe and accept this truth. Water your own seeds with your own love and kindness.*

As she spoke, something broke deep inside me. I felt a swell of tears just beneath the surface. Thank God I'm a man or I would have blubbed there and then. To my surprise as I lifted my hand to my cheek I realised that it was soaking. Oh. I was crying then!! It felt good. As my shoulders shook and the tears flowed out of me it felt as if I had stepped out of a small confined space into the light. It felt as if I was about to enter the most beautiful garden full of flowers, birdsong and laughter.

Amy quietly held out her hand and caught one of my tears. The single sphere of water bounced along her tiny palm and then fell to the flowers growing all around my feet, bending a single leaf as it fell.

*You are alright Phoney, it's OK. Better out than in. Once we get past the tears, we can let the joy in. Now you know the way to your garden of paradise, just remember to take off your huge boots so that you don't crush the flowers.*

## Chapter 7

'That's all a bit biblical I suppose Amy.' I sniffed into my handkerchief.

*Go ye and sin no more means 'off you go and stop being mean to yourself'. Stop choosing fear. Start choosing love and watch your garden grow. Now isn't there something that you need to do, apart from wipe your eyes and blow your nose that is? Isn't there someone you know who might appreciate some pretty flowers? You see my dearest Phoney, we can also water each other's seeds of happiness.*

Amy was smiling at me. Something in the way she looked at me so kindly, so lovingly, so gently, brought a memory flashing back into my mind. It was of my wife, Hazel. Oh my God I was such an idiot. She was the only person who had ever seen through my rubbish and made me feel special, loved and happy to be alive.

'I can't just go back to Hazel, Amy. She threw me out.'

*That's fear talking Phoney. Now. Still yourself. Breathe. Smile deep into the heart of your being. Let love take a hold there. Think of Hazel. Now what flower of an idea grows?*

I looked down at Amy and carefully stepped backwards. In the centre of a flourishing new growth of lovely flowers were my two huge footprints. Proof that I had been there and witnessed a small miracle. I heard someone enter the greenhouse behind me so I turned and quickly let myself out, remarking briefly to the surprised gardener how nice the blooms were.

So that's how I came to find myself a few minutes later, engaged in an animated discussion with a kindly old gentleman in the flower shop section of the garden centre, about which roses are best to send to your wife. I chose the most enormous bunch of pale pink roses that had that delicate old-fashioned fragrance that reminded me of the small girl who had vanished into the cake shop. As he carefully wrapped them in crinkly paper and promised to deliver them after work, I had a sudden bout of panic. Fears rose up. What would Hazel think if I sent her flowers? She would think that I was wheedling after her affections, that I was grovelling, that they were a guilt purchase...

I quietly and carefully did as Amy had instructed me. I leaned forward on the desk with my pen ready to write, and as the old gardener turned his back to label my purchase, I breathed slowly and deeply. I exhaled my fear. I exhaled my anxiety. I told myself that I was a kind loving man. I told myself that I was a good man. I allowed myself to believe that I was safe and loved. I felt a deep sensation of love and kindness arrive deep inside me. It seemed to form a very real warm glow that began in my stomach, and bloomed all the way up to my head. I breathed again and waited for the message for Hazel to flower within my consciousness.

I love you. Michael x

It was simple, truthful and with no ulterior message or neurotic need. No emotional blackmail or manipulation. No guilt. No regrets. No fear. The three words were a gift that I could freely give without fear of pain or rejection. A simple gift of love.

As I exited the garden centre, Amy caught up with me. She was eating a huge slice of cake.

*Well done Phoney. That was real. Well done. You're getting the hang of this. How are you feeling now?*

'Honestly?'

I searched my mind for my true feelings and found that my heart spoke to me.

'Relieved Amy. I feel relieved.'

*Good Phoney. Now we can really begin. Are you ready for a wonderful life Phoney? Are you ready to wake up and see how amazing you really are?*

As we walked back towards town I realised that Amy's challenge made me feel excited, not fearful. For the first time since I'd moved to Glasgow, I found myself noticing all the well-kept gardens and beautiful hanging baskets that adorned the houses. I realised just how much love and careful attention it had taken to make them all flourish. Then I realised how lucky I was to be able to enjoy them.

What on earth was this small and carefree apparition going to teach me next?

# Chapter Eight

Sitting on a hill, overlooking the wide valley that is the city of Glasgow, I felt a deep sense of wellbeing. I watched families playing with their children. I followed the trajectory of dandelion seeds as they floated higher and higher, lifted on the warm breeze. I heard the call of a skylark as it began its tuneful decent. I smelt the fragrance of freshly mowed grass. Beside me a small girl was blowing the seeds from a dandelion clock and calling out the imaginary time. I looked down at my newly purchased walking boots and reflected on the past days.

Surely life doesn't get much better than this? I felt the anxious memories of the past few weeks rise up to meet me. I let them appear but I didn't allow myself to grab hold of the emotions that had caused me so much suffering. I just let them drift into my mind's eye and then chose to let them go off on their way, just like the dandelion seeds that my small spiritual friend was sending high up into the air with each breath.

But then again, it was so easy to drift off and let the mind take over. Before I knew it I'd headed off down a memory motorway of mild embarrassment.

For the first time in years I had begun to think about my physical fitness. It began quite by chance after a meditation session. Our elf-like teacher had introduced us to a concept of something she called mindful walking. This seemed to consist of walking whilst taking very slow steps. She'd asked us to concentrate on every detail of each step that we made. We were supposed to focus on our breathing, notice how our feet met the earth with each step, pay attention to our bodies, be aware of all that surrounded us and maintain our equilibrium.

I hadn't found it easy. I'd felt ridiculous. I kept losing my calm and getting distracted, trying not to bump into my fellow meditators. I'd sulked a bit and had been about to reject the idea all together when my meditation teacher had caught me after the session.

'Michael', she'd said gently to me. 'Michael if you find this practise challenging then why don't you simply take up going out for long walks? The exercise will do you some good and walking is a natural way to restore the body's equilibrium. Don't rush though. Don't rush to get anywhere. Just walk and see where it takes you.'

Of course on the way home I'd taken this to mean that I was fat. Not only had I failed at this basic meditation practise, but my svelte teacher thought that I was unfit and fat. I patted my middle-aged spread and glanced at myself in a shop window. It was true. The past years had seen me stop taking any real physical activity. I had retreated from outdoor living to embrace writing my masterpiece. Somewhere along the way I had also embraced a sedentary lifestyle. I had stopped exercising for pleasure. I hardly went out. My world had shrunk to the flat, my work and the coffee shop.

My reflection stared back at me. I was slouching. I had put on weight. My body ached and my lungs gasped if I had to walk upstairs. It was then that I noticed that the window of the shop I had paused at was actually a hiking and outdoor specialist. And I swear I could hear a faint ringing in my ears of familiar child-like laughter. I checked my back pocket for my wallet and, taking a deep breath, opened the door and went in.

Fifteen minutes later I was the proud owner of the very latest, snug-fitting, waterproof, lightweight, hyper-grippy, foot-supporting walking boots. I knew that I would regret the huge sum of money that I had just parted with but honestly, now that I had been banned from the pub and had all but stopped drinking, it would only take a week or so to save the money back.

So happy was I with my purchase that I had left my battered old brown brogues in the shopping bag and marched out of the shop with my new boots on. I have to admit my feet felt happy.

So that was that. Every day without fail, facing wind, rain, sleet or hail, I would head out of the door and simply walk wherever my feet took me. It wasn't always a success. Occasionally I ended up in vast, grey, frightening housing estates, moving swiftly past gangs of young people who were only just managing to hold onto their fierce fighting dogs. But for most of the time I experienced Glasgow and the surrounding countryside anew. It was as if a completely fresh topography had opened out in front of me. I had never realised just how beautiful so many parts of Glasgow are. I walked along rivers and canals until I emerged onto breath-taking hillsides that afforded an elevated view of the whole area. Some days, leaving the car behind, I would take the train and walk out to the stunning national park of Loch Lomond. As I began to lose weight and feel fitter I found that my meditation practise improved. In the parks and on the hills around Glasgow, a new perspective on life was slowly dawning on me.

This wasn't a city full of fear and loathing. It was a city full of possibilities.

Of course it wasn't long until I bumped into myself coming the other way. At some point on my long walks I would meet my own suffering and doubts. I swear they would sneak up on me when I wasn't looking. So whilst walking, I had to confront my negative feelings and thoughts. I'm terrible with confrontation. Even the very idea of opposing somebody else just freezes me solid and makes me tongue-tied. I lose all of my ability to converse in an intelligent and rational manner. Or I find the opposite happens and I just blurt out random words. So, like so many men I guess, I quickly resort to childish swearing and bellowing. My frustration at not being able to articulate my position means I just speak louder and quicker and then resort to personal name-calling. Soon I was fighting with myself, admonishing my lack of meditative calm, angry at my thoughts and feelings. I felt cross at my recent actions and my stupidity at being thrown out of my own house and estranged from the love of my life. On and on and on until suddenly I'd realise that I was back at my flat feeling even more stressed than when I'd left. Most days I managed to gain some sense of equilibrium by the end of my walk but so often I was left either fuming at myself or at somebody else.

My meditative walking and peaceful state of mind collapsed completely soon after a promotion was announced at one of my business ventures. A highly intelligent and very motivated young man had been appointed as a new member on the board of a media company that I provide occasional consultancy to. I know media consultancy all sounds very grand but basically it just gives me a way to create a higher profile for my writing, and I rather like the buzz and excitement of writing for TV.

The new chap, Markus, had been promoted to provide coordination and financial management. On paper it sounded like a great idea and at the interview I sang his praises. Yet two months later he transformed into my bête noir. At every turn I discovered that Markus had either undermined my position or simply refused to act on my recommendations. I found myself at a loss. I had entered my mute phase. At meetings there was a heavy atmosphere hanging in the air. We could hardly bear to be in the same room. The elephant was so big there was not enough space for the both of us, so I generally left early and headed back to the café to work remotely. I felt utterly shaken and quickly started to obsess about him. I moaned about him to my other business partner in the media company and to anybody who would listen. Yet to all of them he was a complete angel, always ready with a smile and a helpful and humorous suggestion. I was fast becoming alienated from a company that I had helped start up. I lost my sense of humour. I dreaded going into the office and then I stopped being able to sleep properly again. Basically I felt dreadful.

So, on the last Friday of the month I dragged myself out of bed, weary, groggy, and with a slight hangover. I was primed and ready to 'have it out with Markus.' Enough. It was him or me.

Needless to say, when I tripped over my brand new hiking boots and bashed my shins on the table, I wasn't too impressed. I yelped with pain and danced around, hopping and rubbing my shins at the same time. Of course almost immediately I heard the infectious mix of familiar laughter. I spun round, half angry and half relieved to have her back.

'Amy you flipping little minx, you put my boots on the floor for me to trip over didn't you? That hurt, still hurts, yow!'

*They weren't there for you to trip over, Phoney. They were there for you to notice. Seems you have been tripping over for some time now you poor old thing.*

'Where have you been anyway?' I asked as I sat down to rub my shins.

*Nowhere. Everywhere. Watching you practise. Seeing you let your garden fill up with weeds again. Did you miss me then?*

Amy was now standing in front of me, holding up my boots.

'Erm, no. Well maybe. Well occasionally. Look what do you want? I was...'

*Busy? You were busy falling asleep and falling back into fear Phoney. Getting all angry and mean with the people you are working with. I was watching you deciding on being a new mean version of yourself. You've lost your calm, lost your stillness, lost your quiet and want to be a big old meanie.*

'I'm not the one who's mean Amy. I'm fed up with being Mr Nice Guy. Anyway Amy, it's not fair and it's bloody hard sometimes. Life isn't as easy as you try to make out. Sometimes you can't control what happens to you. You can't change other people. I'm only human. I have feelings as well feel you know.'

124

# Chapter 8

Amy stood still. Her head was on one side. She was considering something. Then she threw the boots at me. I caught them in surprise.

> *Put them on Phoney. We are going for a walk. It's a wonderful day.*

Amy was only three feet tall, if that, yet somehow her presence seemed to tower over me, especially when I was feeling emotionally confused. She had crossed her arms and was looking up at me with that gimlet blue stare that she was wont to use on me. I sighed and acquiesced to her demands. I rubbed my shins one last time and put the boots on and headed after my small friend as she skipped towards the front door.

Soon I was out of breath and puffing. Amy set off at a breakneck pace. She bobbed and weaved in front of me, dodging shoppers and tourists, all of whom I seemed to collide with on a regular basis. Amy had the ability to dart between people like a small minnow whereas I felt like a whale in comparison. The effortless calm of going with the flow had deserted me along with my good humour. As we marched along I vaguely wondered if the two were linked somehow. Soon we were heading far out of the city. Amy walked me for miles, not saying a word. We walked alongside the river and then out of Glasgow until we were at the foot of a huge ben, a massive hill. We paused at the bottom of a steep muddy track while Amy turned briefly to regard my sweaty and breathless demeanour with a sardonic look.

> *You have to keep on walking Phoney. Up we go.*

Amy began to skip up the steep incline a few feet in front of me. I was not as fit as I thought I had become. I couldn't keep up with her rapid and childlike ascent. Amy hopped from foot to foot, plucking shoots of grass, picking dandelions and skipping after butterflies. I kept on grimly putting one foot in front of the other, wondering if my heart would give out.

Eventually we reached the summit. It was very high. Even though the weather was unseasonably nice the wind was strong up here. I bent double, gasping for breath. I looked at Amy. She was still skipping round and round me.

'How come you are not even slightly out of breath?'

Amy stopped skipping and plumped herself down in the long grass so that only her head was visible.

> *I put down all the weight I was carrying at the bottom of the hill Phoney. You are still carrying all of yours. In fact, by the time you reached the top you had managed to pick up some more. Mumble, mumble, murmur, murmur, grumble, grumble...*

Amy was imitating me grumbling away to myself, bent double as I staggered up the hill. As usual she was spot on. I didn't appreciate it because my lungs were fit to collapse.

'Oh nice. More metaphors.' I was still finding it hard to breathe.

> *Stand up straight Phoney. Breathe slowly. Now look.*

I stood up, trying to find my balance. The walk had cleared my head but my heart was still pounding. I put my hands on my hips, straightened my back carefully and tried to focus on the view. Amy turned to look up at me while she chewed on a long stem of wild grass.

> *Do you see it Phoney?*

I blinked into the wind and tried to take in the view. Breath by breath I slowly managed to regulate my heart rate enough to be able to take a good long look at the sprawling city spread out far beneath us.

> *So Phoney do you see it?*

Chapter 8

I paused and looked again.

'See what?'

*It Phoney. It.*

'What's it? What do you mean?'

I could see the streets, the factories, the spires, the roads, the parks. I could see it all.

'See what Amy?'

*See what really is. See the suchness of stuff. See just how things really are. See the simple beauty of the world.*

I took a moment longer to try to regulate my breathing and used the time to focus on what Amy was saying to me.

*Phoney you need to learn the next step of how to end all this suffering. You have to learn how to see truthfully, honestly, without any made up thinking. If you don't you won't be able to lead yourself and other Phoneys out of suffering. It's time to learn Right Seeing.*

'Huh?'

A huge wave of anger flooded over me. I felt confused and patronised again by Amy and now, seeing the city below, I was reminded that I would soon have to face my enemy at its centre. That was the 'suchness' of the situation; I had to go head to head with Markus. Amy looked so god damn cheerful I couldn't help feeling resentful. It was alright for her. She was a master of this stuff - that was if she was even real in the first place. I felt confused, tired, angry and upset. I started to turn and head back down the steep climb to confront Markus. I felt ready for a fight now. Well done Amy!

Then I tripped. I fell headlong and clattered down the incredibly steep incline of the hill. I bounced, undignified, over low bushes for a few metres until I hit a large clump of thistles. That made me really yelp and momentarily I lost all thought of battling Markus and focussed on plucking thistles out of my hand. Of course from just behind me I heard that cascade of laughter that I had grown to recognise. Through my own pain and frustration, as I plucked thistles out of my hands, my posterior and legs, I could see my small torturer once more doubled up. She was lying on her back and kicking her legs in the air whilst laughing so loudly that the ground seemed to shake. Tears were streaming down her face. One of her bright red welly boots flew off and hit me square in the chest. That made Amy laugh even more, and she was literally holding onto her sides for dear life. The sight of her unhinged mirth distracted me again. It was so maddening. I have no idea what gives Amy such an infectious laugh, but to my exasperation I found that her hysterics seemed to shift my black cloud of anger and pain just far enough for me to smile.

'Did you trip me up Amy?'

*Ha, ha, he he, hic...no Phoney, that's why it's so funny... you always trip yourself up. You just don't look where you are going. Ha ha...*

'Right I'm off. I've had enough. I'm not in the mood to...'

*Come here Phoney, there's something I want to show you.*

'NO!'

*YES!*

Amy had leapt up and was suddenly serious. She fixed me with her steely blue eyes and pointed back up the hill.

*Now Phoney!*

Chapter 8

I sighed. Amy was already marching back up to the brow of the hill. As I climbed, limping slightly, grateful for the grip of my new boots, Amy stood staring out across the valley, hands on her small hips, her hair blowing in the wind like a miniature red tornado. I arrived at her side. She looked up at me and grabbed my hand. Then ever so softly she gave me the same order again.

*Look Phoney, see with your eyes, see with your heart, see with the whole you. Breathe; let go of any idea of what you think you are seeing. Allow yourself to simply see.*

I stood facing into the wind and allowed myself to return to my breathing just like the day at the duck pond. I was vaguely aware of the small warm hand in mine as my breathing regulated and I felt a deep calm come over me. I took a long slow breath, in and out, and then let my gaze fall on the view that surrounded me.

My mind became silent. My head stopped whirring. Then, a place of peace opened like a deep well inside me. It grew and grew until it expanded out from me as far as my eyes could see. It was as if there was no beginning and no end. It was as if I was no longer seeing the view with my eyes but rather being part of the view. I had no beginning and no end. The world in front of me, around me, behind me, seemed and felt wondrous, magical and yet so real. It was as if I was seeing it for the first time. It was as if I was seeing it through new eyes. I had flashbacks to when I was a child, just lying on my back in our garden, in the sunshine on the grass, staring at the shapes of clouds. I became aware of Amy's voice - it seemed almost like music that rose up into the air and swirled inside my mind.

*You have dissolved the separation between you and the world Phoney. You have let go of the blocks. You have stopped using thoughts and descriptions and ideas of what you think is there. You are seeing what really is. This world can be your heaven or it can be your hell. The only thing you have to do is choose to see it.*

A full flock of starlings began an astounding swirling flight in front of us. They darted up over rooftops and trees and chimneys, changing direction as one. Suddenly I felt them, I became aware of them. It was as if they were fish shoaling through the air, swimming through the air. They appeared as one mind, with each bird losing herself for a short time into the collective.

*Oneness Phoney, there is no separation in heaven. I am one, you are one, we are one. The birds do this to remember. We are doing this today so that you can remember. The millions of cells in your body continually do this so that you can exist. Without oneness, without heaven, nothing would be. As you drop into separation you fall asleep and become fearful. Your lions rip apart the fabric of your world. You become isolated, lonely and angry. You try to reach out to re-create connection with violence. Rather than seeking love you seek anger. Love releases you into oneness. Anger only creates division.*

She paused and then shouted out the name Markus. In an instant my amazing vision shattered. I found my mind whirring back to confront my new colleague. I felt my anger rise up again. The shock of the switch in emotional realities made my legs buckle. I sank to the grass and put my head in my hands. My body was shaking. Yet again tears were stinging my eyes. I sniffed, still feeling some resentment towards Amy.

'Why did you do that? That was mean.'

I felt my head being forced upwards. The small and serious face of Amy thrust itself into my blurred vision. Her warm rose-scented breath filled my senses.

*I only spoke a name Phoney. You reacted. You fell back into separation. You fell back into your own hell. You chose to fall.*

I sniffed and wiped my nose on my sleeve. I felt small and vulnerable. I wrapped my arms around myself. Amy sat directly in front of me and began to smile.

*Oh poor Phoney. Don't worry, I am going to teach you how to make it all better. I am going to show you how to practise living in heaven. Now listen carefully.*

I wiped my eyes, cleared my throat and glanced around. Nobody was near us. I sighed and met Amy's steely gaze.

'Erm...be gentle Amy, I've had a bit of a week you know.'

*I'm always gentle. Isn't it time for you to be gentle with yourself? All of the cells in your body have to get on. They have to be kind and loving to each other, all of the time. If they didn't you wouldn't be alive. You would get cancer or something nasty and die. You have to let go of that part of your mind which keeps on wanting to beat you up.*

'You just mean that I am the one hurting myself. But that's not true. This hell that you mentioned wasn't down to me. It was down to that back stabbing little b...'

*Phoney – no swearing! Right seeing must be supported by right speech. Now listen. Humans forget their oneness. They all fall out. They think that they are separate. They treat each other awfully. When they are together they forget why they're here. They do it for all the wrong reasons but that is for another day. Today you need to wake up to right, loving and compassionate seeing.*

'I don't hate anybody Amy. I just get confused.'

*That's spot-on Phoney. Don't worry, everybody thinks they are doing the right thing according to their perception of the world. The trouble is that for most people their perception of the world is based on fear.*

'You mean they think they are seeing lions when in fact we are all antelopes?'

*That's right Phoney, but it starts earlier than that.*

Out of her jacket pocket Amy produced a small hand mirror. She held it up to my face.

*Look Phoney, what do you see?*

I looked. I saw grey hair, a tired and stubbly face covered in tears with red marks from thistles, all mixed in with mud from me wiping my eyes with my dirty hands. I looked awful.

'I dunno Amy, I see a complete blubbering idiot, I see the phoney that you are always talking about. I see a weak and confused man.'

Amy reached up and wiped a tear of self-pity from the corner of my eye.

*Now Phoney, stop your nonsense, breathe like I told you.*
*Look into the mirror and stop your drivel.*

I held the small mirror up to my face and stared into it. I started to breathe slowly and deeply. As I breathed outwards I let go of my confused feelings. I began to allow the calm of earlier to slowly return to me. As always in Amy's presence my emotions quickly managed to right themselves. I looked carefully into the mirror and let go of my thoughts. I stared at the mirror. Soon I was just seeing a face in front of me. I stopped even recognising it as me. I noticed how tired the face looked, how sad and forlorn it was. Suddenly I felt a deep surge of compassion for the poor creature looking back at myself. I felt so sorry for him. He seemed to be suffering just like I had been. His face showed a thousand small battles and a thousand small defeats. Every line spoke of some weary memory. Every crag and crease of his features revealed some frightful confrontation. Yet his eyes seemed to speak deeply about a man who cared, who really was trying to do his best. Here was I sitting so peacefully now, so contentedly in Amy's presence and he looked so sad.

*Now you have identified with him Phoney, forgive him.*
*Encourage him. Love him Phoney.*

I found myself so sorry for the man looking back at me that my breath caught for a moment. I could see all his hopes, his belief that he was trying to do the right thing. I could see how hurt and sad he felt when he failed to achieve the hoped-for outcomes of his actions. I could feel his pain. I could see his suffering. I realised that all he wanted to hear was that he was a good man. He just wanted to be seen and acknowledged for the way that he loved the world. He was me. I was him. We were one. It was as if we met somewhere far away yet also near, in a still place, a quiet place outside of time. Amy's gentle words made me forgive him for all that he thought he had done wrong. As I forgave him, I forgave myself. In my head I heard a sound not unlike ice cracking on a pond in winter.

The man looking back at me began to change. His features softened, his brows un-knotted, and ever so slowly a kind and generous smile returned to his mouth and then to his eyes. His features began to glow. He appeared different, like I had never seen him before. I seemed grown up. Wise. Kind. And then, finally, joyful.

*You are now One, Michael.*

I was vaguely aware that Amy had used my real name. I smiled some more. The man smiled with me. When I laughed, the man laughed with me. Then suddenly I felt what I can only describe as a huge restoration take place deep within me. It was as if I actually put down the huge load that Amy had told me I was carrying. I put the mirror down and looked at Amy. She was beaming back at me. I picked the mirror up and looked at the new glowing me in the reflection. And then I really forgave him. I found myself telling him that it was alright. I found myself comforting him. I found myself telling him that he was a good man. A flood of words of encouragement, support and advice broke my silence. I continued for some time before falling silent and finding peace in the calm and quiet.

Amy took the mirror out of my relaxed grip and put it slowly back in her small pocket.

'Thanks Amy. I hadn't realised how much I disliked myself. You broke me out of that prison. How come I got to believe all that rubbish about myself?'

*It's even harder for us girls you know Michael. Girls are taught separation when we are really young. Girls are forced to become body aware and then we dissolve into being the object of all male and female perception, the critical gaze of other people.*

Amy and I sat on the hilltop staring at each other. Something was happening to her. She was beginning to glow. Even though she was small she seemed timeless, ancient and wise. For the first time I could see a deep compassionate sadness in her eyes. This was something she really wanted me to understand.

*Women can't cross any floor of a room without feeling the controlling stare of a man or woman upon them. We feel vulnerable and weak. Then we are preyed upon and manipulated through our anxieties and lack of self-worth. We give up. We agree with these darkened ideas of the world. We join in the nasty hurtful game. We believe that we don't really exist as beautiful shining stars anymore. We give in and allow ourselves to be exploited. We allow ourselves to be sold a thousand ways to alter and change our perfection. We are sold makeup masks, hair dyes, smell adjustments. We are even encouraged to damage our bodies with markings and then we pay people to cut us up so we match their image of perfection.*

It was a big outburst from Amy. She had used a lot of long words. I realised that she felt passionately about this. As she had been speaking the image of my beautiful daughters had flashed across my mind. I felt a surge of protection for Amy, for them, for my wife, for all the women that I had ever had the pleasure of knowing.

Chapter 8

'That's really awful Amy. I mean I have two daughters and I would hate for them to feel like that, to be weakened like that, for them to lose their certainty of how wonderful they are.'

Amy gave a big long sigh and smiled at me with a deep and gentle compassionate gaze. It was a gaze that let me know that she saw me in all my imperfection as amazing and wonderful. I felt myself glowing under her gaze.

> It's sad isn't it? We are taught comparison from the word go. We have to compare ourselves with our mothers, our sisters, our friends, and teachers in fact everybody. Comparison, comparison, comparison. No positive identification. We are separated and set against each other. We are denied our oneness. Heaven is our birthright and hell is our reality. We get so low and have such lack of self worth that we even sell our bodies. We girls, we women, perpetuate this wrong view of ourselves. We judge each other even more than men.

'What can I do Amy?'

> Oh Phoney, it's not for you to do anything other than practise your own correct view of the universe and your own loving kindness and compassion for all living beings. You have to begin with yourself. Love for others begins with love for yourself. You have to overcome your own separation from yourself to be able to dissolve the separation within others.

Amy picked up a dandelion and to my amazement began to gather the seeds that she had blown into the air around her earlier and re-attach them to the flower's head.

> Your fear of confrontation Phoney is actually your fear of reconnection. Your fear of confrontation with Markus is your fear of realising that you are both one and the same. This fear of connection, this seed of suffering, grows like a choking weed to strangle your own sense of

*worth my dear Phoney. You run off into a lonely space,
wrapping yourself up in isolation to protect yourself from
Oneness. You think that Oneness is pain and suffering.
You think that only in separation can you find peace.
You feel threatened by the idea of Oneness. Oneness is
simply truth. It is the truth of joy, of love, of heaven made
manifest right here, right now.*

Amy had completely restored the dandelion and was examining
it closely as she spoke to me. She looked more like an ancient,
little old lady than a five- or six-year-old child. She spoke slowly,
over-emphasising all the long words she was using. She paused
for a moment as if staring into the flower head was in fact the
entire universe.

'You mean that I am alienated from myself?'

My comment made Amy snap out of her reflection and she gave
me a huge grin.

*Tee hee – yup Phoney, you are a bit of an alien at times.*

'That's not nice Amy.'

*Now Phoney, think of Markus again. Call him into your
mind's eye.*

I didn't want to but I had a feeling that Amy wasn't going to let
me off the hook that easily. I wanted to remain in this wonderful
place of realisation and bliss.

*Come on Phoney. Don't grasp onto any moment, not
even bliss. Don't go back to fear. Let go. Don't worry; I am
going to teach you the Amy Way.*

'Amy's Way? That sounds daft.'

*Oh Phoney you love long words don't you? OK, the Amy*

Chapter 8

*Principle of Perception then.*

'Ha, APP it is then.'

Amy rolled her clear blue eyes heavenward and then turned towards me intently.

*All right, calm down professor, sit on the grass. Now listen and do as I say.*

I adjusted my sitting position and began my breathing practice while I concentrated on what Amy was saying.

*Slowly bring Markus into your mind's eye. Just like when you were looking into the mirror. Don't think. Don't seek any feeling. Keep breathing. Keep calm. Don't use judgement to seek separation and the illusion of safety. Now you see Markus but don't use comparison. Stop all your judgmental thoughts, release them. Let them flow through you, past you, up and out of you. We must never judge anyone for anything Phoney. Judgment leads to immediate separation.*

It was hard because I was really struggling to feel anything but negativity towards Markus. I tried to look with neutrality. It was amazing how clearly I could see his face in my mind's eye.

*Now see the real Markus, Phoney, see him with your own inner eye. See his truth. Identify with him. What do you see?*

I looked carefully. I saw a young man full of ambition and fear, blinded by his own idea of self-importance.

*Good Phoney.*

'But aren't I judging him?'

*No you are seeing his suffering for what it is. Now identify with him. The secret is to identify with each other Phoney. We mustn't fall into the habit of comparison. The need to compare ourselves with other people all the time is a need built of fear.*

'So comparison is neurotic? Are you sure?'

*Of course it is, it's our sly little self-doubt peeping out of the corner of our perception to see if we are better than someone else Phoney. Those fears only surface because we don't believe that we are fabby in the first place. Women have whole magazines designed to keep them in a constant state of unhealthy comparison. Remember what I showed you Phoney?*

I scratched my head as the world around me just made a bit more sense.

'So you are saying that the path to happiness is to identify with those around you, not to compare yourself with them?'

*Comparison creates instant separation Phoney, just like judgment and blame. Remember, separation is a lie, the great big lie. If we think that we are separate then we can choose to be meanies.*

'Is that why we create all those labels then, black, white, yellow, good, bad, Christian, Muslim, communist, capitalist? Do we create them so that we can be mean to each other?'

*Yup, unless it's just to identify someone from the crowd so that you can buy them an ice cream. Now focus on Markus again Phoney. You may have been guilty of comparison. Concentrate, identify with poor young Markus. Remember when you were like him. When you felt and acted like him. Call the memories back and let forgiveness dissolve time and space.*

Not sure of her directions I persevered until I could see myself,
a young lecturer, new to the university department. I was full
of my own ideas and was railing against everyone above me.
I thought I knew best in all things. I could see that I thought I
had all the answers. I was so dissatisfied with my superiors and
their shortcomings - I even felt contempt for them. I judged them
and fought intellectually with them every day. My self-belief was
bolstered by my prolific rate of study and writing. How much
better my academic ideas, research and papers were to my
superiors. I realised that I had been quite ghastly, that I'd been
completely tied up in my own ego.

> *Good Phoney. Now see the roots of your suffering. See
> how you were really just filled with fear and operating
> from a view of the world that was not true.*

I did. It was actually very easy. It was true. I had just been terrified
of being found out, terrified that I was just bluffing, terrified that
I had to fight for my position. I was so unsure. I was, as Amy had
said, living in a world of fear.

> *Now Phoney, understand your suffering and forgive
> yourself.*

I saw the younger version of myself confronting the professors
and saw him with furrowed brow being a complete idiot. I saw
him judging himself and those around him. I saw him comparing
himself to great minds and great writers. I saw him comparing
himself to his father and mother. I saw him unable to function
with any real happiness. I saw him going home and using ready
and easily available drugs to expand his mind when in fact he
was running away from the feeling of terror that gnawed at his
soul.

Then I remembered the mirror. I asked my younger self to sit
down in front of me, to stop his incessant writing and working.
Then, just as I had been shown earlier, I forgave him. I sort of
held him in my mind's eye. I loved him with my whole being. I
told him it was OK. I forgave him. I realised that he had no idea

what he was doing. Then, in front of me, my younger self looked up from his writings and smiled directly at me. I felt a flood of warmth, happiness and healing surge through me.

*Well done Michael.*

Amy actually sounded proud.

*You have forgiven yourself. You have healed a rift across time and space; you have dissolved separation within you. Eventually all perceptions dissolve - in the end none are real. How does it feel?*

'It feels nice Amy.'

We both laughed; for a man who loved words that was a pretty lame description.

'I feel ...whole.'

*Good Phoney. Now, call Markus into your mind's eye and identify with him and forgive him, release him from your judgment and your idea of fear and separation.*

I did as she requested. This time it was easy. Suddenly I could see the excited, ambitious and talented young man working in the office. I know this sounds odd, but as I forgave him I felt a flood of love and compassion for him. Suddenly I realised that I was there to provide a safe place for him to escape his own prison of fear and anxiety so that he could flourish. It was Amy's 'watering the right seeds' again.

*That's right Phoney. Let only your love water the seeds that lie within you and within everybody.*

The vision passed and I let go of it just as Amy had instructed. I noticed that I felt light and carefree and that an old fear had left me. Every time I called Markus into my mind's eye I had only respect and compassion for him. Who would have thought it? This 'Amy's Way' stuff was powerful healing.

I sat back on the grass and let my mind soak up the view. Amy had moved some way off from me and was eagerly blowing dandelion clocks like a young child again. I could hear the gentle sound of distant children's laughter and I felt truly part of the world that I inhabited. The sun had come out. The grasses swayed in the breeze. I felt a deep and wonderful childlike joy bubble up through me like a spring of clear water finding its way back to the desert.

\* \* \* \* \* \* \* \* \* \* \* \* \*

The next day I went into the production office. For some reason, maybe because I had slept so well after my day on the hilltop, I didn't feel at all stressed or nervous. I had meditated on the train. I hadn't had coffee. I just went straight into the building and entered the production office. Only Markus was there.

He looked up as I went in. 'Hello mate' he said and then turned back to get on with his work. That was that. Nothing more, nothing less. It was just a simple greeting and a momentary acknowledgement of my presence, and then back to work.

I never experienced another cross word or negative moment with Markus again. For the entire duration of the time we worked together, we got on famously. In fact he grew to become one of my closest friends. Amy's idea of oneness had somehow worked its magic.

Much later I learned that my business partner had in fact been playing Markus and myself off, one against the other. I forgave him of course...well after I had practised the 'Amy's Way'.

Every night for weeks afterwards, whenever I felt angry or recognised that I was being judgmental about somebody, I practised Amy's teaching. I even began to share it with some of my new meditation friends. Day by day I realised that I was experiencing a new relationship with my work colleagues. I noticed that whenever I was with them I didn't bring division into the room; rather I brought a sense of community or team or even, dare I say it, family and friendship. The shift was small, it was subtle, and as soon as I noticed it I let go of it, anxious not to water my own ego and grow more weeds of suffering.

As the weeks went by our department at the university began to show noticeable change. We came up with more ideas, developed more courses and began to get admiring glances from the other faculties. More and more graduates wanted to continue with us rather than move to other departments. I realised that I had never noticed just how bitchy and backstabbing academic institutions were. I had never noticed that in myself. I had never noticed it in our department. The more I became aware of it, the less I judged. The more I practised 'Amy's Way' the more I found myself identifying rather than comparing myself with my colleagues.

Soon after my mini pilgrimage up the hill with Amy I visited my daughters. I got them to discuss how they felt about themselves and their friends and women in general. I was amazed at how much they opened up to me once I broached the subject. I was quite shocked to hear how badly the girls at their schools and colleges has treated each other and how highly competitive it was even at parties and social occasions.

Without even asking questions I soon came to realise that everything Amy had said about being a woman was true. Even my daughters were discussing tattoos, how they could change their bodies, their looks and their personalities. They all read from any number of terrible women's magazines that on the one hand celebrated beauty yet on the other hand printed huge pictures of female celebrities and pilloried them if they revealed any cellulite or failure in their personal lives. Flicking through the magazines I felt sick.

Chapter 8

In the airport on the way home I looked at the covers of men's magazines with a different eye. Each one had a young woman desperately thrusting herself forwards in some stereotypical sexual pose whilst selling music, cars, bikes and even engine parts.

Everywhere I looked in the airport I saw airbrushed images of women selling goods and cosmetics. Each message was the same: 'You are not beautiful unless you have this product'. Each item was being sold by deliberately undermining women. Making them insecure so that they would buy products to make them feel secure. It was like a chemical and cosmetic protection racket. It was a device for divide and rule. The images were designed to create separation. The critical comments in the magazines created separation from any sense of real inner beauty a woman might have and pitched women against each other.

Was this what Amy meant by living in a view of the world based on fear? Is this what we do to each other as human beings, undermine each other so as to exploit each other? Do we create a fearful perception of ourselves just by accepting other people's fear-based views of reality? Just by projecting our own insecurities onto other people do we force ourselves to judge them and then end up in what Amy called 'separation', a real and living hell? Oh my poor daughters.

I became anxious for a moment until I remembered how, on my last evening with them, my daughters had introduced me to their small group of friends. I had bought them all supper and was curious to see how they all got on and if they were emotionally crippled by all these terrible and negative perceptions foisted on women.

To my great and profound relief, I immediately saw that my daughters had found a small selection of wonderfully imperfect women, just like themselves, who all provided emotional support for each other. Their mutual love and good-humoured compassion for each other seemed to give them the strength to overcome the self-doubt that they all suffered from time to time.

I realised that this small group of close friends were already practising what Amy had taught me. They all identified with each other's suffering and worked together to overcome it. If one felt low, the others gave them positive encouragement and support. They didn't judge each other and shared any insights they had, usually about boys and other less friendly women. And of course they also told stories of how they could fall out with other spectacularly sometimes, usually at a drunken party!

I remembered how I had listened with amazement as they had shared their stories with me. How mature and grown up they all seemed, yet still so young. I was glad that they all agreed with Amy's version of the world and that they were doing their best to see through it. Maybe young people are already learning to see through this illusion of self-doubt and suffering.

As I left for the airport later that evening my girls gave me a huge hug and commented on the difference they'd seen in me. Standing between both of my teenage daughters, I felt as if I was with Amy again. They both stared long and hard at me and said that I had changed, that I was nicer, that I listened to them now, that I was trying to understand, and that I hadn't embarrassed them in front of their friends like 'I USUALLY DID!' Then they both frisked me for any available cash I had, gave me a warm hug and ran off to be with their friends once more.

In the departures lounge moments later, I saw woman after woman picking up the horrible magazines that oppressed them and I silently gave up a small prayer for all daughters, sisters and mothers in the world.

There was no getting away from it; Amy's idea of right-seeing was beginning to make a lasting impression on me.

# Chapter Nine

I spent almost a week practising the 'Amy Way' of seeing the world.  One morning I woke to find that three small pictures had returned to the shelf in my small living room. There was one of each of my daughters and one of my wife. Underneath the pictures of my daughters was a small note scrawled with a child's writing that simply said, 'Well dun Phoney ☺'. Under my wife's was a bright red, crayoned question mark.

There was no way I could call Hazel before I had checked in with myself to see if I was ready. I felt happy and proud and then scared. Breathing quickly, I tried to monitor my emotions as they arose, just as Amy had showed me. I realised that I felt terrified of rejection and felt worried, anxious, nervous, vulnerable and needy. We had actually parted, or taken a little break from each other, on such good terms that I had no idea what to do. Usually women threw me out screaming, shouting and hurling abuse. This time I had just received a quiet suggestion that I might be better off on my own until I had finished whatever it was that I had to do. Perhaps I had taken this as my usual sign of rejection. Maybe Hazel had not even really ended it with me – maybe she just knew I needed space? Maybe she hadn't. I was grasping at straws and very quickly slipped into meltdown.

I had continued to send Hazel pink roses every week. I had written short cards telling her that I was now trying to sort my life out, that I was meditating, that I had taken up exercise. Hazel hadn't replied but, one evening, I had come home to a flat that had been cleaned and the fridge had been stocked. There was no way Amy would have done that. All she ever did was eat all my cakes. In fact all I ever seemed to have in the fridge these days were lots of small chocolate cakes in case my diminutive guide showed up. Hazel had just thrown out all the sugar-based munchies, which I assumed was to encourage my diet and fitness regime. (Though maybe she had been checking in on me and decided that the cakes showed I was lying.) Maybe she just saw I needed help. Anyway, I bought her double the amount of roses that week and put a huge 'Thank You' on the card. Surely this was a good sign?

But if things were getting better, why did she avoid my texts and phone calls? Maybe she was just humouring me. Maybe she was just feeling sorry for me. Maybe she was...

*Just waiting for you to get it Phoney.*

I jumped, my thoughts shattered. Sitting on the windowsill was Amy in a bright blue dress, stuffing my biscuits down her throat in a gleeful fashion.

'Huh, oh hi, erm, what...?'

*Maybe Phoney, maybe she is just waiting for you to see her.*

'Huh, well that's what I was just thinking. Hey don't eat all of those - you'll make yourself sick... if you can get sick. Anyway, that's just it; does she actually *want* to see me?'

*It's not you visiting her that's important Phoney.*

Amy jumped down, crossed the room and clambered up on the table until her small chocolate-smeared face was inches from mine.

*It's you joyfully seeing HER that she's waiting for... maybe.*

I don't get what you are trying to say Amy.

Amy had left a pregnant pause after the word 'maybe' that had alarmed me. What did she know? Maybe Hazel didn't love me anymore. Maybe she was seeing someone else. Maybe she wanted a divorce. Maybe she…

'Ow'. I shouted and leapt up, sending my teacup spinning. Amy had jabbed me in the eye with her finger.

'Ow bloody hell, ow you…'

I let rip a long line of profanities and expletives, enough to send Amy into hysterics.

*No swearing Phoney – I'm gonna have to teach you Right Speech soon or else your neighbours will disown you – sorry about the eye but you seemed to have something in it.*

'What do you mean I had something in it? What I had in it was the end of your finger!'

At this Amy started laughing again. Her laughter drowned out my indignant swearing until eventually she came to a wheezing full stop and my poor eye ceased streaming.

*No Phoney, what you had in your eye was wrong seeing again. It was full of it. Full of rubbish. Full of fear.*

'That's not fair Amy; I have been practising every day. And I don't judge Hazel, I never judge Hazel - she's wonderful, probably the kindest and nicest person I know and…'

*You were seeing Hazel from your usual place of fear Phoney. You weren't seeing her from a place of truth. You had gone all scaredy cat and weak and silly.*

'Well I love her and…'

*She is waiting for you to get it Phoney.*

Chapter 9

"But I know that I love her Amy.'

Amy stood up on the table and grabbed my cheeks. Her small powerful fingers held my head firmly and she stared into my eyes.

*You think you do Phoney. If you love her then why are you so scared and stressed out?*

'Because I might lose her, obviously Amy!'

*How can you lose someone Phoney if we are all one?*

'I erm. I don't know, that's not the point. Hazel and I are obviously not one Amy, not at the moment anyhow. I'm here and Hazel is in our house, at this moment doing something without me. Spatially Amy we are not coexisting. I want her back. I don't know if she wants the same, that's why I'm nervous.'

*Phoney, you have loads of weeds of suffering choking up inside you, poor old thing. So stop watering them with fear and try love instead.*

I stopped and began to mop up the tea that I had spilled all across the table. I took a few deep breaths. I had secretly hoped Amy would show up to help me but I had forgotten that she always made me do the hard work. This wasn't going to be easy. My mind was a mess again. I finished clearing up then sat down on my chair and took a deep breath. Amy had moved to her window perch and was breathing on the glass and drawing love hearts in the condensation. I waited for her to finish and returned to my gentle breathing technique again.

I held Hazel in my mind's eye and thought about her. I could see her clearly. She seemed fine. What was I supposed to be seeing?

*You are scared of losing her 'cause you don't know that you are one yet Phoney. You want to be with her because you need your mummy.*

'You - what!!!'

*It's your fear that blinds you Phoney. Your fear comes from many places, but the main one is that you were separated at birth from your mother.*

'What on earth are you going on about Amy? Of course I was separated from my mother at birth, all children are; it's a universal truth. It has been since the beginning of time. The umbilical cord is cut, baby cries, life starts... that's a ridiculous reason! You've really lost it this time Amy.'

Amy had begun to annoy me. Now she was sitting on the windowsill deliberately sucking her thumb, noisily. As I finished speaking she pulled it out of her mouth with a loud popping sound. She looked pleased with herself.

*That's how it all starts Phoney. I know you had a difficult childhood but that is the very root of suffering right there. Once you broke free you had to breathe for yourself, you had to eat for yourself, you had to create safety for yourself and you had to create love for yourself.*

'So you are saying that the original desire for a mother is still there deep down inside me?'

*Of course it is Phoney, you are all really scared that you can't survive on your own. You all fear that no one will take care of you. You crave your mother's breast and look for it in every woman you meet. You still crave someone to take care of you. It is the same desire, based on your fear seed and you keep on watering it. You just fear that no one notices the little sparrows falling.*

Amy put her thumb in her mouth again and started sucking loudly. My anger levels were building quickly and pretty soon I felt incensed. She was clearly mocking me. I tried another tack.

Chapter 9

'So you are saying that all relationships are just some neurotic urge and so are all doomed to failure?!'

Amy pulled her thumb out of her mouth again and laughed as she managed to increase the volume of the popping sound.

> *Many relationships are, yes Phoney. You see, if it's all about need, then you - or both of you - are still living in the old fear reality that is 'we are not OK unless we have someone to love, to make us feel good'. Your fear is that you won't survive without someone to take care of you. That's why Hazel filled the fridge for you. Not to show she loves you, which maybe she does, but to show you that that's how you expect her to love you.*

I felt my mouth go dry. Amy wasn't reassuring me or helping my positivity levels at all. I had hoped that Hazel's surprise cleaning and fridge filling had been a good sign, a sign that we were on the road to recovery. Then I heard Amy laugh - she was pointing at me and laughing. I stopped and looked down at my hand. I was actually nervously sucking the end of my finger.

'Unfair, Amy. Unfair.'

> *He he, don't worry Phoney, I'm here because you still need me, so it's OK to want your mummy.*

'I don't want my MOTHER!!!'

The volume of my voice shocked us both.

Amy got down from the windowsill and crossed the room until she was standing underneath my downturned head. She reached up and took my hand and then led me back to the chair that I had overturned when I had leapt up and shouted at her.

> *I know Phoney, I know, it's alright, we'll talk about that another day. Now sit down and have a biscuit with your*

*tea, they really are quite good.*

Somehow a new cup of tea and a single chocolate biscuit had appeared on the table in front of me. I felt about six years old. I sat down and took a sip of tea and then nibbled my biscuit. Amy had definitely touched a nerve. She  leant forward and her face was the picture of concern and gentleness.

> *When a relationship is based on fear, it's doomed Phoney. It can't be real. It doesn't have a strong foundation. It's built on sand, on mud. The weight and the pressure of the relationship will cause it to sink.*

'But I thought that relationships should be based on love and caring for each other's needs? If we don't need each other we would never come together.'

> *Caring and loving is part of Right Action but, being with someone out of need is not Right Seeing: it is not a healthy view because it comes from a reality based on fear. Relationships based on neediness just water the seeds of suffering Phoney.*

'So, Hazel...?'

> *Hazel wants to know if you are able to wake up and have a healthy relationship.*

She's testing me?

> *She's communicating with you Phoney, very carefully. She is a clever lady.*

'What's she saying?'

> *She's asking you if you can live without her yet.*

'Huh - but I don't want to...'

# Chapter 9

*It's not a question of choosing Phoney; it's a question of why you are choosing.*

'I don't understand Amy. I'm choosing her because I love her.'

*Well you pushed her away, you acted selfishly, you denied her unconditional love and now, suddenly, you want her back.*

'Erm...well, I was under a lot of pressure, I didn't mean to....'

Amy was giving me that look. It was the one where she raises her eyebrows and challenges me to speak truthfully.

'OK, maybe I got caught up in my own stuff for a while...'

*You've been caught up in this stuff for years Phoney.*

'So I have to exist on my own, nurture myself, that's what you are saying?'

*No Phoney, you forgot your last teaching – we are all one. How can you ever be on your own?*

'But I am, Amy. I am sitting here on my own, night after night. I'm lonely, I miss Hazel.'

*That's OK Phoney, we can all feel lonely. You just want Hazel back because you've noticed that you are fearful of being alone. That's not lonely. That's fear.*

'There's a difference?'

*Yes, choosing to be with Hazel from a place that's not based on fear is different. Choosing to be with Hazel knowing that you no longer need to cling to another person for your own happiness is a healthy choice. It's a truthful choice. It's an enlightened choice.*

Amy pulled me over to the window and wiped away all her smears and love hearts.

*Look Phoney, see the sun, see the clouds, see the trees? You couldn't survive on this planet without them. Fact?*

'Erm...fact?'

*Yes, you see you have just as strong a connection with them as you did with your mother in the beginning. The sun, the rain, the earth, the planet - all of it. She is your mother and she nurtures you all the time. It is impossible to be apart from her. We are all linked as if by thin energetic umbilical cords. Your belly button is linked to your mother, your father, the sun, the earth, the farmer who grows your food. You don't just have one, you have thousands of them.*

'But you just told me not to want my mother, I mean want anybody to nurture me - that I had to do it all myself."

*No Phoney, the belief that you have to do it all yourself is a Darkening, a weed of suffering that has grown up in you. You believe it and then try to overcome it by looking for your mother in all the women you meet. Oh and don't worry women do this with men as well.'*

'So what is the right view then?'

*You have to see it Phoney, wake up to the fact that the whole universe is part of you, is there for you, all of the time. The idea of separation is an illusion, a nightmare that can only occur when you are asleep. Now that you have woken up, Phoney you won't have any more nightmares.*

'But, if I see everyone as my mother all the time, that means that I'm always a child. I won't grow up. I will just let everyone continually do everything for me.'

*Many people don't grow up Phoney. Many wither on the vine. Many stagger through relationship after relationship never being nourished. Time after time they fail in love because they want the other person to be the source of their nourishment. Many are stuck with the glue of fear onto other people, expecting them to supply all their needs. But listen, if you realise that the whole world is your mother, what does that mean?*

My mind was whirling but something in Amy's voice triggered an idea deep inside me.

'Erm, that I can be an eternal child and never worry for my needs, ever?'

Amy jumped down from the windowsill and did a small dance around the room.

*Come ye as a little child – yes Phoney you can – but you ARE part of everything. Your own true nature is also that of the mother. You are your own mother. The universe is your mother. Hazel is your mother but she doesn't want to be a mother that is created out of fear-based neediness.*

'So I've got to see everyone as if I am their mother and, at the same time, as if they are my mother?'

*Yes Phoney, you're getting it. This is the core of Right Seeing. This view brings endless unconditional love to water your seeds for growth, happiness and enlightenment. As you go out into that big old world out there you will be truthful, whole, real. And you'll make a difference.*

'So I can't be an eternal child then, I have to mother everybody?'

*Ask and ye shall receive. You will be both Phoney. As you all learn to love and nurture each other as the universe loves and nurtures you, so you can all be like me, a happy child, free to dance and play safe in the knowledge that you are safe and that you are loved.*

Amy kept up her dancing and started to keep time by banging her spoon on the table. She was hopping from one foot to another, her face full of joy.

'But what about being a grown up? I mean, being an adult. Being responsible? Creating things, working to provide, all that stuff?'

*Ah, your third side. From the foundation of love and the knowledge of oneness you will have all three aspects co-existing inside you in harmony. They will be like one big happy family. Just like all the cells in your body working together to make you. As you wake up, you grow up with the knowledge that there is enough, that you are not alone, that you can truly mature into being the man that you dream of being. Maybe even fulfil your destiny.*

I was silent. I paused. What Amy said had made sense. She always made my head ache, but in a good way. Whenever we started a conversation I never knew where it would end.

'So Hazel wants to know if I can truly see her without need, without neediness, without fear, just as she is, so that we can choose to be together, erm...if she, if we want?'

*Or not.*

'Or not?'

My breath caught again. The moment of doubt gave me an unwanted flicker of panic.

*Practise and breathe Phoney. Once the 'Or not?' question does not scare you then yes, maybe then you have answered Hazel's question about the two of you.*

'Huh, hang on Amy, I was getting there. Let me take a moment.'

I sat down again and sipped my tea slowly. I put it down and began to breathe unhurriedly. I let myself become aware of my emotions, which had now become calm as I breathed gently and deliberately. I allowed myself to quietly ask the question, 'What if Hazel doesn't want us to be together again?'

I felt a small internal jolt of fear, a small hit of adrenaline. Then I quietly let myself focus on the fact that I was okay as I was; that I was okay on my own; that I couldn't ever really be on my own; that the universe and I were one. As I quietly breathed and reflected on this truth I felt a deep sense of wellbeing rise up through me. I noticed that my heart had stopped pounding. I saw that my fingers had stopped drumming on the table. I realised that my tummy had relaxed the knots it had wound up earlier.

Ever so quietly I heard the quiet prompt from within me: 'Ask again.'

I asked again and this time I felt a massive shift deep within me. It was as if something dropped right out of the middle of me. It was as if a huge plug had been pulled. Something most definitely just left me. I felt an immense state of calm flood through my body. I became still.

I'm not sure how long I sat in quiet meditation but it had fallen dark in the room when I felt ready to open my eyes again. As I did I had to smile. Somehow a large single white candle illuminated the table in front of me. Amy was ever so quietly carving intricate shapes into its soft wax . As I watched I realised that I was still tranquil and calm inside.

Amy looked up at me and smiled. In a very gentle voice she said:

*Now you are ready to ask the question that has been troubling you Michael.*

I didn't respond but just maintained my regular breathing. Amy slowly turned the candle so that the side she had been carving faced me. On it in small letters was the word, 'Hazel?'

*Ask yourself the question Phoney.*

Amy leant forward, whispering gently to me.

*Go on, stay in your place of calm and ask the question.*

I knew what she meant. The question formed effortlessly inside me.

'Do I need to be with Hazel?'

And not a single molecule of my being stirred. Not a single flicker or pulse, not even a murmur of emotion - nothing.

I looked straight ahead at Amy. Usually this lack of a response would have freaked me out but Amy held my gaze.

*What is your answer Michael?*

'No.'

I whispered the answer to Amy. My voice seemed to come from a very faraway place and rose effortlessly. I felt no shock or sense of loss, just the realisation that I did not need to be with Hazel. It was odd. It was peaceful. It was neutral.

*So now Michael, now you are really free to choose. Now you are not reacting through fear. You are not responding to a craving. You are experiencing your freedom.*

# Chapter 9

I can only describe the liberating freedom I experienced as space, endless space, inside me, around me, in all directions at once. There was not a ripple on the millpond of my mind.

*As I am here to help you my dear Michael I am going to ask the question for you, right now. The real question. The question of your heart.*

Amy had turned the candle again. This time I saw that she had carved one of her love hearts into the white wax. It was beautiful; it was filled with the most intricate and delicate designs. Somewhere deep inside me I recognised the blend of Celtic and Arabic art.

Amy leaned forward and slowly reached out her finger towards me. Then she touched the centre of my forehead and, staring into my eyes, she asked the question.

*Do you choose Hazel?*

A ripple scurried across the calm of my mind for an instant but I managed to keep still. The question seemed to float in front of me. It was somehow neutral, safe and inert. Then Amy prompted me.

*Use the Amy Way of Seeing, Michael.*

I let my breath rise and fall and then used the reflective technique that Amy had taught me. I could see myself sitting, unmistakably calm, in my mind's eye. I could see that I was momentarily liberated from any kind of need. Then I allowed myself to see Hazel standing in my mind's eye. She was also standing free from need yet I could see that she was even stiller than myself. She was waiting. Waiting for what? Waiting for me. The truth was obvious. Waiting for me to decide. Waiting for me to grow up enough to get it. Waiting for me to be able to get past my own suffering so that I could step into a real relationship. That was her great gift to me. I could see how generous it was. How enlightened it was. How loving and compassionate it was.

> *So many people never hear the calling Michael. So many are lost in their fears. Now Michael, answer her.*

So there and then, in my kitchen, for the first time in my life as a grown up, I chose to be with a woman. I allowed myself to choose Hazel even though we could not be separated by anything in the universe. As I chose Hazel I felt so calm with no accompanying fear of 'what if', 'but' or 'maybe'. Just a quiet, simple 'I choose you.'

Amy leant towards me.

> *It's time to move forward now Michael. Your journey back to each other can be gentle and without fear and neediness. You must let go of outcome though my dear Michael. Hazel is still free to choose whatever her heart delights in. She is also dealing with her own stuff. You have to let go of any idea of outcome, any idea of a happy ending. You must just let what will be happen simply. You must accept the truth and make your heart ready for it. Now call her.*

I picked up the phone that Amy was proffering me. It was already dialling and ringing. Hazel picked up on the third ring.

"Oh hello Michael, I was just thinking about you. What's up? Are you alright?"

My vocal chords bounced back into life and I heard my voice being deep, gentle and calm.

'I couldn't be better. I really feel as if I am starting to make some progress and just wondered if you might like to come with me to the meditation centre tomorrow after work?'

'I would love to Michael. I'll see you there. I've wanted to see what it was all about for ages. So, tomorrow at seven?'

'Brilliant Hazel, I'll see you there.'

As the phone went dead I looked up to see the small smiling Amy vanish into thin air. She sort of faded away until, for a fleeting moment only her smile was left, not unlike the Cheshire cat.

On the table in front of me was the best part of an intricately carved, flickering candle gently capitulating to the warmth of the flame. I put it on a saucer to save the table and looked at the photos on the shelf. I gazed at Hazel's and I felt a thousand questions rise in my mind yet I breathed them away easily. I smiled as deep within me I realised that something quite profound had taken place. It was as if my past and future had been healed and all that was left was the wonderful moment of the present.

And that is how, the very next day, Hazel accompanied me to the meditation centre and then began her own journey towards becoming a world-renowned meditation master and teacher. Yup, Hazel got it straight away. Thing is, that fact filled me with a simple and immediate happiness.

# Chapter Ten

Hazel and I took things slowly. It was as if we were dating for the first time. We met to go walking, we made meditation dates, and we began to exploit the rich seam of theatre, dance and music that the great Celtic city of Glasgow had to offer. We strolled through the park, walking mindfully and marvelling how two people could exist so closely with each other and yet feel and cause no discomfort or pain. We talked and talked like never before. Hazel was amazed to discover how much I had changed since I had moved out. Yet, at the end of each date, I would kiss her on the cheek and head back to my little flat. I had made my choice. I had to let Hazel make hers.

If only things were as tranquil at university. I had been given loads of student seminars to deal with. I also found to my surprise that more and more students would show up at my office, not to discuss work but just to sit, share a cup of tea and confess their worries. This was nice. This was new. This was something that seemed to naturally and gradually evolve out of my new mindful and easy-going approach. Occasionally the visits were unwelcome as I was very busy but, the more I stopped rushing around, the more work I seemed to be able to finish.

The more informal meetings I had with students, the more I became alarmed and began to lose my sense of calm. As students opened up to me, looking for advice, I became concerned and then horrified at how many of them seemed stressed, anxious, worried, confused, depressed and even borderline suicidal. More often than not I was only able to be a supportive pair of ears for just a few minutes. I began to seriously feel out of my depth. I shared my concerns with some of the other professors and lecturers but they just shrugged it off as the 'challenges of student life that were the making of young people'. My colleagues saw the student's obvious suffering as the stuff that built character. I wasn't so sure. I saw more and more frailty and insecurity than I did joie de vive or character building.

It was late one night, after a prolonged session of marking exam papers that I was left to lock up the old department building. I had realised that I was going to miss my meditation class and anyway I was exhausted and ready for my bed. I texted Hazel to decline her offer of supper - yes we were often dining together now - and I wrapped my long black coat carefully around myself and headed down the hill towards my flat. The wind tugged at my scarf and I could sense there was rain in the air. The first smells of autumn were being carried in from the trees in the park. I inhaled their nutty fragrance and enjoyed the respite from traffic fumes. I had grown more and more grateful for the glorious parks as they allowed me, a city dweller, to notice the subtle changing of the seasons. I found the open areas and the proliferation of mature trees deeply grounding.

Ever since Amy had opened my mind to stillness in the park I would actively seek out some of my favourite trees and quiet corners . As I simply stood, breathed gently and mindfully and let my gaze fall onto the trees I found my whirring ego would become quiet. I came to believe that it was because trees were living creatures who gave no reflection of humanity back to me. There was no replication of my own human concerns, worries, fears and desires. I could observe them, be impressed by them and not get troubled with my own self-important thoughts.

As I walked past the park I allowed my pace to slow. The first golden leaves of the lime trees, the linden trees, were dancing high up in the sky, lifted by the cold breeze. I allowed my gaze to follow a solitary leaf as it danced over the park gates and slowly boogied its way towards the ground. It was then that I saw her.

The figure was bundled up in a coat not unlike mine. She caught my attention because she was hanging onto a lamppost with a fierce intensity. I was used to seeing students in varying degrees of sobriety at all times of the day but this person, this girl, was motionless, frozen. I dithered and slowed down. There was nobody around. It was late. I sighed as I realised that I would have to walk right past her. Not wishing to break her focus, or gain her attention, I prepared to lengthen my stride so as to move past her with some speed. But, drawing alongside, I heard her gasping, crying, and moaning and as I slowed down with concern, I could see that her partially covered face was streaked with tears.

I came to a stop a few feet from her.

"Erm, excuse me, are you okay?'

There was no reply, no reaction. The girl just clung on tightly to the lamppost and continued to stare at the ground in front of her. I cleared my throat and raised my voice to ask her again. The wind picked up a bit and whisked my greeting away. I tried again, moving a bit closer. My heart began to pound. There was something faintly worrying about how terrified the girl appeared. Suddenly she gave out a small moan and collapsed onto the ground. As she fell, her scarf came away from her face. In a flash I realised that she was one of my students. Oh hell. That kind of meant that she was my responsibility. This was not going to be pretty. What should I do? Maybe she had taken some drugs, maybe she had been attacked or even worse, maybe she had...

*Help her now Phoney. Come on. Quickly.*

I started. I hadn't seen Amy for days and yet here she was, draped in her bright red jacket, standing over the poor girl with a look of such concern on her face that I leapt into action.

The girl's name was Sarah, I was sure of that, so I bent down and gently shook her shoulder to try and rouse her.

'Sarah, are you OK? Can you stand? Are you hurt?'

*Of course she's not OK Phoney. Come on, get her on her feet, take her back to the department. Thaw her out.*

'But she might be hurt Amy.'

I dimly remembered some basic medical training that had cautioned us never to move somebody who had just had an accident.

*She's physically okay Phoney. At least she will be if you hurry up. Come on or somebody else might see her and then she'd be mortified.*

Amy's instructions didn't compute with me. Maybe the poor girl was having an epileptic episode.

*Look Phoney, I am your spiritual guide and I am telling you to help her up and get her indoors. NOW!*

Amy kicked my shins. I gasped and my head rang with panic. I wanted to call Hazel, or an ambulance, but instead found myself following Amy's instructions. I carefully bent over the girl and gently helped her to her feet. I just kept on repeating over and over to her; 'Keep breathing, in, out, in, out, breathe in, breathe out.' To my relief Sarah immediately took my advice. She sounded as if she was in a labour maternity training class, but hey, it was working. The breathing seemed to help her and somehow we managed to walk slowly together back towards the university building. We moved deliberately and purposely. The girl was shaking yet she seemed to recognise me. She seemed to trust me. That was a relief. I was worried that she might have reacted violently to my presence.

With Amy leading the way we made good time back up the hill and in a few minutes Sarah was seated in one of my armchairs, warming herself and sipping from a hot cup of tea that Amy had made appear whilst I got a fire going. Quite how she did it I wasn't sure and I was too worried to even ask or marvel at its appearance. Sarah still hadn't been able to speak but she had started to respond to my questions. She shook her head when I asked if she was epileptic. She shook her head when I carefully asked her if she had taken anything, any drugs or alcohol and then when I cautiously asked her if she had been attacked. She welcomed the hot tea though and snuck her feet under herself as she sat in my big old leather armchair.

It was then that I had my first really big shock in weeks.

'I'm so sorry Michael.'

Students were on first name terms – that wasn't shocking.

'I know it's late and I'm so sorry to bother you. I'll be alright in a minute. It must be way past your little girl's bed time.'

That was when I nearly choked on my tea.

'Huh?'

Sarah smiled towards where Amy had curled up in front of the fire, devouring a huge chocolate muffin that one of the students had left me earlier in the day.

'I er, huh, well, um, er, yes, we mustn't be too long, erm, but she, erm, can you, see my ...erm young niece...I mean how are you feeling now Sarah?'

If the poor girl had been feeling okay she would have noticed my stammering confusion. As it was she just sighed and began to stare into the fire.

*You look like a goldfish Phoney. Shut your mouth or you'll scare Sarah.*

Amy hadn't even turned round but I could hear her voice in my head.

'Huh, erm...'

I tried to focus my attention onto just thinking my words in my head and monitoring my poor student at the same time.

'How can she see you?  I thought, I mean, I just thought that...' I spoke to Amy in my head.

*Well I am real aren't I, if Sarah can see me?*

Amy was mocking me.

*Now come on. See clearly Phoney. You had better think fast, you have to get me home to my beddy byes soon.*

Amy was ever so slightly freaking me out. I took a deep breath.

'Why are you here?'

*Obvious isn't it Phoney? You need my support. Now come on I'll help you. Ask Sarah how long she has been experiencing panic attacks.*

'Huh?!'

I must have exclaimed out loud as Sarah turned towards me. She still looked dazed. She smiled at me.

'They have been coming and going a lot this term. They just happen. All of a sudden one will start. I don't know when or why but they just happen. May I have a piece of cake as well please?'

Sarah seemed relieved to be able to tell someone about her condition. My mind was just wondering how she had managed to hear the private conversation between me and Amy. I hadn't asked the question or spoken out loud. This was beginning to confuse me. Another chocolate muffin appeared instantly right in front of me on my desk. I had no idea how it had got there. I quickly passed it to my student.

'Oh thanks Michael, I find cake helps me but then I feel so guilty afterwards.'

My student started to cry a little but she tucked into the cake as if she was ravenous.

Amy was looking at me from her place on the floor and smiling at my look of incomprehension.

> Cake, Phoney, is full of yummy carbs - great for getting rid of stress and  soaking up the adrenaline. And cake, especially choccie cake, just has to be the best comfort food in the world don't you think? Now ask her some more, come on you are being useless. Just imagine she is your daughter – remember – doh, come on Phoney – what does she need?

I felt my own stress levels rise. That's all I needed was one of Amy's training sessions while I had to deal with a traumatised student who was somehow hallucinating along with me. I took a long slow breath. I passed Sarah some tissues and wracked my brains. Come on, identify! Identify with her.

I cast my mind back a long way and managed to remember when I had felt similar sensations. My unconscious mind flashed up an unpleasant memory that I had tried to forget. It was the moment I had found out that my first wife was leaving me for my best friend. Rather suddenly, in the midst of a party, the penny had suddenly dropped. My world had imploded. I remember standing in the crowded party in a fog of drink and probably drugs, experiencing an uncontrollable rise of fear and anxiety. As I froze like a rabbit in the headlights it occurred to me that everyone in the room knew that I was being dumped and that they were all part of some great conspiracy. All the familiar faces of my nearest and dearest friends took on the guise of assassins and betrayers in my mind. I remember that I had been torn between staying and leaving or slumping to the floor. I even considered having it out with my wife or just ignoring my extreme discomfort and hoping that nobody noticed. It was one of those moments when I was actually glad that we were all young and in various states of inebriation. None really noticed my emotional shift and if they had they would have just put it down to a bad chemical reaction. I remembered how that whole experience had left me shaking to my core for days. I had forgotten the party though because the next day my life had really turned upside down.

I gulped some tea. My heart rate had increased just with the memory of that terrible evening.

> And back in the room Phoney. Come back to us. Breathe it out, let go of the memory but use what you have seen to identify with Sarah. Come on, she's almost finished her cake. Come on!

I looked at Sarah and my heart sank. She turned and looked straight at me and I knew that kind of student gaze - it meant that she expected me to have all the answers. My poor old mind whirred slowly, conscious that two women, well one young woman and one small girl, were looking at me expectantly. I took a deep breath, adjusted my face to smile mode and gave it my best shot.

'OK Sarah, I'm glad that you are feeling a bit better now. I'm going to call you a taxi, erm I'll pay for it. It will be my pleasure, and then you can go straight home and get a good night's sleep.'

Sarah smiled at me gratefully. It was always a financial challenge surviving as a student.

Amy snorted with derision.

'Your little girl seems to have a cold,' said Sarah sleepily as I rapidly dialled for a taxi. I knew it would only take a minute as the rank was just outside the main entrance of the university.

Amy gave another snort and then poked her tongue out at me and pulled a face. She said nothing. I was on my own.

'Erm, the taxi will be here in a moment, so you might want to put your coat on.'

I stood to pass the now-warm coat to Sarah who gratefully took it and turned to leave. As she did there was the beep of a car's horn from outside the building.

Amy calmly stood up and moved towards me. Sarah dreamily tousled Amy's hair.

'What a lovely girl, erm daughter, erm niece you have Michael.' And then she turned to leave.

'Ow. Shit!'

Sarah turned back with a look of mild puzzlement. I covered up the fact that Amy had kicked my shins again by pointing lamely to the corner of my desk.

'Erm... look Sarah, when these panic attacks happen you should try and just focus on your breathing and let go of all the anxiety you feel.'

Sarah paused and looked expectantly at me. Outside the taxi beeped its horn again. They were used to students languidly stumbling out of places and the local taxis would cheerfully beep the horn several times before pulling away.

"Erm... try meditating and seeing what the thoughts are that scare you so much.'

I was pleased with myself. I went to open the door and stuffed a tenner into Sarah's hand for the fare.

Sarah paused.

# Chapter 10

'I'm not sure I understand.'

'Erm, breathing techniques, they erm, they are great for dealing with stress and things like that.'

Sarah was just about to re-enter the room when the taxi gave a strident beep of the horn.

'Look, come back tomorrow and I can explain some more to you. Come by in the morning before lectures.'

I added this in the full knowledge that most students never made it out of bed before midday.

'I never knew you were a Buddhist Michael,' said Sarah thoughtfully as she went to leave once more.

'Thanks for the tea and bye bye erm...'

*Amy.*

'Yes, bye lovely Amy. OK Michael I'll see you at 9am.'

Then she was gone. I stood motionless, nearly holding my breath, until I heard the cab pull away.

I span on my heels.

'Will you stop doing that Amy! It flipping well hurts and I'll have to explain to Hazel about the bruises ...what are you laughing at now?'

*Well Phoney, what a great teacher you are...not.*

Amy was chuckling to herself and then sat down in front of the fire and looked for all intents and purposes like a normal six- or seven- year old girl.

I flopped wearily into my armchair. My tummy was rumbling. The girls had eaten all the cake. I felt my brow furrowing into a juggernaut of exasperation.

'I tried my best, what was I supposed to say? Oh anyway, now what have I done? She's coming back first thing tomorrow expecting me to have all the answers. Nice one Amy. See, that's what happens when you try to help a person.'

> *She just needs to know Right Thinking, that's all. You can show her how to breathe properly. Easy, peasy, lemon squeezy.*

'Hang on Amy, what's 'right thinking'? You haven't told me about that.'

> *Well actually I kind of have. Look Phoney all these insights connect up you know. They all blend nicely with each other just like the ingredients of a great big choccy cake.*

'Yes well that's all well and good but I don't have the right ingredients to help that poor girl. Besides she's not the only one you know. A lot of the students are hanging on by their fingernails. And it's usually the bright ones! Now she will expect me to have all the answers.'

> *Stop panicking Phoney. Don't lose your practise. Keep breathing. Let go of all of the weeds. Oh, well done for identifying with her by the way. I was quite proud of you. That's why you are feeling stressed. Some of the memories got through. You had a bit of a Darkening. Poor old Phoney.*

'I don't want your pity Amy, I want your help. That poor girl is going to come back tomorrow expecting me to enlighten her. Now she thinks I am a Buddhist monk or something.'

> *Ah now you are getting close Phoney, it is about what she*

*is thinking. It's really all about what she's thinking. It's about the thoughts that she entertains, just like unwanted guests at a birthday party. They all rise up and terrorise her. She is full of internal gremlins all trying to scare her out of her wits.*

'She's full of gremlins?'

*Yup, she's stuffed full of them and they are terrorising her. You have quite a lot too actually Phoney.*

'Gremlins?'

*Yes they latch onto thoughts, often quite innocent thoughts. They really mess up a decent thought. Thoughts are often troublesome anyway.*

'So you are saying that Sarah is plagued by small supernatural creatures who are attacking her thoughts?! Was it the ...erm... gremlins that caused her to freak out at the lamppost?'

*I thought we had agreed not to mock mental health issues Phoney, and yes gremlins are real until they are not. See, it's easy. Go find some of yours then you will be able to understand. Go on Phoney, go looking. Snare a gremlin.*

'Go searching for small imaginary thought monsters? Come on Amy, I'm a grown up.'

*I never said they were imaginary.*

'Do you mean like your lion and antelope stuff that you told me about ages ago? That's what you mean isn't it?'

*Think of a thought Phoney. Make it a nice hopeful one. Make it about something you would like to happen.*

I sat up in my chair and straightened my back. I realised that I was tensed up tighter than a boa constrictor ready to pounce. Amy always managed to mess with my head.

*Your head is a mess in the first place. I keep telling you to keep it clean, now go on think a thought.*

I sat and breathed gently and in a flash I found myself thinking about having a real dinner date with Hazel.

*Great, now stop.*

I literally froze.

*Now what's the next thought that occurs? Don't try to find it, let it pop up to meet you.*

It happened immediately. 'I would probably just mess it up and make it worse and send us back to the beginning because I wouldn't be able to stop gushing about how much I love her and then I'd lose my calm.'

*See Phoney, wow, look at poor old you. One nice calm, fluffy little thought and suddenly half a dozen gremlins all over it in a trice. All attacking it, biting it, darkening it, weakening it, munching it all up. Poor old Phoney.*

'Huh, oh I see, erm, but hey that's just erm doubts, I mean, seeds of suffering. My thoughts travail against me with their constant intent on unsettling my equilibrium just like the many headed Hydra...'

*Shh Phoney, you are being all professory and conceptually again. No this is the key to Right Thinking. It's all fear, False Expectations Appearing Real, that's what the gremlins are. Now take a nice breath and relax again.*

# Chapter 10

Under Amy's gentle and rather firm supervision I found that my equilibrium returned fairly easily. My image of Hazel resurfaced as a picture of calm and happiness.

> *You see Phoney, just one poor, innocent little thought can get attacked by a legion of gremlins and then you can spend all day getting chased by them, just like with the lion. Before you know it you are exhausted and stressed out and all your energy has gone.*

I rubbed my eyes. I had a compelling image of Sarah hanging on to the lamppost, surrounded by gremlins. I didn't tell Amy, but I had the unsettling feeling that my gremlins were actually forming an orderly queue waiting to pounce on me. Literally lining up waiting to ruin my day.

> *Because many children have a rotten time they go through their big grown up life always expecting the worst. Gremlins are those thoughts. Most thoughts have a second thought, if you are not meditating and being mindful that is.*

'Er, you mean like a qualifying thought, a thought that evaluates the situation, that checks the path ahead?'

> *Well done Phoney. Yup, there you are wandering along your happy little path and then you see an old bendy stick up ahead. What happens?*

'I don't know, I erm, I pick it up and throw it for my dog.'

> *Don't be silly Phoney, you don't have a dog – yet. Anyway, think. Use your imagination, that's what it's for. Imagination is for tuning into reality like a radio. Now go on. It's getting dark. You are in Africa. You are walking along a path and you see a long brownish stick in your path. What do you think?*

I rubbed my eyes again. Amy's love of colourful animal imagery often helped me but this time...of course!

'I know, I've got it. I'd think that it must be a snake.'

I was slightly embarrassed by my childish outburst but Amy seemed to enjoy it.

> *Well done Phoney. Yup that's what you do. You let your habit energy run you. Your poor old damaged self expects the worse and so up pops the gremlin. Suddenly an innocent stick becomes a snake.*

'And that's what Sarah was experiencing? Her second thought was a snake thought?'

Amy took a deep breath and scratched her nose, then she smiled.

> *Okay Phoney, yup snake thoughts, or gremlins, they all jump up to chase the original thought.*

'But Sarah wasn't thinking about snakes?'

> *Maybe not Phoney. You were a student once. What stressed you out?*

'Erm, exams, other students, money, studying, deadlines and.. .'

> *So?*

'Huh, so what?'

> *So it's easy peasy isn't it? You think the thought 'exam'. Then your fear habit horse hurls you down the path to self-destruction. Your poor old neutral thought 'exam' is ripped to pieces by gremlins. Exam equals fear, pain,*

*suffering.*

'I was anxious about exams for sure, I mean all students are anxious about exams.'

*Are they?*

'Huh?'

*Are they?*

'Oh I see, they are actually anxious about failing the exam.'

*Hooplah – he's done it, well done. Back to the good old seeds of suffering. The belief that I am going to fail.*

'So Amy, tomorrow I need to get Sarah to point out her gremlins?'

*Actually no Phoney, that's not what you need to do. It can help people to name their gremlins though.*

Why?

*Because then they can notice when they leap out to strangle a thought and can say 'No!' to it and then command it gone by using its name.*

Really?

Amy started to laugh.

*No Phoney, part of Right Speaking is being compassionate to all living things.*

'What, oh come on Amy, it's getting really late and I'm tired. I'm not going to be nice to my gremlins.'

I suddenly became aware of what I was saying. At that point Amy started to roll on the floor, chortling. Her laughter was infectious. I began to smile and then chuckle. Amy had a great way of making me not take myself too seriously.

*Thy ego runs from the laughter of love.*

I stopped.

'Huh?'

*You have to name the gremlins Phoney, write them down, so that you can learn to recognise them when they come calling. Look. I'll call out a word and you think of a gremlin word. Okay?*

'Erm, yes, I guess so.'

*Great, now get a pencil and some paper and write them down. Use your imagination. Ready?*

'Ready.'

*Dream*

'Drowner'

*Hey well done Phoney – Dream Drowner – that's definitely a gremlin. Now people have lots of money gremlins, think of one for that.*

'A...er, Wealth Waster.'

*Wowsa Phoney – go on get some more.*

Over the course of the next half an hour Amy and I laughed our way through many a gremlin. I was proud of some of mine;

# Chapter 10

Marriage Murderer, Performance Pummeller, Health Hijacker, Imagination Incinerator, Conversation Corrupter, Family Flattener and Education Eraser.

Amy stopped me as I started getting too fancy. She liked short words and eventually persuaded me that simple words like 'doubt' and 'fear of failure' and short sentences like 'I am not worthy' were best to describe my gremlins. In fact the longer we went on, the more I realised just how many gremlins I had.

Eventually we came to a stop. Amy became serious and looked straight at me.

> *Listen Phoney, these gremlins are real nasty. The more we let them take up residence in our minds the stronger they become and they invite all their friends along too. Soon your poor old body gets so stressed, the feelings turn into real symptoms of pain and suffering. Poor Sarah had a real attack of the gremlins. To her they were real. You have to share with her how to turn the volume down with Right Thinking. She has to love her gremlins. She has to thank them for their service and then let them go. Let them know that they are no longer needed. Let them know that they are of no service any more. Let them know that they can go back to sleep.*

'How do I do that?'

> *The same as always Phoney. Returning to the breath, putting your attention on the lovely cool air passing through your nose and into your lungs and then the lovely warm air going back out. Follow each breath from the beginning to the end. Remain with the body – return to it from the battlefield of the mind. Reflect on joy. Notice how good it is to be alive – deeply, gently, wonderfully.*

'OK, I think I've got it.'

*No you haven't Phoney, well maybe you are starting to.*

'Huh, but I thought...'

*Tomorrow you are going to start something new. You are going to practise some Right Action.*

'Right Action?'

*Yes my dearest Phoney. Right Action often follows Right Thinking.*

'What do you mean? I've invited her here, nice and early. I'm ready to listen, to advise, to prompt. What more can I do?'

*Yes Phoney, if that action had been based on a thought of compassion rather than fear then you wouldn't be in such a funk now.*

Amy yawned and stretched like a small red haired cat.

*Poor Sarah is going to need help and support Phoney, more than just from you my dear. You said that there were literally hundreds of students suffering like her.*

Amy was deliberately staring at me, a small determined and beatific smile on her face. A slow realisation was dawning on me. From beneath the fog of my mind I suddenly realised that I had been suppressing a compassionate thought for weeks. I looked around my largish study. I smelt a set-up job. It felt as if Amy had just framed me.

'No!, No Amy, I don't have the room! I don't, I can't.'

*Imagination Incinerator, Idea immobiliser – nah! Gremlin alert Phoney! Gremlin alert! There's a snake on your path. With the rise of every negative thought you must always question it. Take away its authority; its certainty of being right. Stick your tongue out at it. Always ask it – 'Hmm, now, 'Is that really true?'*

I smiled. Amy was pulling on a pretend beard just like my maths teacher used to do when I was at school.

'Is what really true?'

*Is your gremlin thought really true dear Phoney?*

Then, as if on cue, the fire died out and Amy vanished in front of my eyes.

As I went to put the old Victorian fire guard in its place to stop any spitting embers I noticed that somebody – guess who? – had written the words 'Is it really true?' on the mirror above the fireplace.

\* \* \* \* \* \* \*

I slept like a log that night. I was exhausted. No gremlins chased me. I woke up calm and confident. My session with Sarah went very well. In fact I felt quite inspired by it.

The poor girl quickly confessed that she had been experiencing irrational panic attacks, which had been getting worse and worse. She told me that when they began it was as if she literally turned into a block of ice, unable to move and unable to process the world around her.

I quickly shared with her my experiences of panic attacks and then gently relayed to her the lesson that Amy had delivered to me the night before. We both sat with paper and pen and wrote out a list of our gremlins. Sarah's gremlins were the ones that Amy had guessed at; they were all about failure and not being good enough, even though she was one of our best students. It amazed me how plagued by self-doubt she was.

I remembered how a concerned Amy had shown me that many women were denied ever feeling whole or able to really love and enjoy themselves. Sarah was no exception. She opened up some more and told me about her demanding parents, who, recognising their daughter's natural talent, had encouraged her to try hard academically but at the same time had pressurised her so much she had developed a strong fear of failing and disappointing them. She was definitely divided inside. She was unable to experience university as a great big collective. She felt isolated and all alone with her overwhelming sense of anxiety. Her gremlins were easy to name and we had a good laugh as we ceremonially put the lists into my open fire and watched them disappear in flames. I really enjoyed the experience. It was like being with Amy but with the roles reversed. Then I put some gentle music on and actually managed to demonstrate how to still the mind, how to become calm and dissolve gremlins if any showed up.

As we worked through our gremlins, it occurred to me that this was a great practice, a great way to begin the day. I realised to my surprise that I enjoyed spiritual companionship. The togetherness thing that Amy had been talking about felt kind of good. Realising that I had to be careful not to give out the wrong signals, I recognised that any meditation practise in university would have to be an openly declared intention. My room wasn't small; I often held seminars in it. There was room for a couple more students, if they wanted to come of course. I was actually delighted when Sarah agreed to join me for what I quickly called 'an open access meditation and relaxation class before lectures' every other day in my chambers.

The word spread quickly. I had no idea just how 'open' I had to make the practice sessions. In no time at all I had upwards of thirty bright sparks solemnly filing into our department before the cleaners had even finished in the morning. To the exasperation of Clair Welch, our head of department, we soon ran out of space for everyone to sit, even if students didn't mind the floor. I thought that Clair would seriously fall out with me; the cleaners had begun to complain. So, with Amy's prompting I invited her along to one of our sessions. To my surprise Clair took me to one side after the session and gave me permission to use one of the lecture theatres for the time being. To the shock of my colleagues she gave our morning sessions her wholehearted endorsement. Apparently Sarah was fast becoming the department's star student and had told Clair that her success was all down to her being able to manage her stress due to the early morning sessions. And of course, as star students are wont to do, she soon had the whole thing organised properly with leaflets distributed, and even began to serve breakfast. This in turn increased the turnover of our small department café to the point that we could buy some much-needed modern equipment.

Oh, and of course, soon I wasn't needed at all. The funny thing was that on the day I realised that I was superfluous to requirements, the day I felt as if my job was done, Sarah and the students got the early morning 'Wake Up' meditation sessions officially recognised by the University. The students now ran it and it went from strength to strength. I was actually quite relieved to slip away into invisibility again. Sarah had started to ask me when she was next going to see my nice young niece again. Apparently she had only trusted me that night of her panic attack because she saw I had a child with me. That was a blow to my ego that I really didn't mind. I guess that was probably why Amy had made an appearance. Then again who knew when it came to Amy?

# Chapter Eleven

Why is it that storms hit us just when we think that everything is fine and plain sailing?

One day we can be enjoying the millpond calm of life, drifting around with good cheer and sunshine thoughts. The next moment all our optimism and inner joy gets flushed down the proverbial plughole. My personal tornado flung me so far out to sea that my little ship of sanity was nearly capsized for good. It felt that it had been drawn into such a powerful whirlpool of despair and depression that I might drown. Even the weather reflected my inner landscape of grey and misery. It began to rain and didn't stop for weeks. The whole city felt overcast and gloomy.

Just as I thought that Hazel and I were getting on an even keel she rocked me to my core.

'Michael', she said, putting down the large glass of fine red wine that I had bought to woo her with over a fine supper in one of the best restaurants in Glasgow. 'Michael, I just don't feel ready to get back together with you and I'm not even sure if we are good for oaoh othcr.'

The wine in my mouth turned to vinegar and I put down my glass with a trembling hand. Hazel took a deep breath and then continued.

'You see Michael I've been thinking about us and, well, it's just that, even after all your hard work...'

# Chapter 11

She paused. She frowned. It was obviously hard for her to say. I caught sight of the smallest tear in the corner of her eye. Oh my god. This was not going to be good.

'...even after everything, I just don't think that you know how to be happy.'

I caught myself before I launched into one of my usual defensive rages.  I breathed just as Amy had taught me, I sat motionless. Hazel continued slowly, gently and this time the tears really began. That panicked me. Everybody in the restaurant would think that it was my fault. Maybe it was. Oh hell.

'You are never happy. You're not really here. Most of the time you are just moping because you are missing your kids, or you're immersing yourself in work, or well, I just don't think that I can make you happy and that's not good for me'.

Hazel accepted a new napkin from a passing waitress who gave me a filthy look as if to say, 'look what you've done you idiot man.' Why do women always have to cry? Especially in public? Especially when they are with me?

My mouth went dry. I opened and shut it like a struggling goldfish. Hazel blew her nose on the expensive linen napkin; I was going to have to leave a really big tip.

"I do love you Michael, it's just that...' she paused, as if surprised that I hadn't spoken at all. Then Hazel, realising that I had gone mute, gave me such a look of pity that my heart almost broke. She continued:

'The fact you are always grumpy and miserable and depressed, that just makes me doubt myself, just makes me feel like I am worthless. I don't want that in my life again. I'm not sure that anyone can make you happy Michael. I'm sorry. I have to go. I can't stay. Thanks for dinner. Goodbye darling.'

Then she was gone. My beautiful and caring wife got up and, with all the grace she could muster, glided out of the restaurant and out of my life.

The moment she left, the attentive waitress was at my side. In a trice she had presented me with the bill, a clean napkin and a very large whisky. 'On the house love', she said and headed off to preserve the restaurant's atmosphere. I was grateful for the down to earth and intelligent Glaswegian service. I realised that I was crying. In public!!! Damn!

All waitresses worth their salt are experts in reading body language and she clearly knew that I had just been dumped. In moments I had been carefully and expertly escorted off the premises. The waitress had presented me with my half-finished bottle of wine and leftover food, wrapped and boxed. As I stepped out into the incessant rain she squeezed my arm and wished me good luck. How the kindness of strangers can be so bitter sweet. My tears mingled with the rain and I hunched my shoulders against it and headed for my cold and empty flat where I quickly swallowed the remainder of the bottle of expensive wine before passing out on the small single sofa bed.

Three days of a steady alcohol-fuelled binge passed before the familiar scent of roses wafted past my nose. I was lying in a dishevelled heap half on and half off the sofa bed.

*Wow, you smell sooo bad Phoney. You smell like a brewery and a distillery and an old tramp at once. In fact you pong so bad I think you might have wet yourself.*

My hand reached to the floor and found an empty bottle. Without opening my eyes I flung it in the direction of the voice. I heard it smash.

*Wow, violence, depression and a hangover from hell. You really are in a bad way my poor old Phoney.*

# Chapter 11

'I don't care about your stupid games Amy. I just don't care anymore. I don't want you here – just go away. You lied. You said everything was going to be alright. You said that Hazel and me we were....were...oh hell my head!'

I felt my head begin to slump towards my hands again.

> *Don't sulk, Phoney. You know that you're glad to see me and you know that you want me to help you.*

'No I don't, that's the last thing I want. Your help just sets me up for a fall. Now go away.'

Amy laughed and began to deliberately kick the side of the table with her chair. The steady bang, bang perfectly matched the sound in my head.

> *Oh dear. Phoney's all at sea. No he's not, he's actually fallen overboard and isn't even trying to swim. Thing is Phoney, the occasional storm hits even the strongest boats you know and even the best captains have to hang on for dear life. The difference for a mindful captain is that he sees the storm coming. The mindful captain steers the ship directly into the storm so that it doesn't broadside him and tip the whole boat over.*

I groaned at yet another Amy metaphor and let my head of self-pity rest in my hands half under my pillow. Amy came back through to the bedroom and whispered into my ear.

> *The thing is Phoney that the mindful captain doesn't even look at the storm, he sees through the storm to the calm and light the other side. He never breaks his concentration and he never doubts his survival because he knows that peace, joy and happiness lay on the other side.*

That really annoyed me; in fact even the thought of the sea was making my tummy queasy.

'Well this captain apparently isn't happy or clever enough so despair shipwrecked him. Now Amy please get out of my head or wherever it is that you come from and vanish.'

I was trying to shout but the volume of my own voice hurt my head. It sounded like sandpaper being scraped along the rump of a camel. Amy ignored me and brought her mouth so close that her breath tickled my ear.

*The mindful captain of the ship doesn't steer his boat by out of date charts and maps Phoney. He knows that if he does he'll hit the rocks and sink. The mindful captain only uses the maps that are right up to date. The mindful captain stays present and always maintains his happy smiley face.*

My stomach knotted every time Amy referred to my state of happiness and I felt myself scream with frustration. I even entertained the idea of swatting her away but thankfully the idea of striking anybody, let alone a woman or child, repulsed me more. I swear Amy knew because she kept on prodding me with her little finger. My voice rasped at her as I tried to shout.

'Bugger off you nasty wee demon. You know that I'm not happy. You know that I am a miserable old sod. I'll never master all this stuff. I thought I was happy. Well Hazel doesn't agree so please flutter off back into your little cave or wherever it is that you devil children come from.'

*Ooh somebody's forgotten right speech again.*

Amy had gone back into the kitchen. I could hear a tap running. Her voice carried through the small flat.

*You are only miserable because you keep on watching miserable old movies when you should be paying attention to the real story of your wonderful life unfolding all around you.*

'Hey you little sod...'

A glass of ice cold water hit me square in the face. I swear that Amy must have somehow chilled it at the polar ice cap. The intensity of the shock jolted me out of my fug and made me gasp for air. I tried to curl up on the bed again and buried my face in the duvet.

'Just go away Amy, I don't want to see you!'

*Yes you do Phoney. You love me and the more you struggle the stronger I'll become, you big dafty.*

Then, before I could formulate an abusive reply, a deluge of ice-cold water hit my body. I shot upright with such force that I thought my head would break. Arms flailing, I fell off the sofa bed and rolled dangerously close to a pile of smashed glass. The broken neck of the whisky bottle was in my eye line and seemed to mock me with its refusal to disintegrate on impact. Suddenly I was awake and focussed, my whole being on red alert with my heart pounding stronger than if I'd consumed a triple shot espresso. Amy stood over me and cheerfully prodded my nose with the end of her welly boot.

*You are a rotten liar and a terrible drunk. It's time to stop both these habits of suffering Phoney. Come on, get dressed we are going to work. You stink and the flat is a pit. Go shower and then clean up.*

I have no idea how Amy does it but within moments I was meekly complying with her instructions. Something inside me gave in. Two hours later me and the flat were clean and tidy. I just wish that the inside of my head could have caught up. It felt as if a small army of heavy metal drummers were practising in my skull.

I sat heavily on my chair and sipped from a scalding cup of coffee. Amy took up her usual position by the window and was staring at me with her arms crossed.

*Right then Phoney, it's time to get you trained in Mindfulness. It's time to teach you how to time travel without hurting yourself and other people. Right, bring your coffee; we're going back to school.*

That's how, one hour later, I found myself in the small projection theatre in the basement of our film and television department at university. It was a Saturday but I had the master key and let us in. I meekly followed Amy as she skipped down the stairs clutching a valuable roll of film that she had somehow discovered behind a pile of old books. Amy made me spool the ancient film onto an equally ancient projector and then dim the lights – I was glad of the enveloping darkness as my head was still pounding. Moments later I had started up the old projector and in the gloom the back wall was illuminated with a very old print of an early Russian film. I pulled up a chair beside Amy who was stuffing popcorn down her mouth. So that was why she had made me stop to buy it on the way up. Popcorn and mints. Popcorn for her and mints because she said my breath was still smelly. I sighed and slumped in my chair. I still felt terrible and the flickering old film didn't do much to lift my spirits. It was a typical Russian agitprop film. Boy meets girl, meets tractor, falls in love and works heroically for the collective good before dying and renouncing the idea of a bourgeois god. Great.

We sat in silence for over an hour as the old projector clicked and whirred. As soon as the film ended, Amy turned to me.

*Play it again Phoney.*

It was not a request but an order. I protested.

'Oh come on Amy. It's not the kind of film you can watch twice. It wasn't even popular when it was made. The Russian people of post-revolutionary Russia just wanted Mickey Mouse and

# Chapter 11

Walt Disney. Why don't you? As a small girl aged six or seven, shouldn't you want something less dreary? Besides, you've eaten all your popcorn.

*Put it on Phoney.*

I sighed. My head hurt and I was still tired; at least I could sleep through it this time.

I rewound the film then pressed play. I had barely sat down when something caught my attention. There was something wrong with the film this time. Somehow the images seemed all muddled. The faces seemed to distort. The backgrounds faded away and then I got a real shock. There on the film was a small girl who looked just like Amy, running through a vast cornfield.

'Oh my God Amy, what's going on? I didn't see that before...I mean you are in the film...how can that be? It's the same reel...'

*Shh, Phoney, it's just the titles; look, here's the real story.*

I froze. I was really losing my mind this time. There was no mistaking it. I could see a much younger version of myself playing in the park with my young children. I gasped with the shock of recognition.

*Just keep breathing like I showed you Phoney and watch the movie.*

I couldn't do anything apart from observe. I was transfixed. I watched myself frolicking with my daughters in the park, playing silly games until they were shrieking with laughter. Then I saw myself taking them on holidays, sitting all alone in the car while they slept soundly in our small tent after a great day at the beach. I saw myself making mucky murals with them and then cooking huge roast dinners which they tucked into until they were fit to burst. The film kept going and I saw myself walking them to their first day at school; in the audience at countless school plays; providing present-laden Christmases; going for long walks, teaching them to swim, climb trees and ride their bikes; painting pictures and modelling with clay; then snuggling up with them at night and telling them exciting stories. I watched as Hazel took them shopping, buying them everything they needed; taking them ice skating and pony riding; reading books together; endless rounds of laughter and pretend fights on beds, couches and chairs. Then, far too quickly, the film reel whirred and clicked to the end.

An hour had sped past in no time at all. My face was once more a damp rag of tears and smiles.

Amy turned off the projector and then clambered onto a chair to switch on the overhead lights. I was sitting motionless, unable to move. I didn't want to return to reality.

*How are you feeling now Phoney?*

I still couldn't answer. I realised that yet again there were tears rolling down my cheeks.

*Come on Phoney, how are you feeling?*

Amy prompted me while she made shadow puppets against the back wall.

'I, er, actually feel quite wonderful. Thanks for that Amy.'

It was true. As I wiped the tears from my cheeks I realised that they were tears of happiness, not pain and suffering.

'That might have been the best film I ever watched Amy. Can we watch it again?'

*No Phoney – sorry we can't but I'm glad you got to see it all. Wasn't he just the nicest, most loving daddy any little girl could wish for?*

'Huh, erm, well, they did seem happy and they were having fun but...'

*No buts Phoney. They are happy and you are having fun.*

'Well I guess so, but ...'

*No buts Phoney! I wanted you to see your past life, the one that is making you so sad and depressed.*

'It didn't make me depressed Amy, it made me very happy. Thank you.'

Amy slowly approached me and sat on the ground at my feet.

*That's because that was the real film of your past Phoney. It wasn't the tragedy that you keep on playing over and over again. It wasn't a film about guilt and suffering. It was a film about happiness. Your old film is constantly running and it holds you in the past Phoney. It does make you unhappy Phoney, it makes you very sad; it tears you apart and steals all your joy. It's an old film and it has to stop playing. Come on Phoney, how did the true film really make you feel?*

'I told you. Very happy.'

Amy looked up at me in just the same way that years ago my daughters used to do as I told them stories of fairies and dragons.

*There were other feelings Phoney. Think, what were they?*

I took a deep breath. My hangover seemed to have gone. I concentrated. I focussed on my emotions. I counted them out to Amy.

'I felt happy, contented, blissful, filled with laughter, joyful, ecstatic, pleased, contented.'

*And?*

"And?'

*And?*

'Erm....oh I felt relieved.'

Amy jumped to her feet and gave that little victory dance of self-congratulatory pleasure that she employed whenever she had made a breakthrough with me.

*Exactly Phoney, you felt relieved. The short film of your life brought you relief. Why?*

'Huh?'

*Why, dear Phoney? Why did the lovely film of your life with your children fill you with relief?*

I took a deep breath. I wasn't sure what Amy was driving at but she had my attention. I had forgotten my devastation of earlier in the week and was ready to go deeper with my small guide. As I focussed, a thought occurred to me.

'I felt relief because the girls were having such a great time?'

*Almost Phoney. Think deeper.*

'Erm, um, I was relieved because the girls had a great time with me?'

*Almost Phoney...just a bit further.*

Amy sat at my feet again. She put her head onto one side and stared at me with unsettling concentration. Her eyes were kind and focussed. Then I felt a slow realisation dawn on me.

'I was relieved because I wasn't a complete mess-up?'

> *Yippee Phoney – see – you were a great dad, you did well; you did all you could and your kids love you for it.'*

Amy leapt up again and did her little dance. I stood up as well. Suddenly I needed to straighten my legs. Amy laughed out loud and produced a small harmonica from her pocket. To my amazement she started to play an intricate jig. She played it loud, she played it like a virtuoso. It was fast and infectious; as Amy played, she danced around the small room. To see her so happy and impish made me smile. Then, to my surprise I joined Amy. I began to dance around the room behind her. My feet couldn't resist the melody. We began to whirl around the room, knocking over chairs and tables, laughing aloud with such recklessness I began to laugh at my own behaviour. This just made Amy play faster. The jig was hypnotic; it was the best thing I had ever heard. I wasn't sure how long we kept this up for – it was probably only a few minutes before the music stopped suddenly. I had been just about to pull off a particularly spectacular high kick when I spied the surprised face of one of the departmental janitors. I turned to see what Amy was doing but she had vanished. I was so puffed out and laughing so hard that I could barely speak.

'Sorry Professor, I just heard all the noise and I thought, well... that maybe students had, you know...'

"Yes of course, I was just leaving, erm rehearsing for a, erm, workshop, something that I want the students to try..."

It was plain to us both that I wasn't telling the truth so, as we were obviously both embarrassed, I put the poor janitor out of his misery by quickly picking up the film reel and making to leave. I was so glad that Amy had made me wash, shave and eat plenty of mints. I didn't need any rumours circulating about me being drunk on the premises. So many lecturers had been politely asked to leave over the years due to excessive alcohol consumption and I didn't need any of that kind of attention. I didn't want to lose my job and janitors were unionised and highly political creatures. I shook his hand and left. At least he would only consider my behaviour erratic. That was to be expected by students and faculty staff alike.

I strolled back to the flat not even minding the rain, and stopped at the local shop to buy some real food plus a fresh supply of cakes and biscuits. It was just as well, because as soon as I entered the flat I saw that Amy was there.

'I never knew you could play the harmonica, and so well Amy.'

I put the biscuits down and Amy greedily opened the packet.

> *Actually Phoney, neither did I. Wasn't it fun though? You were hilarious, and I've never seen you laughing so much. You found your joy again Phoney and that makes me happy.*

I went to make some tea and stopped dead in my tracks. My shelves were now completely filled with photographs. All the photographs I thought had been thrown out! Loads of pictures of my daughters, of Hazel, and of us all together lined the shelves. It was quite a shock. I made the tea and sat down. For some weird reason my bon homie was evaporating.

Amy looked at the pictures and then at me.

> *Ah, see how quickly your joy leaves you Phoney. Now listen. This is the hard bit. You have to master mindfulness. You are going to need to make this your most important number one practice. Every day for ages – maybe forever. It's time for you to live in the present Phoney. It's time for you to be happy. You have to master time travel. Otherwise you might lose Hazel.*

# Chapter 11

At the mention of Hazel my emotions dived into a spiral. I hadn't had anybody to share my pain with and for the next hour, over two cups of tea, one packet of biscuits and three small cupcakes, I spilled my guts to my small and imaginary friend. For once she just listened. Eventually I came to a juddering stop.

'So Hazel can't be with me because she says I'm not able to be happy.'

Amy gave me a long, slow, chocolaty smile.

> I know my dearest Phoney. That's why I'm here. That's why I'm going to teach you how to be a joyful time traveller. But first you have to learn how to truly be here. If you practise mindfulness then you can remain in the present and stay in your happiness. Life is all about joy, oh and cake of course.

'Erm, I am here Amy, I am present aren't I? I'm here, right now, sitting beside you.'

> Yes you are now Phoney but for the last hour you have been dwelling in the past. In fact for years now you haven't really been present.

'Huh, of course I'm present.'

> Now listen Phoney, what Hazel said was true. You can't be happy now because you keep on playing all your old movies and those movies make you sad.

'But the movie made me happy; we even danced!'

> That's 'cause I made it for you Phone. I showed you all the good bits. I showed you what was really there, all the good stuff. You always play a movie full of lack, full of the suffering. I showed you the real film of your life. When you play your film it's always a tragedy.

'But, it was a tragedy Amy. I really messed up. I never meant my little family to break up. I never wanted the girls to suffer a broken home. I never wanted any of that to happen. I fought to keep it all together I...I...I failed.'

*That's not the right film Phoney. That's not how it was. You keep on wanting to watch the wrong film. Every time you watch that old movie of how bad it all was in the past, you squash all the joy out of the now. You didn't fail Phoney, you did the best that you could with everything you had and you were a great Dad. Look nothing is going to make sense until you learn how to time travel back to the present. Now sit down and begin your breathing.*

I sat on my chair with my back straight and allowed Amy to instruct me.

*To be mindful Phoney, you have to return to the breath. Mindfulness begins and ends with your breathing. Now be with your 'in' and your 'out' breath.' Just let that be for a moment.*

I did and soon my breathing was returning to normal.

*Now follow your breath with your attention, with your mind, all the way in and all the way out.*

I did as she told me. My breathing grew gentle and I found I could follow each breath as it entered and left me.

*Now let yourself become aware of your body Phoney. Notice how it feels. Relax any parts that might be hurty or tense.*

I let my attention expand to observe and feel my body. It was aching from our excessive dancing and my tummy felt full of knots and aches.

*Because you are away all the time living in the past or future, chasing after your habit thoughts, being chased by gremlins, you forget about your body. You leave it behind. Your body knows where the present moment is. It knows where your 'now' is. Now Phoney, release the tension in your body. Relax your tummy, relax your body.*

I did as Amy requested. Bit by bit my aches and tensions unravelled and dispersed.

*Now you must generate the energy of joy and happiness Phoney. Notice that you are alive. Be thankful for that. Notice that you are breathing, be thankful for that. Be thankful that you can feel, notice all the things that you have that are good; your health, your daughters, your job, the rain, the sun, the food on your plate, the cakes.*

I smiled at that. It worked. The more I allowed myself to be grateful for all that I had, right here in my little flat, the more my earlier sense of joy and happiness returned.

*Let your only prayer be that of gratitude Phoney. See how fortunate you are to have this amazing gift of life. See how lucky you are to have such a brilliant spiritual guide as me.*

My smile grew larger as the sense of peace and happiness flooded through me.

*You keep playing old movies in your mind Phoney. They are old events, old happenings. You keep on watching these old movies then you begin to react to new events as if they were old ones. Now then, let's find some gremlins. Now you are safe in the present, now that you can feel your joy, look gently and carefully to see what gremlins are chasing you.*

Maybe it was Amy's presence, her clarity, but in moments I could see in my mind's eye the presence of some real gremlins. I had the feeling that I was a failure, that I had let down my children; that I would inevitably fail again.

> *Well done Michael. That fear of failure, that's your old energy habit, your old gremlin popping up to munch up all your joy.*

I could see that clearly now. Every time I thought of my kids I felt like I was a failure. I felt guilty that I had been the cause of all their suffering.

> *Now replay the movie that I showed you Phoney. Watch your own life with compassion and understanding. As you replay the thoughts simply let go of all those gremlins. Don't fight them. Don't resist them. Don't run from them. Just love them. Thank them for showing you the painful stuff. Tell them that you are older and wiser now. Tell them that you are choosing to be different. Let them go back off into the past. Choose not to judge yourself Phoney. If you judge yourself you just create separation, separation from your joy.*

I replayed some of the earlier fun-filled movie in my mind. I saw just how happy I had been with my girls; just how amazing the time was we had spent together at weekends and holidays. I let myself see just how loving I had been and how hard I had tried to get it right. I realised that I never had to choose to get it wrong again.

> *Well done Michael. This is good. Now come fully into the present moment. Open your eyes but keep breathing and keep concentrating.*

Amy was sitting in front of me. She was cross-legged and had a look of pure bliss on her face. She was almost whispering.

> *Michael you made your home in the past. You have to*

*choose to make your home in the present. You have to let
your younger self be healed. Tell him that he did a good
job. Tell him that he was a kind and loving man. Tell him
that he did the best with what he had. Forgive him. Now
release him back into the wonderful tapestry of your life.
Let go of all your pain and suffering.*

I did as Amy suggested. I could see my younger self just as I
had appeared in the old movie earlier. My hair was darker, my
face less lined and I was thinner. I smiled at him. In my mind I
told him that he had done well, that he was a great dad, that his
children loved him and that he was a success. I opened my eyes
to find that Amy was disappearing in front of me. She was going
transparent.

'Don't go Amy, not yet.'

As Amy vanished, her voice remained in my head.

*Keep practising being present Michael; mindfulness will
restore your joy. Practise bringing the Kingdom of God
into your life daily – oh, and don't forget to laugh and
dance. Next time we can go see Hazel.*

My heart leapt ever so slightly. A slight shadow danced for
a moment across my mind but I quickly managed to send it
packing by returning to the present moment and my new-found
happiness. Yet again I really felt as if I had learned something
truly restorative. I felt a tremendous weight had lifted from
my shoulders. An age-old fear had left me. The greyness, the
darkness of my mind had vanished.

I stood up and went to the pictures on the shelves. As I continued
to practise being present I looked at the various photos of my
daughters from birth up to the present day. I realised that as I
looked at them I didn't feel any guilt; only a celebration of life and
a deep sense of gratitude.

# Chapter Twelve

# Chapter 12

As the days followed I came to fully appreciate being present. Being mindful in as many daily situations as possible began to bring me a greater and deeper sense of contentment and happiness. I realised just how scattered I had been. I began to understand just how much of my unconscious mind, my store mind, was occupied with my past films. So many movies of my past were constantly playing and just about all of them left me with a feeling of guilt or lack of self-worth.

Amy's lesson had freed me from a mountain of guilt about my parenting and my acrimonious split with their mother, my first wife. I took to calling my daughters more often. I only called when I felt truly present and able to be the very best of myself. To my amazement I found that in no time at all I had established a new and vibrant connection with them. They both began to open up to me and let me know how much they missed me. Of course, as teenage daughters are wont to do, they hit my pocket hard but before long we were planning visits and even holidays together.

My new life, full of my practice of returning to the breath, of meditation and mindful being, was making a huge impact on my sense of peace and wellbeing. There was just the one fly in the ointment. I felt as if my heart was broken. I couldn't understand why Hazel had chosen that special moment in the restaurant, the moment when I was sure that we were to be together, to formally leave me. Everything had been going so well. As I had become more skilled in being a healthier version of myself, our relationship had seemed to go from strength to strength. At work I had never been more content or more popular. I was writing again and my articles were being published. My new courses were proving to be popular, my seminars and lectures were filled to bursting and my students were passing their exams. Even my small media company had managed to get me loads of consultation work; my reputation seemed to be growing. Yet deep inside I missed my wife.

I sat at home or in the park practising mindfulness. I would sit, stand or walk slowly with my back straight and my mind relaxed. I reflected on not being needy or afraid of loneliness until I felt completely self-sufficient, yet my poor old heart still ached for Hazel. I never missed my meditation class but I sensed a seed of resentment beginning to grow. I couldn't help thinking that all these spiritual adepts and masters had it easy. They never had to live in the real world, the world of work and reproduction, of children, colleagues and wives. They could sit and practise all day whilst the simple-minded peasants fed them food in return for dubious blessings.

The seed of resentment was creating a shoot of new growth. It began to wind upwards towards my joy. As the days passed I began to feel more and more adrift from my happiness and peace again. The weed of bitterness twisted its way up inside my head until some of Amy's gremlins started to growl at me. One evening, after returning from a busy day, I absentmindedly bought a bottle of wine with my food shopping. I didn't realise until I was back at the flat. I put the bottle on the table and picked up my large wine glass, ready to fill it. And then I paused. It was the same wine that Hazel and I had shared that fateful night. My heart jumped and an alarm bell went off inside me. It seemed to come from the new place of peace that had been growing in my soul. I put the bottle down. I knew that if I started to drink from it I wouldn't be able to stop until it was empty. An image flashed through my mind of me hunting for Hazel in the bottom of the bottle. I saw that the only thing I would find was my own self-pity. I needed help. I needed Amy. I...

*Hello Phoney! Well done - ask and ye shall receive.*

I smiled and breathed a huge sigh of relief. I quickly picked up the bottle and put it back in my empty cupboard.

'Oh I'm so glad to see you. I was just about to hit a bit of a tricky patch.'

*Take it next door.*

'Huh?'

*The wine. Take it next door to the new couple that have just moved in, as a house warming present. Go on. Now!*

I raised my eyebrows and realised that Amy was correct about the new couple in the flat across the landing. I had exchanged a few pleasantries but nothing more. I looked at Amy. She was sitting on the windowsill, staring out at the rain and ignoring me. I sighed. Oh well, the wine was expensive so I suppose it would be a great gift. I opened my door and then gave a gentle knock on the one opposite. I heard some laughter and then the door was thrown open to reveal a hallway piled high with packing cases and cardboard boxes. A youngish man and a bright-eyed woman with rolled up sleeves and dirty but happy faces greeted my gaze.

'Erm, hello neighbours, just wanted to say hi and, well, just thought that you guys might appreciate a small drink to settle you in.'

The man replied with a delighted laugh and took the bottle.

'That's amazing! Marie and I were just saying that we had nothing to toast the new flat with. Thank you so much. I'm Stewart and this is Marie my wife. I would invite you in but there is literally nowhere to sit down at the moment.'

I introduced myself and then had a thought.

'Hang on.' I replied and darted back into my flat. I returned with a mug, my large wine glass and a bottle opener.

'Here guys, you might need these, sorry but that's all I have.'

I felt shy and a little awkward. I wasn't used to spontaneous demonstrations of friendliness. But I needn't have worried; my new neighbours were full of the joys of their new flat and buzzing with excitement.

Marie told me that she was a designer and Stewart revealed that he was starting his new job as a life coach. As I wasn't entirely sure what a life coach was I smiled encouragingly and wished them both a good night and hurried back to my own flat to find that Amy had raided my fridge for cakes as usual.

'They seemed nice.'

Amy laughed with her mouth full of cake, looking very young and mischievous.

> Hmm, thought you might like to meet them. Now then Phoney, it's time for some serious soul mining.

Her youthful face vanished and her eyes became old, wise and steely blue. She seemed to transform from a small child into an intense little old lady in the space of a few seconds, reminding me of an ancient fairy person that I'd once seen in the girls' story books. I sat down and waited for her to finish a huge mouthful of cake. Amy kind of ruined her wise-woman effect because most of her face was now covered in a sticky mess of chocolate and cream. She gave it a slight wipe, which only made it worse, and then fixed me with one of her looks.

> I'm glad that you are managing to remain in the present Phoney. You have been practising very hard, and for the right reasons. You even saw your own weed of suffering growing and caught your gremlin. It was right to call me though. It's time to go deeper Phoney. It's time to deal with what scares Hazel.

'Hazel?! Hazel's scared of me? Anyway, she's gone.'

# Chapter 12

*Scared of you Phoney? She has her own fears you know.
She is practising her new path and she has just had a
huge realisation and now she's scared.*

'So this is your fault. All this bloody religious stuff has scared
Hazel! Ow!!'

Amy had jabbed me in the face with her bony index finger.

*Naughty gremlins, naughty words. There's no blame
culture here Phoney. It's all about taking responsibility for
yourself and Hazel is finding her own power. Now shush
and listen.*

I couldn't shush. I was angry, upset and confused.

'Hang on you little minx. You are saying that I scared Hazel off.
Just as I'm finally finding some peace and happiness. Just as I'm
being a better person and...'

*My dear Phoney, you are not a better person.*

'Well that's nice, now you are being mean.'

*No Phoney, you must not strive to be better, that's just a
conceit of your poor old gremlin-led ego. Phoney you are
quite perfect as you are.*

'Don't change the subject, and besides your flattery won't work
and I know you are lying. You saw the mess I was in a few months
ago, that's why you showed up wasn't it?'

*Phoney, you are perfect as you are. You simply began to
see that you could evolve.*

'From being imperfect to...'

*No Phoney, you are always perfect. The truth of you is beautiful - you are a creature of light and a child of the universe. You are made out of stars and you are powerful beyond measure. You simply chose to evolve.*

'Evolve from what to what?'

*All life is in constant change Phoney. Nothing remains the same. Everything changes. Evolving is going with the flow. Being present. Letting change be part of your life.*

Amy demonstrated this by varying the colour of her dress as she spoke. Her small cotton dress changed from red to orange to yellow then green, blue, purple and finally white. It was a good trick and it distracted me momentarily.

*You began to wake up to it, that's all.*

'Woke up to what?'

*You have been waking up to the fact that the universe is constantly evolving and changing all around you all the time.*

'You mean it's impermanent? What's that got to do with me waking up and Hazel being scared of me?

*You have chosen to enter the flow of life with your eyes open Phoney. Now that you have chosen to do this you can be the active designer and creator of your own universe.*

'What the...?'

*Well, the universe is always changing whether you are aware of it or not my dear Phoney. Now that you are aware you can choose to change and go in the direction that you would like and for the reasons that you choose.*

# Chapter 12

*You can co-create. You can choose happiness, joy and an ending of all your suffering.*

'Rather than what?'

*Rather than remaining asleep and letting your karma dictate all your life's outcomes.*

Amy had her ancient eyes on again. She seemed like a little old wise woman and less a small child of six or seven.

'Hang on Amy. What's this karma thing? You've never mentioned that before.'

*Oh it's the law of cause and effect. It's all the energy stuff that makes up the universe. You have begun to understand it by looking deeply into your suffering. You found the seeds of suffering. You watched how they can grow into nasty spiky weeds to strangle all your joy. You saw how you were walking backwards and living in the past. You saw how you then called up loads of gremlins to wreck your happy life and also how you abuse yourself with wine and drugs to forget and fall asleep again so that the whole cycle begins anew.*

'That's karma?'

*That's the great wheel of life. It's the energy that sends you round and round in circles, time after time, year after year, life after life. Always the same. Always different.*

'It's a circle.'

*Yup a great big flat circle.*

'A flat circle?'

*Yup, it's not good because the flow of the universe is a*

*great big spiral. It spirals up and up and up. Well that's if you accept the idea of time and direction. Hmm better that you did at the moment Phoney. Here, have some tea and cake.*

I felt stunned. My mind seemed to have completely taken a leave of absence. I was vaguely aware that not a single thought was stirring anywhere in my consciousness. I took a huge slurp of the tea that Amy had somehow made appear in front of me and helped myself to some cake. The tea and the 'too-sweet' cake seemed to reboot my brain and I scrabbled for a response.

'OK, Amy, karma. I still don't understand what that's got to do with Hazel and me, if there is any Hazel and me left that is.'

*Easy peasy Phoney. Hazel is awake now. She doesn't want to go all the way round again and end up in the same old place. She has seen deeply into the root of her suffering and she wants to choose happiness as her guide, not the need to make someone else happy.*

As usual I had to argue my point. It was fast becoming less of a defence mechanism and more of a way to slow Amy down so that my poor old mind could keep up.

'But I've been practising self-sufficiency. I'm different. I feel different. I really do Amy.'

Amy leant forward to me and her eyes softened.

*I know you have my darling Phoney, it's just time to deal with your karma. That's all. You see you can't go deep soul mining until you are strong enough. You can't dive into the ocean until you have learned to swim. Pearl divers have to practise for ages before they can hold their breath long enough to swim to the bottom of the ocean and find the pearls.*

# Chapter 12

'I thought you said we have to keep on breathing.'

*Exactly Phoney. You've discovered that you can breathe underwater and don't need to fear the depths. So are you ready?*

Although Amy's metaphors were making my head swim I did feel that I was glimpsing something deep inside me. It was just that every time I tried to look deeper, whatever it was vanished from sight.

Amy started to move around the flat, swimming with her arms.

*Each lifetime all your karma returns in a new form, a new reality, one that you can solve, heal and unhook from. This can only take place in the present my dear Phoney. Just like when I showed you the truth of your being a daddy. You had to be absolutely present to view the illusion of the past, heal it and heal your karma.*

'My head hurts Amy, how was I present and looking at the past in the same breath? If there is only the present how can the past even exist?'

*It doesn't.*

'Huh?'

*It doesn't exist Phoney. There is only now. It's just that you believe it exists. In every part of the closed-off and asleep areas of your mind you still hold all of these beliefs, events and experiences as true. You haven't woken up to the fact that the real you, the wonderful divine, light-filled being that you are, is the real Truth. This revelation is the genuine blessing that every living being has at their fingertips all the time. It is the gift of heaven on earth, the experience of heaven, right now.*

Taming Amy

Amy had stopped her swimming movements and was cheerfully munching on a huge muffin. I was amazed that she never put on any weight. Her unconventional teaching methods seemed to be having an effect on me though. I felt truly, deeply awake and present. It was as if my whole head had vanished and there was just a formless energy field expanding out in front of me.

'So if I am awake enough to unhook my karma from the past then I can be free from it in the now, in my new reality of the present moment?'

*Yup, well done Phoney. Words do make it all a bit confusing.*

I paused and wondered if I would ever be the same again. I realised that the whole concept of a permanent state of being, any real or lasting personality, was an illusion that I had just woken up from. I still felt a bit discombobulated and tried to anchor my thoughts again.

'So Hazel then?'

*Let's not worry about Hazel Phoney. It's time for you to go meet some karma. It's time to be brave and see how your suffering materialised in this lifetime.*

I felt very spaced-out yet very clear at the same time. Yet somewhere deep inside me a doubt rumbled away like an old dog snoring in front of the fire.

'I'm not sure that I'm ready Amy. I feel vulnerable at the moment. I feel confused. That's why I called you and...'

Amy hopped up onto the windowsill and pretended to be a great orator as she waved her hand about and addressed an imaginary crowd at her feet.

*Confusion is not an ignoble state ladies and gentlemen.*

Chapter 12

*Vulnerability is strength.*

She jumped down and walked towards me, staring intently up into my face.

> *Now Phoney I am going to need you to choose to be very still and practise really hard and whatever happens, don't panic. There's no need to worry because I am here. You are safe and you are loved. Phoney, do you understand?*

When someone says don't panic I always panic, well at least a bit. I decided to trust Amy and got comfortable in my chair. I put my only cushion at my back to keep it straight. I began to breathe gently and mindfully. I relaxed my whirring mind. Meanwhile Amy had managed to transfer the large carved candle from the shelf where I had placed it to the centre of the table and it was now glowing in front of me.

> *Now close your eyes Michael.  I am going to count you down from one to ten and when I do you will travel back to your karma. Ten, nine, eight...*

Amy's voice was sonorous and pleasing to my tired old ears and as she started to speak I closed my eyes and began to relax. I focussed on my breathing and the gentle rise and fall of my tummy and chest.

> *...seven, six, five, four...*

It seemed like I was descending in a lift, gradually going down and down, deeper and deeper into myself. I felt peaceful and more relaxed than I had been in a long time.

> *...three, two, one...you are here now Michael – what are you wearing?*

The request was unusual. I looked around and then down at my feet. I could see bright red sandals. My feet were ridiculously

221

small. I was wearing a soft white wool sweater and brown shorts. And I was clearly very young.

*How do you feel?*

I felt great. I felt joyful. The world was fun. It was so safe and secure. My thoughts were simple, uncluttered. I was drawing with crayons on a large book of paper. It felt just right.

*Where are you?*

I was in the living room of my old family home. The old fire was crackling; it was late afternoon or early evening.

*What is happening?*

Then I heard my mother's voice from the kitchen. It was a request for me to tidy up, to pick up my drawing paraphernalia because it was teatime.

*What are you doing?*

I was picking up the crayons and putting them neatly back in their box. I was humming to myself. My mother's voice came again, telling me to pick up my stuff. I picked up my large drawing book and looked around. There was nowhere to put it. I peered up at the large table above my head. I reached up and put the book on the table. It was only just on and might fall off again. I shoved it with my small hands and pushed it further onto the table. Then it happened. There was a huge crash. A large lamp with a white glass cover fell off the far side of the table. It crashed to the floor and smashed into a hundred pieces. Suddenly time seemed to speed up. I was aware of the heavy footsteps of my mother entering the room behind me. I heard her cry of anger. Then my world exploded in a deluge of pain and suffering. I was being beaten. I was being hurt. Tears of shock and terror burst from within me. I was lifted and dragged to my feet. Then I was thrust upstairs towards my room and flung into it. The door slammed and I was left shaking, scared, hurt and confused.

*Float above it Michael, you are safe. It's just an old movie. You are happy and relaxed again. If you wish to go further then simply let it happen.*

In the next instance I was standing back in the living room. I was aware that it was a few weeks later. I had done something wrong. Something that I didn't know was wrong. Maybe I had broken something else. I heard my mother's voice. She was angry yet somehow cold and distant. She was telling me that I was going to have the cane. I had no idea what that meant. The next moment my shorts and underwear were being pulled down. I was bent over a footstool and beaten with a stick. It was a huge shock. It really hurt. I was terrified. I screamed and cried. I felt...'

*Float above it Michael, it's just an old movie, you are safe, you are not in danger; See the story, see the characters in your film. If you wish to go on then let it happen - you can return at any moment.*

I found myself lying in my bed. It was another time. I was dimly aware that I had fallen off my bike into a flowerbed and had flattened some flowers earlier in the day. I was terrified. Had she found out? Of course she had. She always did. I could hear slow and heavy steps on the stairs. I knew that they were my mother's. Each creak scared me. Would the footsteps go past my door and into the bathroom or would they come into my bedroom? My door burst open. Suddenly I was being screamed at and punched. A rain of blows fell on me as I lay in my bed.

*Float above it Michael, you are safe, you are loved; you can return now if you choose. If you wish to remain then I am going to press fast forward and your life movie will pass much quicker. You can pause it at any time you want to.*

As Amy's calm voice spoke I felt safe. I floated above the scene, feeling so dreadfully sorry for the small dark-haired boy. He was so scared, so upset. Yet I needed to see more.

> *You are going to see your movie but much quicker now*
> *Michael.*

My life sped up and it was terrifying. Time after time I saw
my child self being punched, beaten, shouted at, caned and
physically, emotionally and mentally abused. There was no loving
touch. No cuddles, no kindnesses, just fear and more fear. I saw
the young boy grow up to be a teenager but with no more safety,
no more security. I saw the same abusive activity being vented on
my small sister. In a flash I realised how much she reminded me
of Amy. I was now scared for the both of us. I witnessed how we
were sworn into a state of secrecy. How we were silenced by fear,
unable to tell our kind and loving father anything for fear of swift
and sudden retribution. How the cruelty became more and more
mental and how the family home came to represent a torture
chamber. Then at the age of sixteen I saw myself finally react with
anger, stop my mother's blows, push her backwards onto a large
couch and then leave home for good. As I looked back I saw my
sister's face and realised that I had abandoned her in hell with
nobody to defend her. There was nothing I could do. I had to save
myself. I left and sought refuge with a friend's parents.

> *Float above it Michael, we are going to look again.*
> *See what you are doing, how you learn to cope with*
> *everything.*

Then I saw myself again. I was about six or seven and seated
on a chair in the middle of my class. I was surrounded by my
classmates who were all sitting on the floor, noisily sucking milk
through straws from small bottles. My disgruntled teacher was
off to one side with a closed reading book on her lap. I was
entertaining the whole class with a funny story. They were all
laughing. I saw how happy I was. Then the room changed. I was
in bed. My torch was flickering but I continued to read avidly
under the bedclothes. I saw myself escaping into book after book
after book. Epic fantasy adventures which gave me a world to
enter that I could manage, that I could control. The worlds were

full of monsters that I could master and defeat. Then the scene moved and I saw my sister curled up beside me - I was a creating a fantastic fairy story to keep her amused. I saw her seeking refuge inside the safety and the wonder of the stories I made up. I saw myself go to college and university and then once more lose myself in books of learning and research.

*Come back to me Michael, I am counting you back into the room. One, two, three, four - your breathing is regular – five, six, seven - you are safe and happy - eight, nine, ten - you are back here, in the flat. Now gently open your eyes.*

I opened my eyes. Amy was perched on the table, inches away from my face, holding out a handkerchief. I nosily blew my nose and wiped my face. The thing was I felt okay, I felt calm, I felt safe and relaxed.

'Wow, that was weird Amy. I could see, hear and feel everything. That wasn't very nice, but at the same time it was fascinating.'

*Shh Michael we are not done yet. These are techniques you can use on your journey yet simply seeing is not enough. What did you learn? What is the truth that will set you free?*

'Erm, that life was tough when I was a kid, that I never felt safe, I never felt loved?'

*How can any child feel safe and loved in that environment? What did you do to cope?*

'I told stories, I read avidly, I escaped from reality as often as I could.'

*You weren't just escaping reality Michael, you were creating reality. You were creating a stronger reality than the one that was hurting you. It was just as real and it kept you safe. The thing is Michael, maybe you don't need to make things up any more. You are safe and you are loved, whatever you might believe at the moment.*

'What does this have to do with Hazel?'

Amy laughed and smiled.

*Oh boy, Phoney's got it bad. He he, don't worry my darling it will all make sense in the end, well probably. Now are you ready for the next bit?*

'There's more?'

*We can't leave little Michael feeling all scared, alone and vulnerable can we?*

'But that was just my film of the past.'

*Yes but your younger self still lives on inside you Michael. All of your past lives do. Come on, you left him behind. It's time to bring him into the present. It's time to heal the rift across time. Use that mighty imagination of yours. Bring him here, now!*

As Amy gave the command, my day got even more bizarre. Suddenly a black-haired, brown-eyed boy of about six or seven stood in front of me. He just appeared. He was wearing a bright red jumper, cords, trainers and an old hat that I recognised immediately. The hat was a treasure from my past. It was covered in badges of all the places I had visited as a kid. I couldn't believe my eyes. I realised that I wasn't breathing. I inhaled. I exhaled. He was still there, just staring at me with his huge eyes. His face seemed curious. I hissed at Amy.

'What am I supposed to do?'

*Tell him that it's alright – go on, you are reaching back*

*into your past. Now give the little version of you all the*
*love and care that he is missing. Go on.*

The moment that I started to speak, I felt soft tears forming in the corner of my eyes. My voice was gentle and full of love and compassion.

'Erm...hello, Hi. Look it's me, I mean you, I mean the older you. I am going to tell you something very important.'

The boy scratched his head and waited expectantly. He reminded me of a younger version of Amy if that was possible.

'You have had a scary time but it's OK, everything is alight. You are safe now, nothing can hurt you, you were always safe but you didn't know it. Thanks for being so brave. Thanks for looking out for your sister. You did all that you could. You were great. You are a good boy and I am very proud of you. I love you very much. You don't have to pretend any more. You don't have to try so hard. We can just sit down and relax and simply be happy together. Let's choose to be happy.'

To my amazement the small boy smiled and his grin lit up the room. He leapt forwards and hugged me intensely. My tears really began to flow this time. I held him tight. I lifted him up into the air. I told him over and over that I loved him, that he was safe, that he didn't have to try so hard anymore, that he was amazing. He kept on smiling and then he started to laugh and before I knew it he had jumped free of my arms and was dancing around the room with Amy. I couldn't stop my own laughter. They both skipped round and round the table, singing and laughing like nothing I had ever seen before. I would have joined them but my small kitchen couldn't have contained this much fun without breaking under the strain.

Then the two small beings stopped and turned towards me. Amy looked at the boy, my grinning younger self, and said:

*Go on then, tell him.*

Then the boy spoke. I guess it was my voice but it sounded so different. So young. So childlike.

'It's OK to be happy now Michael. I love you. I see you. You are wonderful. You are a teacher. You are a healer. This is your calling. This is your gift. All you need to do is remember. You just forgot, that's all. Think of me and remember. The universe is our playground. Our life is all about having fun. Just choose happiness now Michael.'

Then he turned to Amy, giving her a kiss on the cheek. She was delighted and blushed to her roots, not something I thought Amy was capable of. And then he vanished.

*Well look at the smile on your face Phoney. Never seen you looking so happy! That's better. That's some karma released. Well done.*

'Oh – my – god Amy. What just happened?'

*You know what just happened Michael. You remembered how to love yourself. You saw yourself with kindness and compassion. You gave yourself permission to be happy again.*

I was still in a kind of gentle reverie. How could I not be kind and gentle to the younger version of myself? He was just a child, so full of life and potential. I quietly promised him that I would concentrate on us having more fun. I looked at Amy who seemed to be in a dream-world all of her own. She was humming and playing with her hair. It occurred to me that even Amy just wanted somebody to play with.

'So I never resolved my early years then Amy? I never healed my own inner child. Is that why I keep on choosing to be miserable?'

*Your poor little child self was still scared and confused.
You always knew that Phoney. His fears were your fears.
He was the cause of your sadness. You stopped being
happy because deep inside, you never felt safe enough
to be happy. You were trying so hard all the time to create
a safe reality for yourself and others that you lost all your
own happiness. You were spread out through time like
jam on toast.*

My mind flicked back to the movie show that Amy had made
me watch earlier. I remembered how I had immersed myself
in daydreaming, escapist adventures and eventually academic
texts.

'So you are saying that my ego just conspired to create a huge
story for me to be safe in? A story where I was safe, but because I
lived inside this story I wasn't really awake to reality?'

*Yup, all of those ideas about yourself; boy hero, teenage
rebel, juvenile rock god, university academic savant.
You made up loads of stories that didn't serve you. You
believed your karma Phoney. You believed that you were
not safe. You believed that you were not loved. Then you
believed so hard you lost yourself in a story where you
were a rubbish dad, a rubbish husband, a rubbish teacher
and a rubbish human being. Because your mother never
saw you, the real you, the beautiful wonderful amazing
you, you couldn't believe that you existed. You couldn't
believe that a happy and joyous you could exist. You
couldn't believe that you are fabby. I just showed you how
to tell yourself the real story. How to unhook yourself from
the fates, from your karma.*

My heart did imperceptible cartwheels and a smile broke out
across my face.

'So you made me see myself, truly see myself, with all
the love and compassion that I never received from my
mother?'

*Remember what I told you about us girls and how hard it is to be really free to be our wonderful selves?*

'Sure do Amy, I even chatted to my daughters about it.'

*How often do you hear people say 'if only you could see yourself'? Well now you can and now you know that you are wonderful. Just practise seeing yourself clothed in light and love Phoney. Then who knows what might happen...*

I picked up a picture of my daughters when they were really small and playing on the beach. I remembered how easy it had been to see them as the small bundles of joy and possibility that they were. I realised that was a function every parent was supposed to fulfil for their children, no matter how old they had become and no matter what they might have done or believed about themselves.

'So when we are free from all the fears that originate in the past we can actually look at ourselves and see ourselves as amazing creatures full of joy and hope, just like when you see a newborn baby?'

*Free from fear Phoney, we can all truly see ourselves. Free from fear everybody can see just how wonderfully lovely, amazing and full of fun, sunshine and laughter we all are. Adults who are fearful forget to laugh. They grow up without their sense of fun. They stop laughing. They take everything sooo seriously.*

'Why's that?'

*Because fear is serious stuff Phoney. Fear kills. BOO!!!*

Amy pounced on me like a small monster and then darted away laughing. She was heading to my fridge again. I called after her as I saw her climb up and liberate yet another cake from its icy clutches.

'So am I free now?'

Amy clambered down and turned to look at me. Her face had become ancient again. She was glowing at the edges. She had her big blue eyes on.

> *Oh my dear Phoney, of course you are free now. You were, you are, you always have been free. Any cage was of your own making.*

'I made my own cage?'

> *Yup - a cage or prison of fear and doubt.*

Amy began to lick the filling out of the cake with her small pink tongue - she reminded me of a miniature anteater.

> *You mustn't doubt yourself again my dear Phoney. Of course you chose to escape into fantasy like that. Of course you felt like that. Which small child wouldn't have felt like that in that state?*

I supposed Amy was right. I could see a long thread running back through my life. It was a habit of escaping into a narrative of my own making which snaked back through my life. I could see how hard I had worked to maintain it. I could see how I had made it big enough to be a safe place for other people to inhabit as well. I could also see how it had eventually crumpled and failed me. Amy was wiping cake from her red curls as she took a deep breath and looked at me again.

> *So Phoney, the world is full of large adults who still have small children inside them. small children who are still scared and fearful. Grown-ups keep on running backwards to protect the smaller versions of themselves yet they don't know that they're doing it. That's why the*

*small children rule the world. All the unresolved hurts and fears play the adults like puppet masters. You have never been free of your past self because you never took the time to heal him. That's why most adults still squash the joy out of their lives every day, not knowing why.'*

'We squash the joy out of our lives because we are still run by our damaged and unhappy past selves?'

*Bingo Phoney!*

'So I just have to practise loving myself as if I am a small child then?'

Amy made a pretend cradle out of her arms and began to rock them back and forth in front of me.

*Remember Michael, be as the mother - the true, loving, kind, compassionate mother - to all living things. Then you can remain in the flow of life, bringing happiness to all. Want some cake?*

Amy's seemingly eternal appetite for cake amazed me but my mind was still chasing after clarification.

'So is that what Hazel meant? About me not being happy?'

Amy picked up the last piece of the huge chocolate cake I had bought earlier.

*Yes Michael. How can she be with someone who is not able to be happy? People who always choose sadness spread sadness. Those who always choose fear spread fear. Now you know how to choose joy so you can spread joy. It's not your fault. There is no blame in the universe. Karma is not punishment, it's just the suchness of things. It's there for you to use for your evolution, if you wish to.*

'Can I use it to get Hazel back?'

Amy sighed and, swallowing the last piece of cake, looked straight at me.

> Remember the 'Amy Way' my dear Phoney. Just allow yourself to truly BE. All things change when we simply ARE. Identify with the past, don't compare yourself to it. Practise simply being yourself now. Realise that you can allow yourself to be free of your past movies and truly exist in the present.

This was turning into being one of Amy's longest sessions. My poor old mind was racing to catch up but somehow my soul seemed to have completely understood. I wondered if things could be that easy. Mind you, Amy always made things look hard and then showed you that they were easy after all.

'Maybe I haven't healed all my stuff yet Amy?'

> If you want, you can go and watch plenty more karma movies and see how they make you feel. It's easy to do Phoney.

'What? Do you mean that I can just meditate and reflect on my past?'

> If the emotion rings true for a situation in the present then let your mind find the movie in the past, but only as long as you learn from it and release the karma with joy, love and compassion. You must stay mindful or else you might choose to stay in the past or even bring it back with you and end up being spread thinner than marmite on a cheesy cracker.

'So my old habit energy...?'

> It will stop stampeding off with you hanging on for dear

*life. It will evolve and transform into the power of your light Phoney.*

'By being present?'

*Yes, in the here and now. That way you won't project old fearful and negative movies ahead of you. You won't create a crappy future for yourself before you have arrived. Every moment makes the next one Phoney. That is the law of Karma. Simply choose to be happy, joyous, compassionate and loving now and that energy will build and build until it radiates for you in every direction throughout time and space.*

'Wow, that seems a bit flaky and weird!'

*Hmm, well Phoney, you must tell yourself again in the words that suit you but just make sure they set you free, not imprison you again.*

I reached for the kettle but as I turned back to ask Amy if she wanted tea I saw that she had gone. I didn't mind. I felt amazing, really amazing, more amazing than I had felt in years. I could see just how silly I had been for so long. All the rubbish I had believed about myself. I could see how I had crushed the joy out of so many moments of my life. I saw how absurd I had been. Then I started to laugh and laugh. I laughed for so long and so loudly that my sides ached. When the doorbell rang and I went to answer it, I was still chuckling. I opened the door to the happy and surprised face of my new neighbour Marie.

'Hello Michael, are you watching something good on TV? Here's your bottle opener, glass and erm...mug. Thank you so much for the wine. It was perfect. We've wanted our own place for so long and I have to admit the only thing I was worried about was the neighbours. And you are just lovely. Thanks for making everything just perfect. I'm so happy.'

She stood on tiptoes and pecked me on the cheek and with just the slightest of staggers, disappeared back across the hallway and into her new home. I realised that I was blushing and that somewhere deep inside me, a young boy was grinning from ear to ear.

# Chapter Thirteen

Taming Amy

I'm not quite sure why I agreed to look after my daughter Olivia's large and soppy hound. It might have been something to do with my sneaking suspicion that my imaginary friend might appreciate it. Or it might have been the fact that I still craved some regular company, even for a short while. It might just have been the fact that I seemed to have recently become a push over as far as my daughter was concerned. More likely it was the dim memory that Hazel had once suggested that she might like a puppy of her own to keep her company whilst I was away writing my masterpiece. As it turned out, it was for none of those reasons.

As overjoyed as I was to see my daughter, her arrival at my flat was somewhat marred by the fat-footed black dog that insisted on flying around it like an express train. My mind had played a trick. I remembered her dog as a small and easy to handle cute puppy. Now it was huge. To add to the confusion my daughter was horrified to see my bare and empty flat. I could tell that she was worried for my sanity. She viewed my new meditation cushion as proof that I had further lost the plot and fallen prey to some weird religion. I had to calm her down by saying that I was getting ready to redecorate. Then of course she was both sad for me and angry at me for getting myself estranged from Hazel, who she doted on. So much for daughterly sympathy.

The young and maniacal hound was called Daisy and even I could see that she had a kindly temperament. Her tail wagged faster than a hummingbird's wings and if she hadn't been so large I swear she would have become airborne. Plus Daisy proved to be a great distraction from the sudden grilling I was getting from my over-worried daughter. The dog was completely destroying my brand new Tibetan meditation cushion! Pieces of yak's wool

238

flew in all directions and descended on us like the fall-out of a nearby volcano. Olivia pulled some fluff out of her tea and then confessed that she hoped I'd be able to give Daisy some doggy training skills. As she stood up to leave for her festival, the real reason for visiting me, she shoved a leaflet in my hand. I looked at the title. 'How to Train Your Dog in a Week.' That was likely!

'See Dad,' said Olivia, 'you've got over a week before I'm back so I'm sure you can get her trained for me.'

Then she gave one last disparaging glance around my bare flat, kissed me on the cheek and headed outside. Normally when I saw my girls I felt sad the moment we parted. I didn't have a moment to pine this time though. Daisy leapt up behind me, giving me such a shove that I fell over the bag containing her bed, bowls and dog food and landed in a heap by the sink. Before I could feel sorry for myself I had to swerve into action to prevent Daisy from eating up the week's supply of dog food that was now spread all over the floor of my small kitchen.

I was hurt and furious. I gave the dog a swift kick and shouted at her to behave. She slunk away into the corner and viewed me with glaring malice whilst I swept up the food. It was obvious to me that she was spoiled rotten. It was time for some tough love. As I put the last of the food into an empty kitchen drawer I shouted at Daisy for gnawing the leg of the chair and picked up the leaflet.

My daughter had done her homework. The class was in a church hall just around the corner from my flat. In fact right opposite the park. I dialled the number and was greeted by the booming voice of a woman who assured me that as soon as I had learned the voice of command my dog would obey me every time. Due to the time constraints she suggested a week's intensive course for Daisy and me. I agreed even though I felt slightly intimated and unsure of why I would personally need training. Oh well it would be great to make my daughter happy and surprise her. In my mind I imagined Daisy dutifully sitting on command as my astonished daughter picked her up the following week. It would be worth it.

Dogs and cities really don't mix. Well *this* dog and a city didn't go together anyway. On the first morning's walk I nearly had my arm pulled off on numerous occasions as Daisy bounded in all directions. I forever had to pick up soft smelly poo, not a job anyone could really enjoy and one which left me feeling faintly sick. I hadn't been much good with the children's nappies when they were small. My vision of having a new four-legged friend to accompany me on my long meditative walks was quickly shattered. I could barely keep up with Daisy. There was no unhurried meandering. Daisy didn't walk. She raced full pelt at everything, all the time. I dropped the lead once and she shot off up the hill, chasing a squirrel, before deciding to play tig with me for half an hour. Daisy made me late for lectures so I quickly cut myself a long bendy stick from the hedgerow and found that a swift switch of it brought a loud yelp and a quick return to heel from Daisy. I was so annoyed with her that all the way back to the flat I jerked on her lead and scolded her in an effort to make her more obedient. It didn't work.

On my return to the flat that evening I discovered that Daisy had ripped the vinyl in the hall into little pieces. It looked as if she had been trying to tunnel her way out. I was tired and worn out and lost my rag. I gave Daisy a really good cuff round the ear and shouted and screamed at her until she slunk away. I hoped she'd got the message. Then I picked up her lead and dragged her out through the destruction and towards the church hall where the dog training was about to start.

I was determined that every evening that week, I would dutifully brave the wrath of the small but powerfully scary woman who was our dog trainer. I am sure that this lady was passionate about dogs. I am sure that she was passionate about their training and obedience. I am also sure that she was passionate about power.

Ms. Lewis lined us up the moment we came in. Owners and their dogs all stood dutifully in line. Ms. Lewis marched up and down like a sergeant major delivering drill exercise. Ms. Lewis's voice was that of a raging African bull elephant. It seemed to roar even when she was speaking quietly. Every sentence was a barked order. Somehow that seemed appropriate.

She instructed the quaking line of newbie owners about the inherent danger of our dogs. Apparently our slobbering and waggy-tailed pooches could kill, maim and destroy at will. Ms. Lewis wagged her finger at us as she stared up into our trembling faces. We were all suitably chastened and impressed by this confident and masterful powerhouse. I reflected that maybe it was my lot to be forever given instruction by short women.

Then things got fun. Ms. Lewis told us that she was going to teach us the single most important aspect of dog control. We all leaned forward eagerly whilst trying to stop our individual dogs from fighting, playing or mating with each other. Ms. Lewis grabbed hold of the lead of a young pit bull terrier. The hooded youth gave him over to her without a whimper. Ms. Lewis then let the dog off the lead. It immediately ran to the far corner of the hall where it prepared itself to pee over chair leg. That was the moment that humans and dogs met the Voice of Command. Ms. Lewis shouted STOP! In the loudest voice imaginable. Then COME HERE! The young dog literally froze, one leg half-cocked in the air. It gave a small whimper and shot back across the hall to its owner. We all gave an impromptu round of applause. Ms. Lewis glowed just a little bit too much.

'The first thing to do is to find your voice of command,' ordered Ms. Lewis triumphantly as she marched up and down. 'Each of you must send your dogs off and then find your deepest, loudest and most commanding voice. It's very simple. Even a child can do it.'

Ms. Lewis then marched purposely to the far end of the hall and laid out some small doggie snacks.

'You wIll use your voice of command and prevent your dog from eating the offering,' she yelled from the other end of the hall.

Then it was our turn. We bashful, newbie dog owners nervously sent our dogs across the hall, each desperately hoping not to be shown up in case we incurred the wrath of Ms. Lewis.

With red faces we politely and loudly requested our dogs to obey our commands. One after another our faithful hounds wagged their tails, dashed across the hall and wolfed down every tit-bit that they were supposed to avoid. Every dog returned, tail wagging, expecting to be praised.

Ms. Lewis was beside herself.

'Make the loudest and most terrifying noise that you can muster and use the Voice of Command', she commanded us. 'Now do it again. You go first.' Ms. Lewis was pointing at Daisy and me.

I have the lungs of a lecturer that are well used to shouting to the back of  crowded and noisy lecture halls. I felt fairly confident. I cleared my throat, took a deep breath and sent Daisy hurtling across the room. She gleefully raced towards the fist forbidden tit-bit. Then I roared my Words of Command.  'DAISY. STOP!'  I was so loud I think the windows actually shook. The lady beside me whimpered. A small child spat out her sweet. And, to my delight, Daisy froze in mid-flight. I felt victorious.

For the rest of the week I walked Daisy with pride. Whenever we were out and she lollopped towards other people I would roar my word of command. When she climbed onto the sofa bed I would roar. When she ate my dinner right off the work surface I would roar. Each time I used the voice of command Daisy would freeze or at least cower, trembling. I felt my power. I felt my ability to control and I was very pleased with myself. So pleased in fact that I stopped going to the scary training sessions with the foreboding Ms. Lewis and decided that Daisy and I now had a good understanding of how the natural order of the world worked.

I decided I would admonish my lovely daughter if she failed to control her dog on her return. I would lecture her in the mastery of the Voice of Command. I would show her that she had to strengthen her puny female voice. I imagined myself even being able to stop a stampeding bull dead in its tracks if I used the correct voice of command. I was even considering including the technique in some of my lectures. I would of course have been humoured – and then ignored.

As the week turned into a delightful Indian summer weekend I quickly noticed some drawbacks. My voice of command was a tranquility crusher. Daisy would freeze in her tracks and return to me cowering after I barked an order. This left adults, parents, children, old people and even one school's lollipop lady badly shaken in our wake.  During our walk in the park, whole families were momentarily petrified, sandwiches half way to their mouths. In fact, I noticed, that my Voice of Command seemed to shatter any tranquil doggy-walking atmosphere that might have existed. I began to shun public spaces. I started to walk Daisy when there was no one else around. I became a dog-walking recluse.

Things came to a head three nights before my daughter was meant to return from having too much fun. Daisy decided that she had had enough. Every night I had to tramp down the stairs from the flat, along the hallway to the front door to take Daisy out for her bedtime walk. The hallway was long and cold as is the norm in Scottish tenement flats. You don't want to forget things on the way out. You don't want to have to turn back and then drag your dog to the front door. On this particular night I had reached the heavy outer door, put my boots and raincoat on and then turned to see Daisy standing, motionless, at the far end of the hall. I commanded her to follow me but she simply stood absolutely still and observed me, head on one side. I commanded again and again and again but she didn't budge. Cursing loudly, I had to stride down the hallway, cuff her ear and guide her firmly by the collar out into the rain.

The next night the same thing happened. Daisy reached the bottom of the stairs with a full skip and doggy happiness and then refused to follow me out. Again I turned, used the Voice of Command – nothing.  Shouted it – nothing. Roared whilst jumping up and down – nothing. Then in a pique of anger I marched back to get Daisy and 'persuaded' her physically to come outside.

On the third night it happened again. I was ready to reach for any available expletive to impose my authority. Instead however, something in the way Daisy looked at me made me pause and consider my own actions. Why did she keep stopping her full-flight rush for walkies at the bottom of the stairs to then stare at me without budging? Why did she keep risking my wrath? What had happened to my Voice of Command? Had I failed my dog training 1:01?

I took a deep breath and wondered what Amy would say. I looked back up the hallway to where Daisy sat, head on one side, refusing to move. There was something so sad in her gaze that it stopped me feeling frustrated and prompted me to try out my mindful breathing for the first time in days. It was then that I remembered what Amy had said about loving our younger selves and identifying with them.  Immediately I saw myself as the small brown-eyed child again. I saw myself cowering whilst being shouted at. I felt my own fear. I felt my own confusion. I even felt a small amount of anger. As these images flashed through my mind I was aware of Daisy staring at me.

It slowly dawned on me that all I was communicating with my voice of command was anger, a lack of love and zero compassion. It occurred deep within me that I wouldn't expect to be spoken to like that. I would have been shocked at myself if I spoke to another human like that. So in a dim corner of my mind, the question posed itself.

*So why do you speak to Daisy like that?*

I could sense Amy somewhere far off and I knew that her words were ringing true. As I considered Daisy's feelings I felt a shock of shame for all the times I had been harsh, cold or commanding to her. Flashes of an aspect of me I didn't like much danced in front of my eyes. I had become one of the worst aspects of my mother. Maybe even worse? She would never have scared an animal even if she had screamed verbal abuse at her children on a regular basis.

As the turmoil of conflicting emotions passed and I returned to my careful breathing, I became aware again of Daisy sitting calmly at the far end of the hallway. Her head was cocked to one side quizzically. I gently lifted my own head, which had dropped in shame, and softly and warmly invited Daisy to come with me. 'Shall we?' I asked.

Immediately Daisy's tail began to wag. She leapt up and padded happily down the long hall straight past me and out into the night. My VOICE OF COMMAND had become my expression of gentle persuasion.

I was not surprised to see Amy playing in the small garden with Daisy. The two of them were gamboling around like a pair of puppies. Then again, I suppose they were a couple of puppies really.

'So now you decide to show up? I could have done with you earlier in the week you know.'

Amy looked up from where she was rolling on the grass with a delighted Daisy.

*Told you you'd get a dog didn't I?*

'Huh?'

*Daisy just taught you Right Speech Phoney. It's well overdue. You always shout at people and stuff if they don't do what you want them to do.*

'I thought the voice of command was a load of pish.'

*No you didn't, you thought it was great. That's why you used it all the time on poor old Daisy. You only stopped because you were scaring people and embarrassing yourself.*

'Well it's what I was told to do.'

*People who try to command are scared of losing control. Right speech should build love and compassion, not extend fear Phoney.*

'I guess I just became my mother again didn't I?'

*So what does that tell you about your mother Phoney?*

'Are you trying to tell me that my mother shouted and screamed at us because she was scared of losing control?'

*Most command and control people are scared of actually losing control, over themselves and of course others.*

'But I was just a child. How could I have been threatening?'

*Exactly, how could a small child be threatening to a mother?*

Daisy and Amy had both come to sit beside me on the steps leading up to the front door. Daisy sat on my feet and laid her head on my knee as she gazed up at me.

'I, er, I guess it must have been what we represented to her... some kind of fear?'

*Go on.*

The two of them kept looking up at me with their big eyes. I almost laughed, and then an idea occurred to me.

'Maybe she felt that children trapped her, took away her identity?'

*Maybe.*

'Well am I right then?'

*How did you learn to treat your children?*

'I was never like my mother with my kids. That's not fair Amy. I tried my best to make sure I was never like that with the girls.'

*So where did you get the idea that shouting and hitting Daisy was okay then?*

The two of them were still staring up at me with their big eyes. I couldn't get cross. Somehow I sensed that was the point.

'Okay smarty pants. I guess I learnt it from my mother.'

*And where do you think that she would have learnt it from Phoney?*

I smiled at the pair of them as they looked up expectantly at me. My voice became soft as I got Amy's point.

'I guess she learnt it from her mother?'

*And she would have learnt it from her mother, and her mother from her mother before that. On and on and on. The karma extends through lifetimes.*

'So you are saying that the way we speak and treat each other is a behaviour that we have inherited from generations ago?'

Amy gave a delighted Daisy a big sloppy kiss on her head and scratched behind her ears. Daisy was in heaven.

*Right speaking comes from deep within our hearts Phoney. Gentle compassionate speech that neither tries to hurt or judge is how we express love Phoney. Shouting is just us expressing fear, always. Maybe just the fear that we might not be heard; maybe the fear that we won't be noticed; maybe the fear of losing control.*

'So Daisy was my teacher this time then?'

Amy beamed up at me and Daisy tried to lick my face.

*Yes and wasn't she wonderful?*

I took a breath for a moment as the pair of them got up and went to play some more. The past weeks had indeed been humbling. I, the learned professor, had received life instruction from a five- or six-year-old girl, a younger version of myself, and now a dog! It was humbling yet not humiliating. Bizarrely the whole idea was somehow comforting. I called out to Amy and both Amy and Daisy stopped to listen.

'So is that some more karma released then?'

*Just maybe my dear Phoney, just maybe you have released some more. Go ye and sin no more, especially with that frightening foghorn of a voice that you have.*

I was about to argue that my voice wasn't frightening and that I never meant to frighten anybody but the two of them were walking towards the open door.

'But we all shout at our children sometimes. We need to stop them before they hurt themselves or something. That's how we avert a crisis.'

Amy and Daisy turned back and looked at me. They made me chuckle. They were rather cute. Amy stood with one hand on her hip and one on Daisy's head. Daisy kept licking her face as she spoke.

# Chapter 13

*Daisy just taught you that authority can only be given to those who love us and are kind and gentle. If you speak with kindness and love to your children, not with anger or fear, they will quickly learn that you are speaking from a place of concern for their safety Phoney.*

'I always tried to do that Amy.'

*I know you did Phoney. We quickly realise that requests are for our own good when delivered with compassion, love and kindness.*

Amy scratched the delighted Daisy's ears again and to my horror gave her a biscuit. Then she turned to me again, quite thrilled to be almost as tall as me because she and Daisy were standing on the top step.

*No one can assume authority over any living entity without causing harm and beginning a negative cycle of karma. Authority has to be earned Phoney. Got any cake and doggy biscuits?*

Amy and Daisy bounded inside and up the stairs together. I got a sudden pang of guilt for all the times I had shouted at my daughters. By the time I had reached the flat my mood had dropped. As I came in I saw Amy and Daisy both happily tucking in to doggy biscuits, a fact that vaguely disconcerted me. Amy looked up at me and smiled.

*From right thinking must flow right speech Phoney. It is the natural outpouring of compassion. When we speak to each other we must speak from a very deep and happy place. We can't indulge in indifference, coldness, and cruelty without hurting others and ourselves. Don't worry Phoney. You said 'I love you' far more than anything else to your girls.*

I felt my smile return. I realised I was going to miss Daisy.

*You should learn to thank people more often Phoney. Especially when you see that they wanted to command you but instead chose a request.*

'Is that what I have to practise?'

*You just have to practise Right Speech Phoney. Not speaking from a place of fear. Speaking with love, compassion and happiness. Why not? Why would you choose to be anything other than kind and gentle? That's all your inner child would want. That's actually all any adult wants. Look at Daisy; she'll do anything for you now, won't you Daisy?*

Amy tickled Daisy's chin. Her tail wagged. Even though she was taller than Amy and kept licking her face, I could see that Amy was perfectly safe, even if she wasn't real. Daisy went to lay down and Amy moved closer to me.

*Close your eyes Phoney, I want to show you a memory. Oh, and you know that I'm real, you big daftie.*

I sat down on my poorly patched up meditation cushion, straightened my back and closed my eyes. I felt a hot sticky finger gently touch me in the middle of my forehead.

I watched myself visiting a school. It was on one of my earlier careers intervention programs that I had delivered several years ago. I recognized the aging school corridors, now all mercifully demolished and replaced with modern classrooms

I'd been walking down the long corridor ready to leave the building when a loud shout had made me drop my books. It was of such volume that I had jumped a couple of feet into the air with shock. I picked up my books and peered nervously into the classroom that had issued the thunderous bellow. A teacher, who had earlier made a good impression on me in the staff room, had just caused thirty-one young humans in her blast range to physically jump. OK she had received the undivided attention of the whole class but what was that attention worth? I remembered how I had pondered what the shocked roomful of youngsters must now be thinking. The classroom door was open and in the split second that I knew I had available before she noticed my presence, I scanned the body language of her class. Not one face showed any sign of respect or gratitude. In fact I thought I saw thirty young people quietly switch off.

I opened my eyes and blinked. Amy was only inches away from my face, standing on the table.

> *When you shout you create fear Phoney. That's the purpose of shouting. It's aggression. Lots of shouting creates lots of stress. Stress exhausts us. It actually stops us from being able to pay attention or learn anything.*

'I remember how I used to mentally block out my mother's voice and I guess I kind of do that with anybody who shouts at me.'

> *I know you do, dear Phoney. Trouble is that in the classroom that just makes the teacher shout louder. Because she has lost respect by shouting, by creating fear, by making the world unsafe, all she can do is continue to raise the volume of her voice of command 'til the walls shake. The kids then shut down more. It's energetic warfare - or energetic survival of the deafest.*

'You're so right Amy. I remember how stunned many of the teachers were when they visited a special needs school for autistic children. Children that the teachers had previously thought were behaviorally challenging and unteachable were all sitting quietly absorbed in their work and every teacher spoke in carefully modulated tones. They never raised their voices, not once, not under any circumstances.'

> *That's true Phoney. The clever teachers use quietly spoken words filled with loving kindness and delivered with gentle firmness to create a harmonious learning*

*environment. They make sure their words have one simple task.*

'What's that?'

*They use every word to convey inspiration, compassion, mindfulness, stillness and love and safety. We only really learn when we are playing games Phoney.*

'Playing games?'

*Yup, the conditions to play, which is another word for learning, have to be that we are safe and loved. That's all. Learning is easy, humans make it hard.*

'Oh, hey, you might be onto something there...so why do we make it hard for ourselves?'

*Teachers are often fearful people Phoney. They have loads and loads of targets to meet and they don't practise mindfulness. Many of them left home, went to school, then college or university and then back to school. They never got to practise grown up loving-kindness. They are not aware of mindfulness. Head teachers are under pressure to make children into little work robots who pass exams, to make them look good and keep their jobs. So head teachers shout at teachers and teachers shout at their kids just like their parents did.*

I blinked and considered my own school life. I had been lucky to go to a school where not every teacher shouted at us all the time, but I knew that at some points they all did. I wondered if my lectures were ever fun. I doubted it.

Amy had climbed onto Daisy's back and was steering the delighted hound round and round the kitchen. I had to strain to hear what she was saying over the din of a heavy-footed dog pounding the kitchen floor.

*That's what the practice of simple Right Speech can correct in the world Phoney. Fearful people use fearful words to teach fear-based realities. It's the old flat-earth way of thinking and doing things. Children learn through fear and then grow up to live in fear and go on to teach fear.*

'All this just from shouting at them?'

*Right Speech is lovely, warm, gentle and loving speech, filled with humour and laughter Phoney. Right Speech is an expression of love, all the time, even when teaching boring old subjects like yours!*

'That's not right speech Amy, that's mocking me!'

*You are bored teaching it Phoney and your students are bored learning it. Use Right Speech to bring it alive so that it's not boring. Make it inspirational. Good teachers should inspire, not command.*

Amy was right; ever since I'd started on this crazy journey of self-discovery with her my lectures had lost their appeal. Daisy got up and walked towards my shoe. I tried right speech.

'Please leave the shoe now Daisy.'

Daisy did as she was told and drank some water instead. Amy beamed at me.

*See, be nice. That's all we want. That's all it takes. Make it safe to play. Playing is learning. Right speech is how we speak to each other when we are playing. You see it's not just about how loud it is. It's about the deep emotion that you are projecting when you shout.*

'So Ms. Lewis was projecting fear every time she shouted then?'

# Taming Amy

*Well you all jumped out of your skins didn't you?*

Amy headed off to where Daisy had curled up on her bed. She lifted her paw and clambered underneath it.

Amy opened one eye.

*Well done for listening to Daisy. One of the most important parts of Right Speech is compassionate listening. You can practise that tomorrow.*

I turned off the light and snuck off to bed myself. As I lay down to sleep I quietly told my younger child self that from now on I was going to let him play. I slept with a huge smile on my face and enjoyed some very happy dreams.

I awoke to Daisy vigorously licking my face and my front door being hammered on. I sprang out of bed and dashed to open it. My daughter was standing in the doorway, scowling. She looked muddy, wet, and very, very miserable. She marched straight in and went immediately into my bathroom without so much as a good morning. Then I heard the sound of my shower being run.

I chuckled. I knew when to leave her alone. Then I got a shocking thought. Oh my God, that was what I was like when I was upset or cross! As the shower continued to run, I picked up the sound of sobbing. I quickly took Daisy down to the café where I bought large coffees, plenty of cakes and huge hot-filled breakfast rolls. By the time Olivia had emerged from the shower, the feast was on the table and Daisy was lying on her back, enjoying me tickling her tummy.

My daughter's scowl softened and she sat at the table and started to eat. I could see that her eyes were still red. She had found one of my old jumpers and tracksuit and was probably dry for the first time in days. I quietly gathered up the piles of wet and dirty clothes and bunged them into my washer dryer. I sent a silent thank you to Hazel for not only making me buy it but for also making me learn how to use it.

Olivia finished her breakfast and looked up at me.

'Thanks Dad. You're the best. How was Daisy?'

I told Olivia how her dog had in fact trained me and I left in all the mistakes I'd made. I was relieved to see that a smile had begun to make an occasional appearance on her face.

'What happened to you this weekend then?'

She frowned and looked away. I paused. I was trying to remember everything that Amy had said the night before about right speech and right listening. I tried to use what I was saying to show my daughter that I had heard her.

'So it wasn't the great time you had hoped for then?'

'Leave it Dad. I don't want to discuss it.'

'Oh right. You don't want to tell me because the memory of it is still too painful for you?'

As I spoke I tried to remember the last time I had suffered a disappointment and had wanted to clam up. I didn't have to go back too far. I gathered all my compassion, identified with my daughter and just let myself love her. I saw her shoulders drop a little.

'It was me and Dave, we split up.'

That was a surprise. I didn't know that she had gone with her boyfriend. I assumed that she was miserable because she'd got wet and muddy and her expensive festival had been a washout.

'Oh you poor thing. I guess you must be feeling terrible.'

I spoke with careful compassion. Inside I wanted to comment on what an idiot Dave was and try to give her relationship advice. Instead I was still.

'Yup, I'm feeling pretty crap. The thing is...'

Olivia spilled her heart to me like never before. Soon she was telling me everything about her disastrous weekend and her terrible falling out with her boyfriend. I was careful not to pass any judgment but just kept on providing her with a kind and loving pair of ears. I learned so much about her life - much of which would have curled the hair of any parent - and I'd always thought that my thinking was pretty liberal! A member of their group had made a drunken and clumsy pass at my daughter (I swallowed and remained calm) and it had scared her. Dave had not noticed or taken it seriously. My daughter had been distraught. It had all ended in a blazing row because he would not listen to her.

'So Dave just didn't listen to how you were feeling then, love?'

'That's right Dad, I was feeling scared and vulnerable and Dave was a total idiot so I lost it and dumped him and now I'm here.'

Suddenly she turned to me and gave me a huge hug. It was as if she was little again.

'Thanks for listening Dad. I couldn't have told Mum, she would have gone off her rocker! She didn't even know that I was going to a festival with Dave.'

That stunned me. Our daughter had played us both, but I kept listening and maintained my composure without judging or passing comment, just feeling genuinely and deeply compassionate. I had been dumped recently so I knew the pain of that. I had also dumped a few women in my time so I had no vantage point to judge from.

Chapter 13

'So you are worried what your Mum will say when Dave's suddenly no longer around?'

'Yup, kind of. Poor old Dave. He didn't really know what was going on. He's just like you. He wants to see the best in everybody. He thought that Paul was alright but he's horrible Dad. Really slimy and he scared me.'

I thought about it and gently stroked my daughter's damp hair. I could hear my hi-tech washing machine drying her clothes. Daisy came over and, like the evening before, rested her head on Olivia's knees and looked up with big sad eyes. I wondered just how much this dog actually understood.

'So you think that Dave meant well but got it wrong this time?'

'Yes Dad. He should have believed me. He should have got me out of there. He just wanted to make sure there was no scene. Well I gave him a scene alright.'

We both laughed at that, my daughter feeling relieved that she could tell someone and me feeling relief that she was OK.

'So I guess Dave just thought he was doing the right thing but panicked and got it wrong then.'

My daughter turned to me. Her eyes were full of tears.

'But how can I trust him Dad?'

'So you want to know if you can trust Dave to get it right next time?'

'Yes Dad, of course I do.'

'What does your gut tell you?'

I was desperately hoping that my compassionate listening was working. I must have been doing something right as my daughter then began to tell me, at great length, what a great guy Dave really was and eventually how much she loved him.

'I really shouted at him though Dad; in front of all our friends. I went ballistic.'

I winced. My lovely, kind and caring daughter had spoken to Dave in just the same way I would have. I wondered who she had inherited that speech pattern from. I knew I didn't have to look far.

'So you are worried that he might not forgive you for being scared and getting it wrong and now you see that Dave was as scared as you?'

'Dave, scared?'

'Maybe Dave was scared of making a scene, mucking up the festival for all your friends, starting a fight and upsetting you; and he simply made the wrong decision. Haven't you ever got it wrong sometimes love? I know I have.'

'Yup I guess you're right Dad. Oh poor old Dave. Dad lend me your phone, mine's out of charge.'

So, several hours later I waved off my clean and dry daughter with a great feeling of wellbeing and love in my heart. I was sad to say goodbye to my newfound doggy friend and was surprised when a very grateful and muddy Dave turned up to drive them all off on their long journey south.

As the flat returned to its usual quietness I realized that I kind of missed the hustle and bustle. I sat down to gather my thoughts when a text appeared on my phone.

Dad. Thanks for being such a great listener. Thanks for your advice. Omg what did you do to Daisy? She's so well behaved. Can you look after her next time we go away? xxxxxx

I swear I heard Amy chuckle from some far off place.

# Chapter Fourteen

It was a glorious day. One of those days when the warm southerly winds tiptoe through the city, tickling the senses with promises of exotic lands. We were blessed with breezes that had travelled all the way from the Sahara right up to Scotland. Soft winds combined with dappled, autumnal sunshine to make the act of simply stepping into the park one of joy. My usual early-morning walk to the university was transformed into a mindful stroll in paradise. When the gods of weather conspire to gift Glasgow with the very best they have to offer there is quite honestly no other city on the planet that I would rather live in. A quiet amble out into the surrounding hills would persuade even the most sceptical. A gentle glance around with the eyes of those who can see reveals the deep green colour of life joining up the whole world. No sparseness or scorched scrub, just autumnal bursts of red, orange and gold from the leaves of the birch, lime, ash and chestnut.

I allowed myself to walk mindfully, slowly, being present with every moment. I noticed every detail of the surrounding park and drew deep inhalations of the nutty aroma of the last few breaths of the trees before they retreated inside themselves for the winter ordeal. I found myself just standing, looking up through the brightly coloured leaves at the clear blue sky and marvelling at the complex detail of the miracle of life that surrounded me. My breathing was in harmony with my sense of peace and I allowed myself to simply stand and reflect on one particularly beautiful sycamore.

Hearing a rustling sound nearby, I turned slowly to find a red-haired girl of about six or seven in a bright red coat and red wellies. She was happily kicking her way through piles of leaves that had been scooped up into small mountains of fiery splendour along the path. Amy was singing to herself, paying me no attention whatsoever and enjoying every minute of the morning sun. I watched her, smiling with an indulgent pleasure, as she executed lavish twirls and ninja-like dance moves, sending leaves high into the air.

After a few minutes Amy looked up and noticed me watching her. She beamed me a huge smile and began to kick leaves in my general direction as she made a beeline towards me. As she approached I noticed that she appeared different. She was kind of glowing at the edges, and had a softness to her features. Her hair seemed an even brighter red than normal. There were moments when the sun's light seemed to pass right through her, then she would kick up some leaves and move into solidity again. It wasn't long before she stood at my feet looking up at me with a wide smile and eyes as blue as the sky.

*Hello my dearest Michael. Just glorious isn't it?*

Amy said the word glorious as if she was chewing a huge toffee, extending the vowel sounds to make the word itself delightful. If she were an adult I would have thought that she was tipsy.

'Days like this Amy are what it's all about.'

I was smiling; my diminutive teacher only used my real name when she was pleased with me. I needn't have worried - in a moment she'd reverted to type.

*So my dearest Phoney, have you arrived at last? Do you now see deeply into your heart? Have you found the gift that awaits you? Are you ready to pick up your life again and dive into the flow of the universe with a joyful heart and peaceful mind?*

'I guess I am Amy, I guess I am.'

*That's good Phoney. Let's check in with a few things to put it to the test shall we?*

Amy was obviously pretending to be a teacher as she motioned to me to sit down on a nearby park bench. I sat down good-humouredly and Amy hopped up beside me and began to swing her legs, humming away to herself. The view of the whole park stretched out in front of us. As we sat in silence for a few minutes I noticed that many of the people strolling through seemed to be pausing to take in the park's beauty.

'It seems that we are not the only ones enjoying the park today Amy.'

*It's the city, Phoney. The city is breathing as one today. Not many cities can do that. Glasgow can. Haven't you noticed that before?*

'Breathing as one?'

*Yup, everybody has the same feeling, is enjoying the same idea, the same emotion, the same kind of day. It's a sunny-together kind of day.*

Amy kept on humming to herself as she talked to me. It was an amazing feat. Was she humming aloud and speaking to me in my mind or speaking out loud and humming to me in my mind?

'Well I guess you're right as usual, I have often noticed how a mood can zoom to affect everyone some days. Mind you, that's usually when it's a general feeling of being cross or annoyed or edgy or something, but yes, I know what you mean. Why do you ask?'

*We all share the same emotions you know Phoney. Everybody on the planet has the same emotions*

'Do you mean that emotions are universal, some kind of universal truth or something?'

> *Yup. Universes. I like that, 'universes of emotion'. You see my dear Phoney we are all one, we just forget it. Sometimes we remember though. Sometimes we all remember the emotional universe that we all are, at the same time, just for a short while. So we get a great big old universal warmy dormy feeling in our tummies and, for a little bitty moment, we all share the same smile.*

'Warmy dormy? Is that a word? So it's a good thing when the city experiences itself in some kind of collective way then?'

> *Well what did the faces tell you this morning?*

'The faces?'

> *Yes Phoney, the faces of everybody you passed by as you walked? Be still, reflect for a moment. Remember.*

As I let the gentle fingers of the morning sunshine stroke my face I closed my eyes and let myself retrace my steps out of my flat, along the roads and into the park. Amy was right. I could see the faces that I had passed and everybody had seemed to be in a good mood. I had greeted my neighbour with the rhetorical question of 'glorious morning isn't it?' and had been greeted with a smile and a nod. One street later a colleague had passed me and had used the same greeting. As I replayed my short journey I realised that my newfound practise of smiling at people, rather than frowning or ignoring them, had been rewarded constantly by a variety of smiles and nods. I remembered passing a group of my students who had all smiled at me and wished me a good morning rather than hurrying past full of anxiety about late essays. Everyone I had encountered had seemed to radiate the same grateful appreciation of the day itself, of the Indian summer, of the warm breeze and the soft sunshine.

'Yes you're right Amy. Just about everybody I saw seemed to

share my feeling of peace and joy.'

*Not your feeling of peace and joy Phoney. THE feeling of peace and joy. The state of bliss and joy is everywhere all the time. It's inside you and outside of you; it is the deepest truth you have. It will guide you and nurture you as it will every living being on this planet. Every human, every animal and every tree. You've found your joy at last Phoney.*

'Tree?'

*Look at the starlings Phoney. See them dance together. They do this to remember. To link their minds, to reaffirm their oneness. This is the place of joy, the place of deep remembering. We can only truly feel joy in that universe of oneness Phoney. To get there you have to feel it for yourself first, that's all, it's simple. And now you can. Yay!*

I watched the starlings as they swooped and shoaled in their thousands just above the spire of the university building. As I looked down into the park I could see that other people on their way to work had also paused to experience this marvel. Amy was humming an enchanting song - it seemed to soar in time with the starlings as they swooped and paint-brushed their way across the clear palette of the autumn sky. The melody was haunting, it sounded Arabic or Celtic and slightly like a lullaby at the same time.

'So you are saying that joy, the emotion of joy, is the deepest and most important emotion that we can experience, individually and collectively?'

*That's right Phoney. Joy is a better word than happiness. Just like you are feeling it right now. With joy the whole world feels easy; you stop straining and relax into life. No anxiety. No struggle. Just a sense of ease and simplicity. It's the truth that every newborn child knows with their whole being. All children know this. It is their guiding star. It is the light that they steer by and that they learn by. Joy is the truth that sets us all free to play. You could never have felt it before Phoney. You were only able to experience the shades of your suffering, not the brilliant colours of your joy.*

Amy jumped down from the bench and began to do a slow stompy dance in the leaves that had been carefully piled up. My joie de vivre remained as did my deep stillness and sense of peace. I could feel what Amy was saying as a truth that linked up every cell in my body. I breathed in peace and I breathed out peace. I felt my smile naturally take over my face and I sighed deeply and watched Amy as she played directly in front of me. I am not sure that I had ever felt so contented. Amy brought her leaf dance closer.

*All the little beings that make you up Phoney are in love with each other. They all come together to create the most marvellous great big single being that is you. Millions and millions of cells and inside those cells are even smaller life forms that work tirelessly with joy to make sure that you can exist. If you exist so can they. It is a deep truth. Joy is the flowering of life. Joy is the result of love. Joy is what you really are made up of. All of this sitting, all of this practice, all of my teachings have been to help you reconnect, to remember this deep truth. Physical life exists to teach us this truth.*

'To remember my joy?'

Amy picked up a huge pile of leaves and threw them high into the air, which was no mean feat for somebody as short as her.

*To remember that you ARE joy Michael. Joy is your natural and rightful state of being. Not fear. Not suffering. Not pain or anxiety. As above Michael, so below. All the smallest things that exist in this universe work together through love and through attraction, just so they can experience joy. The absolute joy of being. Being joyful.*

*Joyfully being. He he. All the largest stars and galaxies in the universe move in a dance of joyful attraction and oneness. Their dance goes on and on and on. All you have to do is wake up to it.*

Amy was somehow making the leaves that she threw into the air above her head form intricate patterns that seemed to mimic the flights of the starlings. As the leaves slowly fell to earth they danced as if caught in a gentle breeze until most of them covered both our heads - much to Amy's amusement. I smiled; Amy was somehow both young and old at the same time. She was childlike and wise beyond her years. She seemed unhurried yet excited at the same time and quite unaware that she was using all sorts of long words. I hadn't seen Amy in quite such a reverie before and it made me smile. I felt her joy as my joy and as I looked out across the park the whole scene seemed to shimmer and come alive.

'Is that what I am experiencing today Amy? My truth, my joy, my own childlike joy and sense of wonder?'

*Yes my dear. My work is almost done. We just need to look at a couple of final things. Because you live in a city where its people are still open to truth, to an idea of oneness, wonderful days like this can occur. Usually days like these only happen in smaller villages or tribes. Big cities make people live in very small, separate universes based on fear and anxiety. Only the experience of oneness allows the experience of joy to occur. We are all part of each other, of everything. Nothing is not part of something else.*

'So why do I get so many days of feeling miserable and ...?'

*Grumpy! Yes Phoney. We just need to notice our grumps before they arise, before they get up, yawn and then take over our days and our whole lives.*

'So I've just got to notice my negative moods before they get up and take over?'

> *That's what we are going to solve. That's today's final
> lesson. You simply keep on forgetting to notice that you
> fall into a bad habit of grumpy separation. You allowed
> yourself to believe that fear was the guiding principle of
> life. You stopped practising joy. You lost your sparkle. You
> lost your magic. But guess what, it was always there all
> along. Fabby eh?*

'Is that what Hazel meant about me not being happy then?'

Amy was skipping and dancing and twirling but as I asked my
question she stopped, looked at me and frowned for the briefest
of moments. Then she approached me, pretending to be a tiger
or something.

> *Hazel sees you Phoney because she loves you.*

'Well she doesn't love me because she chose not to be with me.'

Amy started to laugh and spin slowly again.

> *Of course she loves you. The truth is a all of you humans
> love each other all the time. You actually can't not love
> each other. It's impossible. You just try so hard to forget.
> You do everything in your power to not love each other. It's
> really funny to watch. You do this because you want to be
> miserable. You choose to live in fear. You choose to create
> fear as your guiding star. Then you work to create stories
> about how different you all are. You divide each other up
> into smaller and smaller groups. You separate, you draw
> apart. Joy pulls you together. Joy is what keeps you togeth-
> er. Joy is what attracts you to each other.*

'So Hazel is not with me because she's fearful that I'm still a
grumpy old sod? She's still scared of me because she thinks I've
lost my joy and if I've lost mine then I will deny Hazel her own

joy?'

I could see my old self and my present self so clearly. It was as if we stood alongside each other in my mind. My old self was grey, grumpy, fearful, negative and critical and my new self was, well, just simply joyful.

I quickly realised that I wouldn't have chosen to remain with my old self for very long.

> *Maybe Hazel knows that she is with you on the universal level Phoney. Maybe she has been waiting for this day to happen, for you to finally wake up and arrive so that she can truly know if you guys can actually be together.*

'She said we couldn't because I wasn't happy.'

> *Well even though you had done quite a lot of work by then my dear Phoney, you just hadn't got the most important bit.*

'Huh?'

> *Well you were still motivated by fear and separation. Come on, be truthful with me, you have been stewing in grumpiness all week haven't you? Today the universe has given you a lift but what happens tomorrow?*

'But I love her Amy. That's not fearful. You taught me not to be needy. I've let go of so much.'

> *What have you been stressing about all week?*

I took a deep breath. My peace and joy was being ruffled. Yet I knew Amy had my best interests at heart and she was always, annoyingly, right.

'Well I've felt kind of adrift. I've felt unsure of where I'm going, what I should be doing with my life. I've not been stressing though. I've felt really peaceful and actually quite happy, and erm...even joyful and contented.'

*Don't lose your peace Phoney. I know it's going to be fun for you now. You're just not sure of what to do and where to go because at long last you have lost your usual reason for doing things.*

'You're right, I feel like I've lost my motivation. I've been practising hard, I've been working hard, my lectures are going well, yet I just don't know what to do next.'

It was so true, yet I didn't want to sound like a whiney ungrateful child. My practice was going so well and I was able to find my peace by following my breathing every morning. Most days my sense of ease and joyfulness would last until at least the late afternoon, depending on the day. I found that being mindful didn't just mean forgetting everything around me but in fact made it simpler to meet the various pressures and demands of the day head on. Yet Amy was right, I was feeling adrift on the calm millpond of my mind.

'Maybe I should just give it all up Amy and head off around the world and just see where it all takes me? I seem to have lost my reason for doing anything.'

*It's okay Phoney. That's because you are finally rising above the clouds and can see so much further now.*

I had to admit that for the first time I was managing to maintain my positive emotional altitude. I felt like I had learned to fly. I had risen above my heaviness and my nagging anxieties... well, most of the time.

Amy made me laugh as she spun round wearing ridiculously large sunglasses.

*A holiday might be fun Phoney! We could go to the cake capital of the world and just munch sweet things all day long.*

I felt a burst of excitement.

'Yes and we could just keep on travelling from cake shop to cake shop keeping fit by mindfully walking from city to city and from country to country. Mind you how will I ever find my motivation in cake shops?'

Amy grinned at me and swapped her sunglasses for a sombrero and a miniature fake moustache. I burst out laughing.

*You are asking the right questions for a change Phoney. Listen, you haven't been watering the seeds of suffering, just the seeds of happiness and now you have lost something that you always had. You've lost your motivation for doing things.*

'I've lost my motivation! Yippee, let's holiday for ever!'

I laughed as Amy and I did a careful dance, which involved her spinning around a lot with me holding onto her raised hand so that she didn't fall over. My lack of purpose did seem absurd yet I had been worrying about it. I had kind of felt that I was stuck, that I couldn't move forwards. I felt slightly aimless and was beginning to feel confused again. Amy sensed or read my thoughts and slowed her dance whilst still humming.

*My dear Phoney, you are confused because you are free now. For the first time. You are free from fear. You are free from being made to do things from a place of fear. You are right; you have always been motivated by fear. You have run after things out of the fear of not enough, of loss, of death, of deadlines, of ego and loads of scary things. You have chased shadows because you were still in your prison. You fuelled yourself on caffeine and*

*adrenaline. Now that you have gone deeper and have
connected with the universal truth of joy you are at a loss.
Am I right?*

I was surprised that Amy actually asked me if she was right or
not, yet I guess she was being rhetorical. You could never tell with
Amy.

'Yes, I guess you're right.'

I sat down for a moment to catch my breath. Truthfully I had
always lacked motivation. I had often built huge deadlines into
my life and then allowed the fear of not meeting them to spur
me on. I guess that I'd been motivated by stress. As I breathed
slowly again and reflected on my life I could see that I had indeed
spent my time continually running away from fears, worries and
anxieties towards scary and impending deadlines. In fact, as I
pondered some more, and Amy made her sombrero turn into
a fez, I realised that even my nagging worry about losing my
motivation was creating a motivation of fear and worry about that
very thought. No wonder I had tripped myself up so often in the
past! Amy gave one last spin and then jumped up onto my lap.
I was quite surprised; she usually kept me at arm's length. She
smelt so fragrant, like a whole flowerbed of roses, an entire rose
garden in full bloom. Amy looked up into my eyes and smiled at
me.

*So Phoney, now that you are real, now that you are free
from following fear, you simply have to remember to
choose to follow your heart, follow your deep sense of joy
and peace. You can let your joy guide you. You can follow
your heart and not your grumpiness and depression and
nasty habits. That way the negative seeds won't get wa-
tered and won't grow and you will be weed free!!*

I laughed as I remembered my damp feet and the spontaneous
growth of flowers in the garden centre. Amy handed me a bright
red and gold leaf that shone in the sun.

*Learn to follow what brings you happiness Phoney, and also follow what brings happiness and healing to others. In fact, bringing happiness and joy to others is the only real way to feel true and lasting joy. Can I have an ice-cream?*

Amy leapt off my knee and rushed over to stand beside a large bush. I marvelled as a small robin hopped onto her dainty outstretched finger and ate some crumbs off her hand.

'So I just need to be diligent in my new found state of peace and joy? I just need to let my sense of peace and joy guide me?'

I heard Amy's voice in my head; I guess she didn't want to frighten the robin away.

*Follow the middle way Michael; don't be too strict or too indulgent. Find the way to practise that suits you best. You have a fear-based tendency to over-do it, to practise too hard. Just chill out and find your own easy way Phoney.*

That was also true. As I watched Amy quietly feed the small bird I remembered how I always tried too hard when I began anything. I had been the same when I was a child and then later at school and university. I guess that it came from expecting a beating at home if I didn't pass a test first time. I sent a mental picture of wellbeing and understanding to my inner child and told him that I wouldn't do that anymore. I smiled as I felt an immediate sense of gratitude rise up within me. I looked up at Amy; she had of course seen everything and was smiling at me. Two small finches had now gathered on her arm. I whispered to Amy so as not to startle her newfound friends.

'So I need to choose to walk the middle path that the Buddhists talk about, the one that lies between excesses of austerity and of concual indulgence? I just need to be careful not to be extreme in anything that I do?'

# Chapter 14

Amy ran out of cake crumbs and the birds flew off, chattering to themselves. I wondered what on earth they were saying about Amy. She turned to me and smiled again.

*It's all about keeping up a gentle state of focus my dear Michael. That means not being too excited, not too dull, not too high or too low. With your breath find your balance in all things. It might take a while. Some occasions will require more balance than others. When I feed the birds I don't sing and dance but I balance myself in stillness. That doesn't mean that I'm not singing and dancing inside with total joyfulness though.*

Amy was mimicking walking a tightrope across the leafy path back towards me. I marvelled at the way she always let me arrive at my own conclusions about things, yet somehow left me realising that she had guided me there all along.

'So I have to choose to be balanced? I guess that means not hanging on to things and making them bigger and heavier than they need to be. Letting go and kind of going with the flow, responding to what's needed. So it's a kind of motivation that isn't motivation then?'

*Yes, look at the wind dancing over those leaves. When the wind stops the leaves are still. They don't try to dance on their own. When those starlings fly over the pond, their reflections skim over the surface. Once they are gone the pond's surface doesn't try to hold on to their images.*

'So I just have to welcome anything that comes along and then let it go once it's passed.'

*That's it Phoney, right concentration. Once the excitement has passed, become still again, all nice and safe and snuggly in your joy.*

'Right concentration? So motivation arises when you concentrate in the right way? What if I am working on something though? It might take me a long time to finish it or learn it. I might need to keep on hanging onto the thoughts, let them play out over days, maybe even weeks?'

Amy plucked a lollipop out of her pocket and then balanced it on her nose. She was absorbed yet I still heard her voice in my head.

*Just choose the one thing that you are doing and concentrate on it in the same still and joyful way. Don't have the TV on, don't think about or do other things, abandon all of your, 'grasshopper jumping-about energy' and be present. Be stable and meet each moment naturally. Make your life effortless.*

Amy spoke the last few words and, as if to prove her point that doing two things at once wasn't a good idea, the lollipop fell off her nose and onto the floor. Amy laughed, picked it up, took off the wrapper and turned to me again.

*It's actually impossible to do two things at once. We might think that we are, but if we try we'll immediately lose our mindfulness and stop being there. We won't exist and the jobs will not get done well. We won't be present in the moment.*

'So I just need to become absorbed in the moment and concentrate on staying there?'

Amy kicked some leaves into the air. One leaf was picked up by the wind. It was as if it was on an invisible wire. We both watched it as it spiralled upwards, dodging trees and branches and even birds. The leaf seemed to be the wind, it seemed to be part of the sky, it was part of the whole view of the park and I became aware that both Amy and I were sharing the moment at the same time. The leaf danced up higher and higher, swirling round and round until it flew over a distant rooftop and disappeared. As it vanished Amy spun round and looked up at me.

*Fun eh Phoney? Being there; with the moment. Really noticing everything about it.*

'There's nothing quite like it.'

I answered truthfully and then laughed out loud as Amy proudly pulled the lollipop out of her mouth and made a huge popping sound. So that's why they were called lolli-pops! She popped it back into her mouth again and sucked hard as she focussed on what she was saying. She took the lollipop out of her mouth and then spoke very slowly and made the long words sound as if she was reading from a book:

*Eventually concentrating in the right way will allow us to touch the absolute dimension of reality.*

'Huh, absolute...dimension...reality, wow did you swallow a dictionary Amy?'

*You like long words for big thoughts Phoney. Look my dear you can learn to walk, look, eat and breathe in such a way that you will rise above all of your scary old fears that are attached to your ideas of reality Phoney. You will rise above any ideas you have of who you are, and who you are not. You will rise above ideas of one and many, me and you, you and them. The thing is Phoney, you will touch the very joyful nature of nirvana.*

I was transfixed. Amy was actually beginning to float just above the ground. She was levitating just above the leaves and the damp grass. Her face was beatific, it shone like the sun and she looked blissful as her red curls floated all around her face. I rubbed my eyes in disbelief and then realised that I was definitely not in 'Kansas' anymore, in fact I hadn't been since Amy had first blazed into my life. My words stumbled out of my mouth.

'Nirvana, heaven on earth, the enlightened state of being! Me, this lifetime - really?'

Amy gave a small chuckle of delight and plumped back to the ground and began to swish leaves with the toe of her boot.

*Yes Phoney, you are now seeing the true nature of reality. Because you can be still and rest in the now, the actual moment of being here, like with that leaf a moment ago, you can see what is real and what is only an illusion.*

I rubbed my eyes again as the world around me began to glow ever so slightly. The whole park seemed to shimmer. I sensed energy swirling around me as Amy spoke.

'So right now my consciousness, my perception, my experience is real and not a made up idea of something? Not just some illusion that I am projecting?'

*Yes Phoney, you will be able to discern what is real and what is just a sign, a symbol, an impression of truth. Your laughter will be joyful. Your joy will have no beginning and no end. You will be free in the knowledge that everything changes all the time. Nothing stays the same. The practise is staying in this wonderful place that we call life and letting our joy flood through us.*

As I slowly looked around, it seemed as if the bright red, falling leaves slowed down their descent from the branches of the trees and began to rise up again. Amy was shimmering and ever so slightly transparent again.

*If you remain in the present then you won't make yourself unhappy. You won't wear yourself out trying to preserve a reality that is false Michael. Remember, the surface of the duck pond does not try to hold on to the reflection of the ducks as they fly over it.*

As Amy was speaking a vivid picture of Hazel came into my mind. I could see her at home, baking. She looked sad. She was wiping a tear from her eye and pushing her hair away from her face as she opened the door of the oven.

'So my problem has been that I keep on trying to hold onto a reality of Hazel and myself together but don't simply let us just be. Erm…be joyful and present? So that is why I feel my joy at last Amy? Is it because I've let go of trying to hold on to things? Erm, stopped trying to hold onto ideas of what is and what isn't?'

*Yup, things don't exist, only now does.*

I watched the leaves dancing in the air again. My deep sense of joy and peace returned. I sensed that I was still at the beginning of something but somehow being where I was seemed OK. Amy read my thoughts and threw another huge handful of leaves up into the air. They seemed to fall exquisitely slowly, making a spiral shape as they danced on the gentle breeze.

*Yup. So, what do you want do then Phoney? What's your Right Livelihood going to be?*

'I'm not sure yet Amy. I'm not sure if I've ever been able to ask that question of myself before, not really, not just from my heart.'

*Well that was your block. You have never allowed yourself to ask the question from a place of joy and peace. Very few people actually do. Now you can allow yourself to ask the question, 'What do I wish to do that matches with my sense of joy and peace?'*

'So I have to align my thinking with being peaceful and joyful and the answer will come?'

*Ask and ye shall receive Michael, seek and ye shall find. It's the truth that will guide you now Michael. Now then, time to go to work.*

'Oh yes, whoops I must rush or I'll be late.'

*No, you can choose to skip all the way there with me and enjoy the journey in a new way happy in the knowledge that you are going to be the very best of yourself when you arrive. It's time to play Michael. It's time to discover your true destiny. Maybe we will need to meet up one more time. Oh come on - I'll race you.*

The world became 'real' again. Amy skipped off down the hill towards the university at quite a pace for a 'wee lassie'. She was laughing with excitement as she tried to skip down the hill whilst kicking up leaves at the same time. I laughed out loud and, without a care in the world, set off skipping down the hill behind her.

# Chapter Fifteen

The next few weeks passed quickly. My inner joy proved to be infectious. Perhaps it was what Amy had said about us all being connected at some level. My sense of humour was with me more often than not. In fact I noticed that my sense of humour had changed. I had lost all my sarcastic wit, clever put-downs and intellectual mocking. In its place I discovered that I could laugh with others, not at them but with them. I found that I could laugh with anybody because I realised that we were all noticing the same absurdity of our suffering and our ridiculous habit of choosing the worst for ourselves. This was the cause of our laughter, self-effacing and compassionate. Maybe it was Einstein's idea of spooky entanglement but I found that the more joyful I was, the more joy showed up in the lives of the people I met and worked with.

And the more I chose to engage mindfully with my day, the more time I seemed to have to practise. The more I practised whilst walking, sitting or even lying down, the greater the number of minor revelations about myself and the nature of reality I experienced. Amy told me that the most important revelations are ones that concern ourselves. She told me one evening over cake and herbal tea that the only wisdom worth entertaining is that which sets us free. She said that when we practise with mindfulness and compassion, our inner enlightenment also works to set the world free. Then of course she sent me into a panic by pointing out that all our negative thoughts create karma, which we then have to release.

I discovered that the more I sat in my inner joy, free from suffering, the more my reality seemed to change - so much so that it left me pondering over every aspect of my life and my work. I let my joyfulness guide me and found that I had a new motivation.  It was simple really, just to leave people feeling better than when I found them.

With regular practise I managed to remain in a joyful and blissful state more often than not. My meditative reflections revealed that so many of my old beliefs about my world were just illusions based in fear. As I practised letting go of them, my mind grew clearer and clearer. I soon discovered that the state of happiness was ephemeral, illusory and always based on some kind of external event or fact or reality. As meditation became part of my everyday life I noticed that I stopped chasing happiness and rather chose to experience bliss. I realised that I had never really examined what I wanted to do from a place of joy. I had always thought that happiness was the destination rather than the beginning, middle and end of any journey. So I sat down and reflected on my hopes and desires and went in search of my own inner truth. What was my path, my destiny as Amy had called it? What did I want to do? What could I do that would benefit both myself and other people?

So I wasn't surprised to wake up wonderfully rested one morning, to find a thick pad of writing paper and a box of pens on the table in the kitchen.

I sat down to write myself a list of my hopes and dreams but always ended up staring at a blank page. What was it that I wanted to do? Where would joy lead me? As I reflected on my goals and motivation, the first thing that came into my head was to go and join the student meditation group again.

That was a surprise. I put my pen down and reflected on the thought. I realised that I missed my connection with my young friends. Their peaceful energy had started to permeate our department, bringing students from other departments to visit us. At seminars and after lectures I had begun to receive a lot of requests from students to join them again. I seemed to have found a new way of relating to young people. I identified with them and their challenges. I strove to make my approach more involving and the learning more applicable to their lives and realities. Apparently my lectures had become far more exciting and inspirational and were always full. I had found so much extra energy that it seemed to engulf the lecture hall. Almost nobody fell asleep now - unless of course they had really bad hangovers - and I'd found a much more humorous and maybe Amy-style way to teach the subjects. One student had even told me that my lectures were the only ones that really made any sense to him. I took that as a compliment but wondered just how bad they must have been before.

The requests to re-join the meditation and mindfulness group, the Wake Up session, became more regular. I hadn't wanted to intrude but I began to see that I did miss the sessions. As I sat at my table chewing the end of my pen I pondered on my dilemma and smiled at my reasons for not going. I realised that I had begun to make excuses as I sensed all was not quite well in the group. How selfish of me. I didn't want the 'negative vibes man'! I chuckled as I realised that I had thought I should remain aloof and let them deal with their own group and its challenges. Yet my joy made me put my pen down, pick up my bag and head for the door. Glancing at my watch I realised that it was still early enough so I headed off to join them for the morning practice. From my place of calm it felt like the right thing to do.

As I walked I engaged my mindful breathing and concentration. I gently waited for the tiredness and sleep to leave my body. I allowed my joy to rise up inside me. I moved gently through the early morning rush of commuters, school pupils and occasional students heading home, letting myself focus on each step and then my surroundings. I allowed myself to let others rush pass, to weave a kind of slow dance in and out of the stream of people, and marvelled at the fact that we were ultimately all one. I paused beside a doorway and exchanged some early morning pleasantries with a homeless man, popping a few coins in his paper cup before climbing the steep hill towards the university. The trees were nearly bare now and the wind smelt of rain and promised a wet day. I saw some tiny tots splashing in a puddle outside the school gates and was reminded of Amy and her abiding love of puddles and red welly boots.

Amy hadn't made an appearance in days, apart from a few cryptic marks on the fridge door that I took to mean buy more cake but she hadn't visited me. The cakes in the fridge marked the passage of time by going mouldy. On reflection I had begun to realise that she had usually shown up when I was stressed or upset or losing it. Maybe that was why my diminutive flame-haired friend hadn't made an appearance. Maybe it was down to me now.

I entered the department building and headed into the lecture theatre. I was early and only a couple of students were there. I recognised Sarah and wandered over to her, humming to myself.

'Hello Sarah, how are you this fine morning?'

'Oh Michael, great to see you. My essay will be finished soon...'

I waved my hand at the classic student-lecturer greeting and smiled.

'So I'm early then?'

'Yes but I'm so glad you're here.'

Sarah glanced at her friend who was preparing to light some incense.

'It's all got a bit carried away you see. Everybody is beginning to get a bit erm...intense, a bit heated.'

Sarah began to chew on her nails nervously. I felt a moment of alarm. Sarah had transformed into a confident student over the past few months - she was first class material now, everybody agreed. I was picking up on her anxiety and noticed some dark circles under her eyes.

'So you're saying that some of the students are taking things a bit too seriously and are causing you some degree of anxiety?'

'Exactly. It's become a bit of a competition. Everybody seems to be out-enlightening everybody else. Some of the guys are insisting on Buddhist rituals now. Some of the Christians are declaring that we should begin with prayers. A couple of nice Muslim ladies are getting nervous and some of the mindfulness practitioners are asserting that we don't speak at all and one yogini wants us to practise yoga at the same time.'

Sarah paused to draw breath so I quietly picked up one of the bells and struck it gently.

'Let's just enjoy the bell for a moment Sarah and let our breathing return to its peaceful level.'

I smiled as Sarah gave a huge sigh of relief and stood quietly with her friend and myself until the very last vibration of the bell had vanished back into the silence of the hall. Within the gap I allowed myself to become still and reflect on what I had just learnt. After the bell fell silent I quietly began to help move the chairs back to make a space for meditation and the girls did the same. We moved carefully, mindfully and remained silent. I sensed that there was a question hanging in the air. I paused and watched the two young women prepare the room. The question was deep inside me. I sensed it rise up from my newfound place of joy until it arrived in my consciousness not as a question but as a statement. Just at that moment both women paused and looked up at me.

'Would it be okay if I re-joined the morning meditation group? I need the daily input of the energy of my fellow travellers. I would love to help your group in any way you wanted.'

Sarah and her friend gave a long sigh of relief and both spoke at the same time, saying that they would love it if I made the effort to join them. I sensed that my presence gave them the confidence to let go of their worries.

# Chapter 15

'So how would you like the mornings to run then?'

'Without any politics,' Sarah answered forcefully.

'Politics?' I wasn't surprised. Over the last few weeks I had purposely untangled myself from the web of political intrigue that ran through the hallowed halls of the university. Politics had begun to seem pointless and self-serving. It was exhausting and usually resulted in more suffering. Amy had once pointed out to my confused head that the word politics had been hijacked. I never had been very good at departmental politics anyway and that was probably why I hadn't progressed too far up the ladder.

As we began to lay out the room I recalled my conversation with Amy. It had happened one morning, early on in our relationship, whilst I was trying very grumpily to read my newspaper. She had jumped up on the table and had pulled down the newspaper to challenge me.

> Don't just hide inside all that smelly old boring and depressing newsy stuff Phoney. You are meant to be looking for good news. You have to find the good news inside you. Politics is all about selfish people looking out for themselves.

'All human interaction is political Amy. Now go away and eat some cake.'

> Politics is when people try to get what they want at the expense of everybody else so that they can be more powerful. Mostly it's just people being bullies who are scared that they won't win and they are not even playing fairly. It's a great big game and they all just play it but have forgotten about why they were there in the first place. It's not mindful or compassionate or joyful Phoney.

I had wearily lowered the paper and stared at Amy across the table.

'So you are saying that in your opinion politics is just about self-interested advancement and plays for power originating from a fear-based reality?'

> *Big words don't make it any different Phoney. Real politics is when people all sit down together, maybe over a nice cup of tea and some cake and share why they are meeting up in a nice open way.*

'That's not practical Amy and...'

> *Yes it is, then the game's not fear-based and people don't get all excited about beating each other up with clever words and backstabbing each other and stuff. Besides, most politicians don't speak truthfully about what their voters want anyway.*

I'd listened to Amy as she got passionate about the subject. To be honest, I'd been quite surprised that she was even interested.

'So then Amy, what you are saying is that true politics is simply the coming together of representatives of interest groups to work out how they might best work together for the common good.'

> *Well that's how I said it. Everyone should all sit down for a cup of tea, forget their fears and let answers pop into their heads. It's easy if you are mindful.*

'You are just being naïve Amy.'

> *You and all the smelly old politicians are just addicted to old habits all built on fear. When people sit together in quiet meditation the best answers always appear. All the best answers to all the best questions already exist Phoney. You just have to listen out for them. You can't do that if you are scared or in competition with someone else. Humans are just addicted to the darkening of politics and won't allow themselves to admit that it just doesn't work*

*properly without mindfulness and love and light and real,*
*truthful compassion.*

As I put out the last few cushions, I recalled how Amy had sent
me off to a local Quakers meeting where the very exercise of
silent meditation on group questions had been practised for a
very long time. The experience had been enlightening. We all sat
in a circle. The question was asked. Then, to my disbelief, about
half an hour later we all stood up smiling at each other in the
knowledge that the answer had been received. It was always a
simple, uplifting answer that held the interests and wellbeing of
the whole group and the individual in perfect balance. No one
shouted, or argued, or tried to battle and bury each other with
lofty rhetoric in fierce debates. It wasn't anti-intellectual either as
many of the Quakers were scientists and academic people but
the answers were always simple and accessible to all gathered.

So, any time I encountered the 'darkening of politics' at
University, I did as Amy suggested and invited people to share a
cup of tea rather than meet to debate in an arena of competition
as inter-departmental meetings so often were. Actually, I avoided
official meetings. Instead I invested in high quality teas and filled
a large container with the best biscuits I could find. I limited the
length of any gathering to the time it took to drink a cup of tea.
Well, it worked for me and seemed to work for my colleagues and
students as well.

'And with some extra training sessions in meditation and
mindfulness maybe we can dump the politics and get back to
meditation without any purpose or intent Michael.'

Sarah jogged me out of my reflection. I decided to suggest that
we take a leaf out of the Quakers' book.

'Politics? Hmm, well you have to speak to express politics so why
not simply revert to how we began the sessions. Silence once
you enter the space until you leave. The purpose of this time is
to simply be present, to become still, to meditate, nothing else.
There is no desired outcome, no aim, no goal, just to experience

the truth of ourselves in the present moment so that we might bring peace to all living things.'

I smiled at my short speech. Maybe Amy had taught me well.

Sarah looked relieved.

'Yes please, that's perfect, you see that's the stuff we need to be taught so maybe you could offer extra sessions as well? We need a teacher.'

I paused and took a few breaths. Sarah's friend went to put a hastily-prepared 'Silence Please' notice on the outside of the door. Sarah looked at me expectantly.

'I might need to ask my teacher first Sarah. I'm a newbie at all this really.'

'When can you ask him?

'Her.'

'When can you ask her?'

'I'm not sure. She may be away on a...erm...retreat at the moment. I'll try and find out for tomorrow's session.'

That seemed to satisfy Sarah and she handed me the large Tibetan bell and a meditation cushion just as students filed into the room. I sat at the front, relaxed and breathing gently, watching and waiting. As each student entered the room he or she immediately became silent as they saw me and then approached a space on the floor and prepared themselves with all manner of cushions and blankets to get comfortable. The sessions were only forty minutes long so I was quite amused to see them preparing as if they were going to meditate for days.

The session passed uneventfully and peacefully. I allowed myself

Chapter 15

to observe the assembled group. I was impressed at the turnout. I noticed how some students were trying too hard as they sat with yoga-like rigidity, some in small groups and some, like Sarah exuding a peaceful and relaxed energy. I could see that some of the guys were sneaking glances at the female students and that some of the female students were sneaking glances back. There were a few gurgling stomachs, a slight hint of alcohol breath in the air (I was grateful for the incense) but apart from that everyone practised peacefully.

I practised a deep reflection on the oneness of the group, on the collective experience of joy and peace. I sensed the energy in the room gradually shift until it felt light and peaceful. As I gently opened my eyes and prepared to chime the bell to mark the end of the session, I smiled. Sitting at the very back was a small and shimmering figure. I felt so happy to see her. Then I had to do a double take as Amy floated above the students' heads and alighted at my feet. She gazed at me with clear concentration and her eyes seemed ancient and wise.

Before I could silently question Amy about her sudden flying skills and ask her exactly what she was doing, she vanished, leaving behind only the unmistakeable scent of wild roses.

I chimed the bell and smiled as the students opened their eyes and prepared to go out into the day. To my surprise some of them offered me short bows; some quietly walked up and shook my hand and some just nodded and smiled approvingly as they left. I realised that they all wanted the same thing. A teacher: someone to guide them just a little bit, to give them a nudge in the right direction. That's what Amy was and had been for me.

As the last person left, Sarah and her friend rose to put the chairs back, blow out the candle and snuff the incense sticks.

'Mmm, the incense smells amazing today Janey,' remarked Sarah to her friend.

'I know...' replied her friend, 'really natural - kind of roses and wild flowers.'

Sarah turned to me and fixed me with her smile.

'Thank you again Michael, you are becoming a bit of a guardian angel for me aren't you?'

'It's my job Sarah,' I replied and realised that a truth was growing inside me.

Amy had told me that deep inner truths create miracles of instant manifestation. I'd just thought that explained Amy's ability to make cake appear out of nowhere.

\* \* \* \* \* \* \*

Right after morning lectures I got a huge lesson in positive manifestation though it didn't feel very positive at first. In fact I lost my cool, got alarmed and wondered if I was going to be sacked. There were no subtleties as a breathless secretary burst into the tranquillity of my room and summoned me for an immediate meeting with the Dean. I marched behind her out of our department, across the quad and high into the lofty spires of the ancient university to the Dean's quarters.

The Dean was a sharp old man and gave me a long hard stare. His spectacles were perched on the end of his long thin nose and he looked like an old bird of prey eyeing up its next meal. His perfect and clipped voice broke the silence.

'Are we expecting some new publications soon Michael? Your department looks to you. You know that?'

It wasn't a request or an observation. It was an order, we both knew that.

Chapter 15

'Of course Dean, it's all planned out and I'm just about to deliver the first draft.'

'Good. Yes good.' The Dean seemed uncharacteristically unsure of himself. We both sat in silence as he twiddled his fingers. I was vaguely concerned and still worried that he was going to sack me yet I recognised something in his manner that I was now able to see very clearly in people. Fear. The Dean was worried about something. Oh lordy, what had I done to unsettle the calmest man in the university? The Dean leant forward and unexpectedly dropped his usual formality. His face and voice softened.

'Erm, look old chap, this university prides itself on its academic qualities.'

'Of course, Dean.'  Oh hell, I was for the bullet!

'Yes, well, it appears that's not enough these days. It's all the foreign students and fee-paying families you see. They are demanding a different level of student support and, well, the board and I are not too sure how to go about it. Apparently a lot of students suffer from stress and depression and a whole range of other mental health issues. All things we didn't even know about in my day.'

He looked expectantly at me. I just sat and breathed and waited for him to get to the point. Part of me wondered if I was about to go on a long enforced holiday with Amy.

'Well the thing is, Michael, you seem to have done great work in your department. I mean in your student welfare programme. Your head of department was telling me how pleased she was at how you have nurtured some of our best students.'

I smiled and realised that Clair, my head of department, had set me up. It was hardly a student welfare programme. My tea-cup meetings and support of the meditation group hardly constituted a wellbeing programme. Still I couldn't help wonder where the

Dean was going with all this.

'Look, this mindfulness thing that you have got them all doing, it seems to work. I checked out the science, it all reads well, seems it's even been accepted at Oxford now. I mean the blighters are actually teaching it. Well, look I know how passionate you are about your subject but, well, how would you feel about setting up a small new department? One that erm focusses on all this wellbeing stuff. You know, maybe write a few articles, invite in a few speakers, set up some programmes. Of course you could still have your lectures, if you wanted, if you had erm...time?'

I was stunned but chose to just sit quietly for a few seconds longer whilst preparing my answer. This was a bolt out of the blue yet it felt absolutely right. I sensed a joyful flicker deep within me. I felt a bit like a child receiving the present that he hadn't even dared ask for.

'Look it would be in the top pay scale,' continued the Dean obviously confusing my silence with aversion to the idea. 'It would have to be just you and maybe one other if the numbers grow like they have been doing. Maybe that lovely wife of yours could work with you and fit it around her writing projects? All properly financed of course. I hear that she is a meditation person as well.'

The Dean was, as always, very well-informed.

'Well, that may work...but she and I are...'

'Great, wonderful, fantastic! Draw up a proposed programme and I'll green light it before the new term. I'll need you to write some blurb for the new University prospectus. We'll sort out your salary straight away and your head of department has agreed to share out your lectures.'

The Dean was relieved to have finished. As I stood up he gripped my hand fiercely. His eyes shone.

# Chapter 15

'My own son, my erm, son... he took his own life you know.'

I was shocked. I rocked back on my feet. The Dean softened again and he clung to my hand for a moment.

'I had no idea Dean....'

'He suffered from depression; of course we had no idea. We just thought he was a moody so and so. Quite brilliant you know. I don't think Janet has ever recovered even though the twins have done so well. Look, it happens all the time and these days we are meant to make sure it doesn't go that far. See what I mean. Your head of department tells me that you are a changed man these past months so...erm...tell me, does it actually work?'

'Mindfulness?'

'Yes, that and that meditation stuff; I mean could it have helped Bruce do you think?'

'Oh Dean, we all suffer mental health issues at some time in our lives and we react to stress differently. But yes, mindfulness can help and in fact maybe it's the only thing that truly can, but Dean, even though these methods are ancient we have only just recently accepted them into our academic processes. I'm sure that...'

'Well just try to make sure we don't lose any more of them, we can't afford to have incidents like that anymore.' He cleared his throat. 'We are all in competition for funding now thanks to that wretched government. Right, good, that's settled. See yourself out.'

I walked down the curving staircase, stunned. I had hardly allowed the thought of right livelihood rise up inside my consciousness and now here was an opportunity too good to turn down. Then the enormity of it all hit me. I had no formal qualifications in this subject; the thought of being liable for the lives and wellbeing of a few thousand students was quite terrifying.

As I rounded the last corner of the stairs a small person looked up to greet me.

*So there you go Phoney. You got what you wanted - a job to make you smile. A job to help you bring peace and compassion into the world.*

Amy pulled on my trouser leg to make me sit beside her.

*Ha ha, you've got a job to help you practise without me. You teach what you most need to learn, my dearest Phoney.*

'But, I'm a beginner at all this Amy.'

*You are a newbie Phoney, and we all are, every day that we wake up and begin to breathe. Every day is your first day. You begin every day. You have a great beginner's mind. You have learned to play again. That's why you will be a fabby teacher.*

I looked at my small friend. She was shimmering slightly. I could almost see through her. Yet she still fixed me with her piercing blue eyes and somehow peered deep into my soul.

*Now don't worry Phoney. Stay present, stay calm and simply keep on practising. Okay, you can get qualifications if you really want but the real truth of why you got this job is that you are perfect for it. Yes you dear Phoney, perfect! How about that then?*

I smiled at my little friend. I didn't quite feel perfect but I felt that I was as imperfect as anybody else on the planet. Maybe I was just as wonderfully imperfect as everybody else, so I guess that was a perfect realisation.

# Chapter 15

*Keep practising every day Phoney. Keep watering the*
*seeds of joy. Keep on returning to your breath. Keep*
*choosing mindfully. Keep up the good work.*

Amy squeezed my knee stood up and climbed a few steps up the
winding staircase. I felt amazing and glanced up and past Amy to
the steep steps that led to the Dean's office. Suddenly I had so
many opportunities.

*Yup you are definitely the right man for the job Phoney.*
*You have been where all those students have been. You*
*know what it's like to be fearful, anxious, confused, wor-*
*ried and maybe even a little full of yourself.*

Amy patted me on the head and chuckled. Her touch felt soft as a
feather. Her voice sounded like the chimes of small bells ringing
in a distant valley somewhere.

*Remember you are simply teaching them to be free from*
*fear. You are helping them to help themselves. Simply*
*being, a simple being. They can jump off into their great*
*big adventures just like you did.*

Amy grabbed my head and pulled it upwards to meet hers. We
were so close I could see the gap in her teeth and smell her
breath of roses and honeysuckle.

*Don't let or make anyone need you, Phoney, don't teach*
*them to be dependent on you. Teach them the way. Make*
*sure they can do it for themselves. Make that your goal*
*if you need one. Be happy that you can wave them off*
*knowing that they will be alright.*

'Will you still show up to help me out if I need you?'

Amy fixed her piercing blue eyes on me and kissed me gently on
my forehead.

# Taming Amy

*You don't need me anymore Michael. You never did.
Besides you will have all the help you think you need from
now on.*

Amy let go of my face and popped her small hands deep inside
the pockets of her raincoat. A small frown flickered across her
face. She looked momentarily sad. She climbed up one step up
from where I sat and observed me for a moment. She stood as
still as a small statue, looking down at me where I sat on the
bottom step. Then Amy realised that she was taller than me and
her usual gappy-toothed grin broke out across her face like the
sunshine from behind a cloud. As one of her infectious laughs
began to take her over, she simply said:

*Goodbye Michael.*

Sending me a theatrical kiss, my little friend, my miniature
spiritual guide, my tiny teacher, vanished from my life.

The rest of the day passed in a whirlwind as I was extricated
from my duties in the department and was given my new large
office. Our head of department was positively purring as she
told me of the generous sum of money we were going to receive
to completely revamp the department building so that it could
include a purpose-built wellness and meditation centre. I sensed
that I had been a pawn in some lofty political game but I didn't
mind. This really could be work that would benefit others.

I realised that if I stayed diligent with my practice and made
sure that it never took me too far away from my sense of joy and
peace and from appreciating the people around me, I might just
succeed. There was just one unanswered question, just one last
area of confusion in my newfound energy field of happiness. I
sensed that something was starting afresh in my life. As I slowly
walked out of the old gothic university building, I realised that I
wanted to share all this new potential with someone. I knew that
I didn't need to, it was just that, oh well, it felt right. As I headed
down the hill towards my flat I remembered what Amy had said
about having all the help that I would need now. Maybe it was

just one of her many metaphors but as I reflected on her words, I felt a small fizz of excitement in my stomach.

As I eventually turned my street corner and headed up towards the entrance to my flat, I felt myself become fully present. The pale sunshine lit up the sandstone walls of the beautiful Glasgow tenements to such a degree that the whole south-facing side of my street glowed as if it were made of pure gold. As I drew closer to the steps leading up to the flat I felt a massive smile break out across my face. Standing on the top steps, just about to press the buzzer, was Hazel. Without speaking I stopped and drank in the moment. Hazel was brilliantly illuminated in the sunshine with her blonde hair creating a burnished halo effect. I'm not sure that I had ever noticed her properly before. As time slowed I seemed to have ages to watch her kind and gentle face as she went to press the buzzer again. I noticed every detail about her. The flicker of hope, the glimmer of worry, the sparkle of kindness and the smallest moment of vulnerability as she half bit her finger nail when she got no reply. At that moment I realised that in all the years Hazel and I had been together I had never been able to be this still, this present, and simply see her as she truly was. As she turned to leave I saw past the flutter of emotions that blew across the calmness of her mind. I saw past her physical form and past any perception that I had ever held of her and, for the briefest of moments, I saw a being of light so amazingly beautiful that I thought she might actually be an angel. Then she saw me and time returned to normal.

'Oh hi Michael, what are you grinning at? You look like the Cheshire cat. Look, here, I was baking; I thought you might like some of these.'

I breathed deeply as time sped up around me, as the background noise of the city fog-horned into my sea of tranquillity and I walked up the steps towards Hazel. It occurred to me that today was all about steps and me looking up at amazing women. She pulled back a tea towel to reveal some of her signature cheese and veggie pasties, all lovingly baked to perfection. My tummy rumbled loudly and Hazel laughed.

'Seems like I arrived at the right time.'

I realised how hungry I was and that I hadn't eaten all day. I carefully leaned past Hazel and opened the door to the flat, still smiling as the magical afterglow of a few moments earlier carried on within me.  As we quietly entered the sparse flat Hazel shyly held out the tray of pasties to me. She looked around at the meagre space and gently sighed out loud. I could see a moment of sadness and maybe even pity cross her face. I stood holding the warm tray of food and Hazel wandered over to the window, which was still covered halfway up with small chocolaty smudges. She absentmindedly held her hand up to one small and perfectly formed Amy-shaped handprint. A long slow smile crossed Hazel's face. She turned towards me, let out another sigh and looked at me as if she was seeing me properly for the first time. We both stood very still, maybe embarrassed or maybe afraid to move. I wondered if Hazel was arriving at some sort of inner revelation or that she was making a decision in that very moment. As we stood, framed in the sunlight that streamed in through the window, I caught sight of a chocolate muffin with an Amy-sized bite laying on the floor. I couldn't help it. A cascade of pure and childlike mirth tumbled out of me. I had to pop the tray of warm food down on the table in case I dropped it. I did a quick hop, skip and jump across to the kettle.

Hazel put her head on one side and continued to observe me, allowing a slow smile to appear on her face.

"OK what's so funny Michael?'

I paused as a thousand answers flashed through my mind. I wiped my hands, which had somehow discovered smears of Amy's last cake attached to the kettle. I breathed deeply again as my chuckles subsided.

'Oh I may have just found the perfect job for you Hazel, in fact I think it might just be the most perfect job ever.'

'That's funny?'

Chapter 15

Hazel was half smiling and half frowning at my inexplicable good humour. A stream of answers raced across my mind's surface and one held and demanded that I express it.

'Oh it's just that I was studying Right Livelihood and how to make a living without harming anything and not eating meat and then you appear out of nowhere with some veggie pasties. Now that's what I call perfect timing.'

Hazel smiled and, after producing a porcelain side plate from her bag, she began to laugh as well. Only Hazel would bring her own eating utensils!  She held the plate up in front of us like a symbolic chalice and glanced around at my austere and empty flat. That sent us both into howls of laughter. We laughed so hard I thought my sides would split.

'Well I noticed that you had thrown everything away. You really have had a major clear out haven't you Michael?'

Hazel regained some composure and put a pasty on her plate and mine. She chuckled again and looked around for another chair. I let her have mine and sat on my meditation cushion in the deep windowsill, enjoying the sun warming my back. As we both sat down there was a moment of awkwardness and then our eyes met and we became still.

I marvelled again at just how beautiful she was. It was as if I could see Hazel's soul, she shone so brightly. I felt an easy smile light up my face.

'It's so good to see you Hazel.'

'It's good to see you too Michael. You've changed.'

I started to chuckle again and gently reached out to touch Hazel's hand.

'You haven't changed at all, and I wouldn't have it any other way.

You are the same beautiful, wonderful woman that you have always been and just seeing you is fantastic.'

Hazel looked straight at me in that unflinchingly direct and fearless way that she has, not unlike Amy I thought.

'You look so happy Michael. Who is she?'

'Huh, who is she?' My reaction was not what Hazel expected though she appeared immediately relieved as I burst out laughing.

'I can honestly say, with my hand on my heart, that there is not and has not been any other woman but you Hazel.'

I smiled. There was no way I was going to try and explain a six- or seven- year-old imaginary female spirit guide friend to Hazel... well, not now anyway.

Hazel relaxed again and grinned. I noticed that she was not fearful in the slightest and that she had only asked to clarify something in her mind. Hazel glanced at the half-eaten muffin on the floor before looking straight at me again. She put her head on one side and frowned slightly.

'Michael, I need to tell you something. I need to apologise to you. You see, back in the restaurant, I was a bit overwhelmed, I was scared and I...'

I didn't let her finish. I just leaned forward across the small table and kissed her – long and gently, with an appreciation and love that flowed from every cell in my body. To my surprise and delight Hazel returned the kiss but then she gently pulled away from me and stood up. She carefully put the untouched food and plates back into her bag and then turned as if to leave.

I chuckled and stood up to see her out. I realised that if that was
the last loving moment I was to have with my wife it had been
worth every second. I stood up and let the moment go. I breathed
out, realising just how much love I felt for her. Hazel reached
the door to the flat and then turned slowly to me with a quizzical
smile.

'What are you waiting for?'

'Huh?'

Hazel smiled again, took a long deep breath, glanced around the
flat and then in her softest voice said:

'I think it's time we went home isn't it my love?'

# Appendices

## Acknowledgements

Amy owes so much to the careful, diligent and tireless editing of my dearest wife Andrea who has encouraged, cajoled and supported me throughout the writing of this book – as well as compassionately providing me the space to gain even the slightest amount of competency along my path.

Many thanks to Dr Damo, for his professional insights and many read-throughs of Amy.

Huge thanks to Kim and Sinclair Mcleod at Indie Authors Scotland for all their generous advice about and support.

Huge thanks to;

Luke & Lina, Becky, Josh & Elliott Peloso, Kenny MacDougall, John Hatfield, Libby Hammond, Martha Leishman, Hillary Storm, Pamela, Charlie & Ruben Grimm, Gerhard Lipfert, Thom Hartmann, Adam Hansen, Richard Powell, Paul Boothman, Pende, Bill & Catriona, Lewis & Eva, Jane Paul, The wonderful Whites and all my fellow travellers.

Author's Notes

The main question readers ask is, 'Why Taming Amy? Surely Amy is the one who tames Michael?'

There is a clue in chapter two but, for those of you who don't like guess work, the answer is a simple one.

The book is a guide on how to tame 'amy' – the amygdala (nuclei) – the peanut-sized part of the brain which activates our 'fight or flight' response. The amygdala reacts to, and is part of, our fear feedback loop as well as inducing negative and positive emotions.

Several years before writing this book and before mindfulness was recognised as a scientific and academic discipline for psychological wellbeing, I was delivering workshops to busy and stressed-out executives and needed a simple way to help them to understand the effect of their amygdala on their bodies and minds. Many of these executives were in a constant state of stress, and were suffering from chronic anxiety, a condition which eventually enlarges the amygdala and can even shrink the prefrontal cortex. The effect of this state of near constant 'flight or fight' lowers the immune system, decreases decision-making faculties and quickly burns up energy reserves. Basically, stress - usually caused by some kind of fear or habit or condition resulting from a fearful state - has profound implications for all psychological disorders. One day, at one of my workshops, an executive mentioned that we were, 'all trying to tame Amy', a phrase that I loved so much I quickly adopted it into the programme which, after much meditation and applied imagination, eventually grew into the title and main character of this book.

Another question often asked is 'Why does Amy eat so much cake?' The simple answer is that the consumption of carbohydrates is a quick and short-term way to help the body mop up, and deal with the huge amounts of damaging hormones our bodies create when stressed. Many eating disorders are symptomatic of the unhealthy way we try to combat high stress levels on a daily basis.

Finally, the spiritual dimension of 'Taming Amy' can be embraced or ignored but the instructions and practices contained within are all tried and tested techniques which have grown out of, and can be found in, many ancient spiritual paths including Christianity, Islam, Sufism, Hinduism and especially Buddhism. It is the Buddhist method that Amy has followed in the book and which can be discovered again by the reader in numerous ancient and modern texts. I am eternally grateful for the teachings of Thich Nhat Hahn my teacher, whose wisdom, insights and teaching metaphors have been an inspiration for Taming Amy.

## Inspirations for Taming Amy

Why Zebras Don't Get Ulcers: Robert M. Sapolsky.

The Miracle of Mindfulness: Thich Nhat Hanh: Rider 1975

Planting Seeds: Practising Mindfulness with Children: Thich Nhat Hanh: Rider 1999

The Heart of the Buddha's Teaching: Thich Nhat Hanh: Rider 1999

Fear: Thich Nhat Hahn: Rider, 2012

The Spirituality of Imperfection:

Storytelling and the Journey to Wholeness: Kurtz & Ketcham: Bantam, 1992

Jack Kornfield: A Path with a Heart: A guide through the Perils and Promises of Spiritual Life: Hyperion, 1996

Change Your Words, Change Your World: Andrea Gardner: Hay House, 2012

Mindfulness Based Cognitive Therapy: Rebecca Crane: Routledge, 2009

Wide Awake, A Buddhist Guide for Teens: Diana Winston: Perigee, 2003

Illusions: Richard Bach: Dell Publishing Co., Inc. 1977

One: Richard Bach: Random House Publishing Group, 1989

Lightning Source UK Ltd.
Milton Keynes UK
UKOW04f0055080815

256556UK00002B/70/P

9 780993 172809